C000066888

FARMHOUSE ACHES, WORKHOUSE PAINS

FARMHOUSE ACHES, WORKHOUSE PAINS

Gerald Green (Horton)

The Book Guild Ltd
Sussex, England

First published in Great Britain in 2005 by
The Book Guild Ltd
25 High Street
Lewes, East Sussex
BN7 2LU

Typesetting in Times by
Keyboard Services, Luton, Bedfordshire

Printed in Great Britain by
Antony Rowe Ltd, Chippenham, Wiltshire

A catalogue record for this book is available from
The British Library

ISBN 1 85776 910 4

'Fruit Ridge' residence of G.B. Horton, 4650 West Horton Road, Sandcreek, Michigan, USA.

Elizabeth Green (1878–1958)

George Horton (1850–1930)

PROLOGUE

Had I been alive and duly observant in the earlier times between 1835–40, I would have been struck by the intense flurry of building activity in parishes through the length and breadth of our fair and happy land. Following the Report of the Royal Commission in March 1834, it was proposed 'that except as to medical attention ... all relief whatever to the able-bodied or to their families, otherwise than in "well-regulated" workhouses ... shall be declared unlawful and shall cease' ('out-relief' was thereafter to be tapered off in practice to tickets for bread and fuel, and restricted to the old and 'impotent' poor under the administration of the New Poor Law).

Prior to this New Act workhouses were administered in isolation by the local Guardians. Some workhouses were housed in slum-like, desolate buildings miles away from decent society, buildings so depressing that they were long ago abandoned by the staff and left to the old and sick to administer themselves. On the other hand, some workhouses were up to the standard of modest hotels, where the newly-arrived inmates would express surprise at the relative comfort afforded, and regretted not going into *that place* years sooner. Indeed, there were records of some families 'living in' over two or more generations. Can you imagine the outcry over such scrounging off the public purse? There were good times and bad times and for some, some of the time might have been considered good – in those days anyway, when the only escape from destitution was to be a workhouse inmate.

Adding his own wisdom to the debate, it was stated by

1

Lord Brough, 'a friend of the poor', that: 'This New Poor Law was like a cold bath – unpleasant in contemplation but invigorating in its effect.' And in an attempt to maintain some dignity, the poor might also remark: 'Poverty is not a crime, it's just an inconvenience.'

In essence this change brought about the merger of two or more parishes into a number of 'Unions', in order to better supervise and control the workhouses under the new Act. 'Guardians of the Poor' were elected to the committee by ratepayers; no one occupying property worth less than £25 a year was eligible, making sure that this voluntary post was occupied by the Great and the Good.

An ideal 'Union', of two or more workhouses, was open to official inspection to check that the Act was being implemented. Each covering a radius of about ten miles from some central town location, was to be the basis of the new system and the sole form of relief for the able-bodied. No doubt about it, this new form of cold-comfort treatment would doubtless breathe new life into the habitual pauper and regenerate him to such a high level that his former slothfulness and disrespect for his employers, and society, would henceforth be abandoned.

Rather than suffer the indignities of this new hard workhouse regime, the indolent would be infused with a new sense of keenness to retain his existing work, rather than go into *that place* and be forced to wear prison-style garb and required to work at the most tedious labour that human ingenuity could devise. And to be confined to live a lonely institutional life separated from his family. A new strict rule had come into force: no breaking up of families; all must come inside; or stay outside and starve without any chance of 'out-relief' (except for some more humane authorities who blindly took a little longer to enforce the harsher New Act rules).

The net widened still further. In future, the entire

responsibility of supporting bastard children would be the sole concern of the mother. The strict 'out-relief' rule would apply: relief for the child would be also considered relief for the parent. The implication was starkly obvious: destitute *unmarried mothers* (in the days before *single-parent* was invented) would be workhouse-imprisoned, along with their unnatural children. Reasonably, the authorities were seeking a sound solution: preventing copulative sinners from roving freely would not only be a kindly act; it would also control the bastard birthrate and reduce the burden of contributions for those who had to pay their rates and taxes. The choice was stark: enter the workhouse together, or starve outside together. This rigid regulation was intended to arouse both fear and panic, which it did, in every town, village and hamlet.

It was also reported that: All Acts which punish or charge the putative father shall as to all bastards born, now be repealed after the passing of the Act. Some relief, however, was on the horizon. After 1844 a mother was allowed to seek an affiliation order against the father. But that could be worthless, especially if he did a bunk to avoid his legal responsibility. In those days there seemed to exist a widely-held view that the common folk should not fornicate to dividing and multiplying lengths if they could not afford the results of their pleasure. Now, any feckless woman (and her tainted offspring) might end up in the workhouse, along with the feeble rest. No wonder one noble lord was troubled to remark, about this procreative slipping: 'It's much too good for the common people!' Alack! Alas! There is no other way to sow the human seed. And the act is far too pleasurable and surely much too good to be considered bad – what a pity it can be sinful...

1

After I arrived in this world, in 1922, and began to think, a doubt started to be a question: the possibility that my alone mother had made me nearly unique, without any claim to distinction (there appeared to be no known dad, not even in the spirit).

Though never christened personally, in or out of church or chapel, this disadvantage seemed not to bother me and any thought of following the 'last minute' catechumen was never even considered. My future would be left to chance; waiting, when the time came along, hopefully not in too much fear and trembling, in a queue with all the other outsiders, fearfully awaiting the last and final verdict, hoping any punishment would not be too harsh or long.

In those euphemistic days, children beginning the age of questioning, but not yet skilled in understanding the answering, were kept in a kind of cosy fairyland, especially when that awkward human reproductive question came along: Where do tiny babies come from?

The answer was returned pat, with due regard for innocence: Babies are found under gooseberry bushes, or delivered in a doctor's black bag. Thus began one of my first childhood confusions, and by no means my last! But I still would ponder, how exactly did I arrive? – left under the bush, or in a bag?

From this early experience in life, came a realisation that under certain embarrassing circumstances, grown-ups, without the slightest hesitation, would tell lies, without, so it seemed to me, a single guilty thought in their head.

Later, my innocence was furtively eroded by filthy jokes regaled by the older, more advanced boys, in a corner of the playground, and snippets of the facts of life they had with great difficulty managed to glean from their ignorant elders (and from the 'dirty' stories going the rounds). The tuition in this regard was, for the most part, less than adequate explanation: no suitable books of instruction for children (or even adults) were available in those tight-lipped highly moral days.

The very thought of using explicit words, with 'rude' diagrams showing a normal function (of this crude kind anyway) would have raised a fearful cry from the protective elders: Well! – The very thought! I never! And, of course, how disgusting! And much more besides...

Most males, in the predicament of lacking any previous skills, or 'user information', with inspiration when they first-nighted (blessedly and properly), held to their ancestors' rationale: this was a trade that did not require a long apprenticeship. But greater knowledge of this unspeakable act might encourage wider abandonment and form the beginnings of the subversion of the previously dutiful classes: much to the discomfort of self-restrained people.

Small wonder in the nuptial bed the innocent bride blushed and blanched, while the desperate groom with every loving intention, flustered and fumbled like someone lost, while trying to do his duty (which he surely must), to prove himself master of the intact maiden-head: unquestionably untorn in those absolute moral days, when good girls had to be undefiled (their fingers always to be held tightly over their ha'pennies, throughout the testing courtship, which could last upwards to ten years – even longer!). And woe betide any 'unmarried' girl who went beyond the acceptable limits of propriety and became pregnant, 'in the pudding club', before taking the solemn vows of membership. The fancy-free and flowing young men were wisely cautioned

5

by their fathers and the male fraternity not to make a mess on their own doorstep and risk the family respectability; highly held in their heads: appearance must be defended at all costs.

In those days now being referred to, of around and after the turn into the twentieth century, ostracism still wielded power over personal conduct. So it must have seemed remarkable that my ancient Horton-Father would have dared to pass on his human seed to sprout me, in the face of common knowledge that the banns would have to be called to avert an impending scandal, inexorably on its punishing way.

That my Horton-Father was at the time an 'unmarried' widower was one thing. But to father a child while in receipt of the old-age pension, at the ancient age of 68 – how disgusting! And perhaps, even worse, producing a healthy child at that! (And my Mam, also knocking on a bit, compounded this event at the somewhat advanced age of 44.) No wonder the local village people reeled, deplored, and went into shock when that couple's lewd fourth mistake produced me in human form: the last of George Horton's extensive brood, of his latest batch of four, all now labelled in a different surname – all beyond the pale.

I gradually began to wonder why the villagers called my father 'Staghorn'. It rang out like the loud bells in Gosberton church tower. What on earth did it mean? Was it meant to be meaningless, or meanness born of envy that such a state of erectile behaviour could actually exist in an old man? Did not the ringing out of 'Staghorn' in our quiet village suggest that animal desires persist strongly, and too indecently long. Perhaps only a privileged aged few are blessed to perform (so surely, he deserved that label). But, 'Staghorn!' – cor! After the first shock passed through my narrow Puritanism – that animals could be compared with humans – my feeling of shame began to remove.

Rightly (and righteously), living or slipping into sin did concern people in those days, especially if the aftermath was fruitful. The vicars denounced fornication as the work of the Devil, without need for further explanation! And the terms 'singles', 'partners' and 'doubles' applied mainly to tennis and whisky. In polite silence I used to listen to the decrying conversations of folk who, unaware of my sinful condition, discussed openly the problems of them (those poor bastards!); unaware that one of them was present and listening in, and pretending to be perfectly normal, even nodding his head in unison, trying to show utmost sympathy for the terrible affront over which they were so woefully agonising, which if left unremarked would condone this poor behaviour. So perhaps you can understand my troublous thinking: Thank God I was born hidden in a pure white skin and not in a branding special colour and most certainly not with the devil's horns sticking out of my head.

My many feelings of happiness from my simple country contentment (which occurred more often than I perhaps deserved – considering my background) would tip the scales against the dreary side of living; the poverty and narrowness of which there was plenty. But compared with other bothers that would invade my life, 'Staghorn' just had to become a bit of a joke – even rough terrain can look serene from high above unclouded skies.

2

Looking like an Old Testament prophet (and often seeming one!), with his searching eyes and flowing black beard, Horton would regularly berate the whole family for its sins, however small they might be. Breaking out with several strictures, usually at the meal table (after a lengthy grace), when we were hungry and couldn't escape, you could safely bet that he would quote some of the Ten Commandments, more particularly those used by adults against children (not the ones they manage to evade), and other frightening bits and pieces of scripture with which the clergy had disciplined him, from his own church attending time, from 1858 when he was four years old and absorbed the Christian beliefs while attending Gosberton Parish Church, in obvious fear and trembling, which was still evident in his old age.

We learnt about the WRATH OF GOD! – which was equated with lightning (to strike us down!), and thunder (the deadly sound of disapproval!).

One day, when I was around eight-years old, I put this 'wrath thing' to the test by running wildly in the grass field, out of human hearing, swearing as loudly as I could: 'bugger and damn!' – many, many times. Such was my wickedness. In trepidation I waited a few minutes; to my relief nothing happened. Not wishing to push my luck, I did not repeat those sinful words again until my nerves recovered.

Although Horton never attended church during the years I knew him (except for odd obligatory funerals), he always encouraged the good habit in others; declaring loudly to anyone he thought in need: Everybody should attend a House of Worship on Sunday.

On that special day, to give him his due, he never worked (except to feed the farm animals): he was fearful of the *invisible* looking over his shoulder, recording any transgressions in the Final Judgement book.

He seemed to have no doubt how he divided good from bad: if there was anything murky, he never dwelled on that. He never swore (except, 'clock-a-daisy!'); never drank 'strong drink' (even at threshing time, the stone-bottle beer for the men was kept in the barn); he never told a lie, except when he promised me a watch as 'big as a frying pan' as a reward for doing simple chores (before I learnt that adults could tell lies without as much as a blanch). The word liar was too strong for Horton: it was akin to a swear word. *Story telling* was the allowed description, and if found out in such an act, we were told to wash our *dirty* mouths out at the pump – even out in the snow on a cold winter's day, so fervently did he ferret evil out.

Only his finest products were sold, with strict attention to accurate weight and measure. A gaze of lingering ownership followed the wholesale merchant's lorry, as it departed with his perfect produce loaded for the market – the simple satisfaction of a job well done.

Now is the time to ask: who is this paragon of virtue, with more than a hint of a doubtful past? Only space and time will tell ... one thing seems certain, he was my father – my growing inmost feelings told me that.

And what of my mother, Elizabeth Ann Green? (Green spelt in the colour way, not with the added olde-worlde 'e'.) Soaked within a strict chapel moral background, how did she manage to produce a clutch of four bastards? How indeed! – in the normal way; but by happenstance, obviously unplanned and surprising. You'll simply have to read on. (Throwing stones was not my way forward. I was born to

9

live; please try your best to suffer me and I will suffer you...)

The animals on the farm loved her. The chickens clucked and followed her around, even into the house (to pick crumbs off the carpet, or the kitchen table) before she shooed them out again. She instructed us not to disturb the many wild birds nesting in the hedgerows surrounding all the fields, as they chirped out their liven songs. There was so much that pleased her. Grunts of delight came from the pigs when she passed by and tipped some food into their trough. The cows gave her an affectionate moo! and leaned their heads over the backyard fence for a gentle stroking as she filled their water trough with sparkling water from the pump. The several cats purred out loudly, especially at teatime on Sunday, after licking out the empty sixpenny tin of Woolworth's salmon, sometimes having to be pulled out if their head got stuck – so tasty did they find the licking. The year we wintered the donkey from the seaside I remember well. It nuzzled Mam so passionately every time she fed it with carrots, which surprised me, that such abundant affection could be shown by an animal. Even the tame, unremittingly fathering rabbits, distracted from their everlasting buckishness, twitched a friendly greeting, and the docile does (during those precious moments free from boundless duty) showed their unconcealed pleasure as Mam stuffed carrots into the wire-mesh window of their cage.

On some treasured occasions, Mam hummed a wordless tune, in what seemed to be contentment, when anxieties appeared to retreat for a time and, to crown it all, she'd disappear frequently, to 'tinkle' on the piano, in the 'room'. There, she played tunes I'd never heard before, in moods I never understood: her escape into other world. And at such times I usually had the good sense to leave her alone, that is, until my childhood cravings demanded attention.

In such grim times we would go through, what else could

a family do but live their lives in hopeful expectation; sometimes desperately reading the tea-leaf signs for better days. And during the grimmest times, before the worst times yet to come, sending away for a sixpenny Cornish 'good luck' charm. Pathetic and laughable that may be. But the stark reality was only too evident; in order to escape from the coming woe, we needed more than inspiration provided by tea-leaf configurations, however favourable they seemed to settle. And the promise of good luck from a few pennies' worth of charm, brought by an elf, fairy or a goblin; wouldn't that stretch the faith of a simpleton? Loud crying out in anguish prayer also failed to relieve our pressing wants: it could be said, we were well and truly up the creek without a paddle, and leaking fast!

Often I would begin to wonder about that well-oiled saying: God helps those who help themselves. It sounded more than jokey-cynicism; possibly the truth.

3

In 1622 (300 years before I was born), the drainage of the Fens began to change a way of life that had long been taken for granted, now slowly being destroyed and forbidden: the freedom to roam and live off the land. The balancing act between nature and man would wobble about, as it had, it could and it would. Progress from the old-ways was steady but painfully slow for centuries, until the motorised vehicle came chugging along; with all its innovative scope, slowly but surely taking over from the horse and human muscle power.

A keen observer of the Fenland scene, John Taylor, the Water Poet, wrote this description of Buttertoft (formerly Goosetoft), in 1640:

> The people here have neither horse or cow,
> nor sheep, nor oxen, nor asses, pig or sowe
> – nor cream, curds, whey, buttermilk or cheese;
> nor any living thing but geese.

Excluding the flocks of geese, which have long since disappeared, John Taylor's description would seem to match my own unfolding Fenland scene as time ticked away towards the twenty-first century.

> Flat, wide-open acres,
> Flowering in rainbow colours,
> And shades of green-pea soup,
> Relieved by gold and yellow.

12

Now crawled all over by
Put-putting four-wheeled things;
The village folk (at full-speed)
Now work with gear and wheel.
Where are the fish and wild-fowl?
Shot, poisoned, or gone missing.

The early drainage of the Fens started to change forever the nature of the land. The surface was lowered, due to the shrinking of the peat as it dried out, which eventually caused flooding disasters in what was fast becoming an unintended, giant embanked reservoir, lower than the surrounding sea. Drainage efforts from around 1638 began to conquer the danger from flooding; but still it occurred. In 1799 many hundreds of acres were flooded. The harvest had to be reaped by men in boats; others collected the tops of the grain as they waded through the flood water.

Nature was harnessed to combat the problem. Wind-powered engines (looking like windmills), with a revolving cupola to face the wind, and giant sails which could be over 60 feet, began to poke up over the flatness of the land. Eventually, some 60 'mills' stood along the bank of the Forty-Foot drain. 'Dykereeve' officials were appointed by the Court of Sewers to supervise the drains and banks and to collect the drainage taxes, usually a few pence per acre. That some of the Dykereens became fatalities, decapitated by the unstoppable swish of the sail in full flight, is quite possible; the fact that there are no such records preserved is not conclusive proof that this never happened.

Along with the drainage came the enclosures of the land; the issue of title-deeds, and miles and miles of hedges and fences. This restricting of the right to roam over the land in freedom caused the wild Fenmen to riot in 1768 and 1773. The taking of wild duck, mallard and teal by the thousands in decoys; the drawing of sedge and reed; the horse breeding,

13

along with the roaming, hunting and fishing, inexorably came to an end. Hedges and fences marked out the new confining boundaries, backed by title deeds – or, as a last resort – the ball from the end of a musket. It was as if a giant steam roller had maliciously flattened the marshes into a dull, tamed state of rich fertile dirt, worked by dogged people. A changed silence came over the land, No longer disturbed by many former wild screeches, the church bells must have sounded even louder, as the subduing of nature moved towards completion – the insatiable human conqueror had arrived.

The land drainage had made a tremendous impact over the centuries, as wide-open marshland gave way to *enclosed* farmsteads. The new yeoman class tightened their belts in hard times and were extra prudent in good times: always conscious that come tomorrow there would be another disaster of storm or flood, along with the normal calamities that farmers learn to take in their stride. The many subsistence smallholders and cottagers had to work long days, eking out a livelihood on a few acres of land. In many cases they were worse off than day labourers, but too proud to admit defeat – such stoics deserved a sainthood!

The breeding places of the malarial fly eventually disappeared along with the fever associated with it, but not for many years (up to the early part of the twentieth century). As a remedy the Fen dwellers made up poppy juice into a paste, to form a pellet the size of a pea (this caused the yellowing of skin all over: one derivation of Lincolnshire 'yellow-belly'). In 1895 a local historian, W.H. Wheeler of Boston, gave his opinion that, 'the effect on the taker and those around them is far less deleterious than excess beer or dram drinking'. This poppy drug, 'laudanum' (locally, pronounced 'lodnum'), was also available in tincture form in pennyworth from the local apothecary, and taken, some years after the malaria had vanished, by those long since hooked and not unhappily dependent.

In low tones of mortification, Horton hinted that his parents had been permanent slaves to it, and not only that; there were also hints of dram imbibing, and the shame that his mother died of cirrhosis of the liver (if not strictly correct, then reputed to be a drinkers' disease). Such wretchedness! – how children suffer and gnash their teeth over their transgressional parents.

But try to imagine; the constant worry of farming conditions; the harsh Victorian winters, when even the local dykes were frozen over. The isolation, when the snow drifted high, up to the waist and sometimes higher; and when that was gone, mud squelching, around the ankles, followed by the hot dry summers, then, sometimes, by too much ran. And the wind and driven rain, without interruption, shrieking and blasting about over the wide open fields, flattening the cereal crop down to the ground, making it impossible to use scythe or sickle, resulting in a financial disaster – even ruin!

But the isolation and repetitiveness of it all, amid the constant struggling (season by season, facing the round of annual gambling). It's enough to make a saint grumble (if not curse), and most farmers are plainly human: country and city living, in their own ways, can be equally stressful, containing the essential conditions to drive some folk to drink and some to early Heaven.

The population of Lincolnshire (Lincolescire) doubled from 200,000 to just under 400,000 from 1801 to 1851, and then slowly increased to 500,000 by 1901. Locally, since the time of the Norman Conquest in 1066, new village names had evolved around the existing village of Gosberton: 'the Risegate' and 'the Clough' came into being. To tidy up the diocese, some of the boundaries were redefined. For example, the Risegate village, formerly part of Surfleet for ecclesiastical purposes, was transferred to the newly-formed parish of Gosberton Clough and Risegate.

The 'Workhouse' for the Spalding 'Union' of nine parishes

15

was erected in 1836, in the Pinchbeck Road, Spalding (number 45a to be exact). It was a prison-like building for Victorian admonishment (and would stand out screaming its custodial dreadfulness for some 136 years, in what was otherwise a respectable, law-abiding road). And also purpose-built were the walls, railings and frosted windows, to confine the fraught and aimless inmates, out of the gaze of the passing public. With further endeavour a Sessions House was built next to the House of Correction in 1842.

Spalding now had a 'triple-chance' in their control of the local population. A workhouse in which to secure the morally, feckless dregs of society and their abominable offspring; a House in which to assemble for the transaction of judicial business, and, if necessary, to lock miscreants away from their wretched villainy. And last, but by no means least, there was already long established a House of Worship, continually struggling to empty the sink of the sunken sinful. Those Houses were ideally purpose-built for processing, flushing and cleansing right round the bend, and out of sight of the suffering worthy.

The essential 'baubles' of future living were not yet easily available; no wireless set, gramophone, motor car – not even a bicycle. So people tended to talk to each other a lot; use Shanks's pony, if they hadn't got a real one, and refused to spend hard-earned money on conspicuous ostentation; although the Horton family did possess a fine piano – the one my mother occasionally tinkered on, the one in 'the room'.

4

Within the space of some 20 years railways spread all over the place, like throbbing varicose veins. Produce could now be speedily sent to markets in far away towns and cities. Under the Great Northern & Great Eastern joint enterprise (later to become the London & North Eastern Railway), a new line from Spalding to Lincoln was opened up from the 1st August 1882, cutting alongside the Horton family farm in Gosberton Cheal. Horton was then 32 years of age; still single and providing cheap labour on the 50-acre rented family farm; living somewhat above the subsistence level of a farm worker; able to afford the necessities of life, but not much else – mainly, because there wasn't much else available.

Down the social scale there were the small-holdings of a few acres (which, as the name implies, were small and took a bit of holding). Further down still were the 'cottagers' who rented or owned their cottage and one field. They grazed a cow, reared a pig and most likely had a few hens or geese, freely roaming; and for most of the year, they worked on surrounding farms as day labourers. Living at subsistence level, many of these struggling people often fell into the hands of the attorney during depressions and found themselves evicted if their mortgage fell into arrears, the rent remained unpaid, or, equally overwhelming, the landlord decided to sell his land and required vacant possession.

George Horton's birthplace and home for many years had been in that mile-long hamlet, oddishly named 'the Cheal', within a mile or so of Gosberton village; its full geographical title being: Gosberton Cheal. No church, parish hall, public house or shop was ever built in 'the Cheal'. No loud noise came from a wireless set (in those days it was not invented); nor was the Hoover, the washing machine, or the refrigerator. The local weekly newspaper contained all the interest and excitement: the marriages, births and deaths; tittle-tattle, village by village; court action over a broken engagement; some minor law infringement, often by a drunk.

In the early nineteenth century, a medium-sized farm of around 120 acres of rich fenland would be considered a large-sized one. These somewhat isolated, proud farming folk often added 'House' after selecting a suitable fore-name for their dwellings, seemingly with great care: White House, Bank House, Wragg House, Marsh House and many others. In Gosberton Cheal a list appeared which showed great flourish: Cheal, Primrose, Ebenezer, Capontoft and Ingleside – fine sounding prefixed Houses where those proud, struggling Chealians lived.

Once again, in the early part of the twentieth century there were large sales of land, and many vulnerable tenants were deeply affected by this. In the period 1906 to 1914, and again from 1919 to 1921, the land-owning squires, or their inheriting children (in professions in far away towns and cities) were getting 'out of land' – in a hurry! Lincolnshire was largely to be transformed from a landlord-tenant relationship into owner-occupiers. Tenants who had previously been confident of obtaining rented land were now dislodged from their tenancies and had no option but to obtain a loan from the bank or the attorney in order to retain their foothold on the land, for themselves and future generations (and some were to later curse that 'millstone around their neck'). Farming, so it seems, is not always as peaceful as depicted in artists' tranquil scenes.

No wonder some of the countrymen scratched their heads in disbelief. Far too many changes in one lifetime for them

18

to absorb. Some would have preferred to walk a bit backwards, but not as far as the cave.

Newly arising was a class of land-owning countryman, the farming entrepreneurs, and proud owners of their land, using bigger, better and quicker machines, with engineers, chemists and accountants, advising them still further how to cut costs to penny fractions, as indeed to survive they must. Not only would they say it, they would feel it in their very bones: 'You cannot stop progress!' How often did I hear those words.

Large retail monopolies would eventually evolve, dictating prices which would hurt – if not destroy. And the city dwellers who'd never been through a farm gate in all their life, would demand their fresh food – at dirt-cheap prices. Wrapped in plastic, in a can, cooled or deep-frozen, with a trade-name boldly printed: *Smilin' Country Pickin'* – with a picture of a farmer in his smock and a cow both broadly smiling, near the boldly marked 'sell-by' date. *Pile it high* and *sell it low!* At lower and lower farm-gate prices to cope with the cut-throat competition.

Yet despite all the continuing progress, way back in 1899 a statement had been made (putting the brake on all future progress?) from no other place than the land of thrust and eternal progress: the United States of America. Charles H. Duell, the Commissioner in the Office of Patents, made the following profound announcement, which some folk may have found quite startling (while others might have found it reassuring): *Everything that can be invented has been invented.*

All the more reason why farmers should hold on to all their outdated farm hand tools and keep them shining brightly; in case the world winds backwards and they are needed once again. A caveman would have treasured them – can you imagine with what loving care he would have fondled them? Even if he couldn't figure out their real purpose, and hacked his unfriendly neighbour to bits with the spade, or impaled his wife on the two-tined fork for being too argumentative.

5

Gosberton Cheal – 'the Cheal' – George Horton's beloved
Cheal; his birthplace in 1854, a place of many struggles
and some successes: of happiness and tragedy (and in course
the odd unmentionable – spoken of in low emotional tones).
It's an oddish name, 'Cheal', rhyming with squeal, which
many folk may have done, faced with the many hardships
of long ago – even extending to our present times – landed
with hard labour, in miles and miles of honest plodding.

The Cheal was listed in the Domesday Book in 1068,
and possibly existed some little time before that. Named
variously: Cheal, Cheale, Cheales, Ceila and Cheel (before
its spelling settled down), it existed along with nearby
Surfleet, Pinchbeck and Gosberton, and was listed by King
William's surveyors. The Cheal was owned by the Bishop
of Lincoln. Atsurr and his brother had two carucates of
land, and two bovates taxable (whatever that means); six
villagers with two and a half ploughs, a meadow of eight
acres and one salt house were also detailed. Sounds like an
up and coming place. Kept alive by the generations, old-
timers referred to 'the Cheal line', 'Ceila' (Celtic): Ce =
boundary, i = in, la = place, thus becoming a 'place in a
boundary' – a boundary line.

Was this the 'line' defining the extent to which the drained
land could be worked? Or was it the boundary line, standing
in an elbow of boundaries, separating the villages of Gosberton
and Surfleet (and possibly Pinchbeck, earlier on)? Other
definitions exist but this one seems most likely to be the
true one.

But the 'stories I listened to,' sometimes laughing, at other times in consternation; especially when it dawned on me that I might forever end up subsisting on vegetables, rabbit and pig meat, eggs from chickens, and solidified suet pudding; forever flattened in the Fenlands, toil-worn, honest but poverty-stricken: hardly different from a slave.

'I see they (the labourers) get here in the morning, they see they get home at night,' was one of Horton's *master* sayings. 'Study capital, not labour,' was another gem which provided much to think about (especially, when my turn came to labour 'for little or nowt'). 'Treat'em mean and keep'em keen!' declaimed some forceful masters. Rufus Welby would run up and down the field stabbing the wind, with a two-tined fork, to punish it for blowing his corn down – the crounsey fellow! Angus Dickens swore that he would never die with his boots on. I never heard how he ended his final days.

And one of the Garners hereabouts used to send his grown son to bed at nine o'clock at nights; thus preventing the lad from courting the girl he loved and any possible complications. Undeterred, he would climb out of his bedroom window and tiptoe away down the lane.

My first master, fully aware of his power, would often bore us with: 'A good boss should always work his men hard; otherwise, they become lazy, and no one would then employ them.'

One farmer once savagely rounded on his labourer, who was riding back to the stable, resting his weary limbs after a hard day's work: 'Get off that horse,' the master shouted, 'it cost me £50 – farm labourers are ten-a-penny!' Alternatively, the kinder version goes: 'I'm pleased to see you riding, it shows you're tired out.'

Those stories starkly described my future prospects: breathtaking, if you only own a bicycle and the clothes you stand up in and you haven't got a home to call your own.

I felt some foreboding and can you blame me? Might it be my fate to be enslaved to a master who regarded the stalwarts of the farming community, the lowly farm labourer, with such utter disdain. As I grew older, many thoughts depressed me and acute awareness angered me, as I began to face the harshness of life on those open, flattening, Fenland acres. I would plan to escape – day dreaming would possess me. I would run away; join a circus; or board a boat to 'Americkee'. Do anything to escape from the dreary round of repetition – start here, stop there – pick this! – lift that! To plod forever in poverty, ageing in dreariness, to an early pauper's grave.

But unbeknown to me it had been postulated in a twelfth-century revelation that: 'Servitude is ordained by God, either because of the sins of those who become serfs, or as a trial, in order that those who are thus humbled may be made better.'

Was that the rational explanation for my humble place on earth: 'to be made better' – not better off!

Although the coming slump of the 1930s was devastating, it was by no means unique, it is recorded that yet another depression in farm prices and poor seasons arrived after the 1870s. One Fenland farmer's wife in 1877 noted in her diary, after attending a forced sale of farm goods and chattels: 'There are many farms given up. We don't know who to hear of leaving next. How long will this agricultural depression last?'

My branch of the Horton family had settled in Gosberton Cheal sometime around the first quarter of the nineteenth century. To John and Lucy were born three children: Lucy, Mary and George (my father to be, in 1854).

John's father, George (my great-great-grandfather), was said to have died a wealthy grazier (on a rented farm at a place called Offleet, some miles away, near Boston). From George to John to George again, with a fair degree of certainty, the inheritance, as it trickled down would not have been frittered away on ostentatious living.

All credit then to my grandfather John (even though he did receive a helpful legacy from his father, George of Offleet), that he survived and remained solvent, after so many tough farming years. John's younger brother, Sam, migrated to the USA and eventually his son (also George) amassed a large fortune: more of them later.

By the time I came along the 'made' period was past and 'gone' (over the quoted three requisite generations). No need for me to linger over what might have been. Rock bottom is a firm place to rise from – it is free of expectant clutter. My clutter was of a different kind.)

Of special interest is the listing of one Robert Sansam, as an agricultural servant in the Horton household in the Gosberton census of 1851.

(Sansam [*sic*], the name coming from Bishop Sam, a Norman. The 'son of Sam' (then spelt Samson) was how the flock honoured their bishop when it came to naming their children. But what a comedown, a descendant of the mighty Norman conquerors now a lowly servant of an offspring of the vanquished English.)

Presumably Robert was a part-time servant, as he owned and worked nine freehold acres; outright ownership was unusual in those days (in Gosberton Cheal anyway). The only other person to own land in the Cheal was Willy Waite: he owned a one-acre cottage field. According to the records, all the others leased their land; so a lot depended on the continuing goodwill of the landlord and the ability of the tenant to pay the rent.

Those precious nine freehold acres would be split at Robert Sansam's death in 1866, age 37. Five acres, one rood and 15 perches, in the Cheal, together with the family cottage (yet another country slum), were left to his wife Sarah and eldest son Branton (more often than not shortened

24

to 'Brant'). The balance, of three freehold acres and two roods, near to Beach Bank in Gobbolds Drove, Robert willed to his other son, John – also assuring him a place in the Fenland farming gamble alongside the rest of the plodding sloggers.

My grandfather John (Horton's father) died at the age of 76, on the 22nd January 1889. Considering, in those days, that 45 was 'old age' (49 for a woman), this was a remarkable achievement. The local doctor, Henry T. Stiles, MD, declared on the Death Certificate that the cause of death was a 'pros abscess', which sounds particularly nasty; especially if it is pussing away internally, is difficult to prick or squeeze and the poison is slowly killing the body. As if not fully satisfied with his description of this fatal condition, the good doctor added an extra medical condition (commonly used in those days to more fully describe any drawn-out 'passing away'): Exhaustion. This was not a surprising addition when 'doctoring' was fraught with desperation, hope and prayer, and hours of dedication with the stricken patient.

Horton often related his memory of the burial scene. The winter was so severe, and the frost in a grip so deep, the grave digger had to use a crowbar and a pickaxe to dislodge the top layer of soil, earning every penny of his modest fee. The family all bedecked in black, funereal mournfulness, shivered around the open grave awaiting to distribute the 'dust to dust', then politely hesitating, before going home for a 'knife and fork' tea. After some family funerals, those in the know would search for a hidden biscuit tin, hoping it might be filled with a hoard of golden sovereigns; failing that they'd listen to the reading of the will, which in John's case was never executed – 'let them sort it out when I am gone!'

John left £816 and a few odd pence. Daughter Lucy took out Letters of Administration and, so far as is known, the estate was equally divided between the three children: Lucy,

Mary and George. Several yardsticks can be used to compare the value of that sum today. The answer would require many comparisons, and then be open to serious challenge. John's legacy was not a great fortune, but £816 in 1889 was a fortunate advantage, even if it was split three ways. Sooner or later (most likely the former), the money would be needed by the Horton children to enable them to cushion their own struggles, in the farming, gambling game. Only too aware of the disasters that could affect them.

To give grandfather John his due, he died of something considered befittingly respectable. Not for him the shame of grandmother Lucy, that regular imbiber, who supposedly slaked herself stone-dead, leaving behind in the Cheal disturbing whispers to sear the family pride of the remaining Hortons. And her family the Westlands, who farmed nearby in Moulton, must also have equally suffered the shame of that branding, yet unproved rumour: the infiltration of her enlarged and lumpy cirrhosed liver, by supping too many drams!

6

After his father's death in 1889, George Horton, at 35, was single, lusty and strong as an ox. However did he manage – you know what! There had to be some romantic interludes within a walking-mile of 'the Cheal'; a girl, kind and understanding, suffering in the same way (you never know, there might be other brothers and sisters I never got to know; although I looked and listened (as one does), no evidence ever came to light of any other secret siblings from those early times – the one exception was yet to come). But those endless 'thudging grips', which must have tempted him sorely; sinfully reminding him of his pressing frustrations. And in an attempt to be helpful, the parson's advice would never waiver: keep sanctity within your life; wait for the Holy Matrimonial thus avoiding wicked fornication, even though it appears to be loving. In truth, it's the obscene work of the tempting Devil, stoking up your sinful desires to blemish the pureness of your life.

The dutiful man was at last his own *master*. Captain Gleed (of Donnington), a local squire and the family landlord, in due respect and sympathy, made a solemn promise of continuation: 'George, I will never turn you out; your family have been such reliable tenants.' In those days such verbal promises were regarded as sacred bonds and as such usually accepted without even a niggling degree of doubt. That was almost all Horton needed: security of tenure, affording opportunity. Plus one more thing: a strong and fertile wife to provide him with sons who would in their turn give him security in his old age, as he had given to his own parents (and some members of his family) over so many serving years. In old age there was no state pension, and poor relief was considered to be degrading; *free* money was for the undeserving, quite often considered feckless, or even criminally inclined.

Horton, lonely without a wife, was still celibate – that was obvious. More in doubt was his chastity at this mature age. Had he already, pleasantly managed to 'cock his leg over' (in a furtive loving fashion) to prove the fertility of his seed? He certainly had some urgent catching up to do. On average he was ten years away from the male actuarial expectancy of death (at around 45). It followed that any children he fathered stood an unfavourable chance of being orphaned before they reached their teenage years. (Yet this ageing man still managed to sow my seed some 33 years later; at the age of 68 – preposterous! incredible! and surely thought impossible?) Yet why such a fuss? Many 14-year-old boys would have been capable of that, if only the facts of life had been more readily available.

Without question, George Horton's concern was now himself. A new situation had arisen: at last he was free of parental obligation; had succeeded to the farm lease; lived alone at home (except for the visiting daily domestic); and he had the benefit of the inheritance from his father (which was largely of his own making, as the loyal family slave). After all those years of frustration, could a probability already have happened: something sinful that now was good. That in the Cheal or somewhere close by, there was a paternity order in force. That there already existed a child (preferably a male, to bear the mantle of the family drudge), and a ready-made wife for the want of rescuing, who would double up her duties in the expected ways, both personal and domestic; thus rolling the paternity payments and the previous servant's wages, into the total household expenses – thereby helping to relieve any extramarital, financial burden of a court ordered enforcement.

But Gosberton Cheal was the last place on earth to be easily sinful – except, perhaps, on moonlit nights, on haystacks, or in cowsheds, when groping and panting would sometimes happen out of prying human sight.

As hastily as respectably possible, there was now need for fertile mating. Like a royal of a kingdom, he needed a female to duplicate himself and continue to extend his family's line. A comely wife was needed; one as strong as an ox; capable of fulfilling a woman's obligations: to yield forth a cluster of children (preferably boys), to provide tied, cheap labour on the family farm. But thoughts, however well intentioned, must not give rise to false assumptions. Even if Horton had created a secret family, nothing from this past ever came to light – not even a spurious claim! On the surface he was a good living man; now a *master* in full confidence of knowing his place in life. What went on beneath the surface, that fleshly bubbling and troubling was expected to be tightly held under the steaming cauldron's lid.

It would be remarkable if fleshly feelings had not closed together, even in the-back-of-beyond, Gosberton Cheal. Quite apart from that, merging-time had come; acres joined other acres; a bit from here and a bit from there, getting ever bigger, wider and longer. The landlords sold; the new thrusting yeomen bought the land. In time, inflation would come back again, which, despite the woeful cries from politicians, can be a good thing, especially when the value of your property increases and the repayments of the mortgage appear to shrink as your inflated income expands. Yes, so it seems, widespread inflation can be bad, but in some respects it's a positive advantage. Politicians are not always right – sometimes they are downright wrong!

7

Events moved faster than expected; a fertile seed would begin its germination inside a mistress's womb. By late October or early November in 1891, less than a decent period after his father's death, in January 1889, the Horton daily-domestic was pregnant. Complicated enough in normal course, the local people would be dumbfounded at the fall from grace of one of their very own.

> Some lovers do intensely tread:
> Forming, performing, readily;
> Imitating a cock's momentum,
> As it lustfully treads the hens.

The Victorians, who could not bring themselves to use that 'pregnant' word. With suitable heavy-headed nodding and anxious, discreet whispering they selected their own telling descriptions, from a longish well-tried list; leaving no doubt as to this poor servant's condition:

In trouble, up the stick or the spout, in the pudding club; in a certain condition; fallen-slipped, tripped, unfortunate, lost, broken kneed/winged, legged, ruined; had strayed or sinned.

In accordance with the strict rule of convention, discreet action was needed. George Horton would have to marry the girl, or risk the sting of a riding crop or the blast from an angry shotgun. Apart from that, the local vicar would voice his pennyworths in pounds.

But never mind the scathing to come, just spare a thought for those affected by Horton's lusts of the flesh, so shockingly performed, soon after his father's death. It was enough to cause the old boy (now spongy dead), painfully to reheat himself and smash through the lid of his highly polished, timber coffin, with his hard domy head. And then to sit bolt upright, before stabbing the air with his rotting forefinger and releasing his feelings in a scream of anger directed towards his son's careless horniness. Making a doorstep mess, indeed! – with (of all the girls readily available) the family's serving wench, instead of a respectable maiden with good prospects of inheriting a few rich acres.

To make matters worse, this was a family mess. Mary Mawer was a member of Thomas Mawer's family who lived in Chesboule Lane, about a mile from the Cheal. Thomas was the brother of Joseph Mawer, who also lived locally, at Station Cottage, Mill Lane (according to the Census of 1891) and was married to Horton's sister, Alice. So this was a potential scandal, awaiting to be respectably settled before the bulging began to stretch her pinny and loosen wagging tongues.

Poor Mary Mawer, that maiden so cruelly violated. Now deeply within the hell of her looming confinement, to the day when her *sin* would be bawling and highly visible. And as the days passed by it became increasingly obvious that, for whatever reason, George Horton was not going to marry the maid. So yet another bastard child was born, a ready target for human scorn, by the respectable folk who would be so deeply affronted by this living proof of lustful passion, sinfully performed.

After all, did not thoughtful William Shakespeare throw a crumb of comfort to all born bastards in the following verse:

Why brand they us with base? ...
Who in the lusty stealth of nature take
More composition and fierce quality
Than doth, within a dull, stale, tired bed,
Go to creating a whole tribe of fops...?

King Lear I.ii

Now that the procreative mode had fully slipped into gear, the pace soon gathered speed. Shockingly, on the 29th August, 1892, some 13 months after the birth of George Horton Mawer, on the 27th July, 1861 – a short, somewhat indecent period to suffer remorse and retribution, to say the least! – that elderly *roué*, George Horton (now aged 38 and considered creeping towards old age) married a virginal maiden, just turned 18 years of age. Alice Mawer was her name, a daughter of Thomas Mawer, the family already violated by the lusty *Staghorn.* That cheeky, overheated devil! In addition to Horton's animal nickname, some villagers would spit out their honest scorn – at that 'dirty old-man' and his disgusting, virile habits. Others might, on the other hand, wink and smile and envy his breathtaking displays of carefree living. Whatever next? Steady on! – such ramrod displays are so unbecoming. (But that name: George Horton Mawer. Registered by Mary's irate father for the birth certificate. It was customary in those days, in case of any temporary impediment against a marriage, to include the father's surname at least. Here we have the full treatment. Then, if later on a marriage did take place, in this case, the Mawer appendage would be dropped from the name, or Horton-Mawer would sprout a hyphen.)

After such a scandal, surely, in too much indecent haste, all now seemed to be forgiven. Thomas Mawer, although injured by the recent violation of Mary, turned up at the register office and signed as witness on the marriage certificate, in nearby Spalding town. At last, Horton was now respectable

32

and responsible, able to settle down on his rented 53 acres, in the Cheal, with that 'never turn you out, George', promise from the landlord, Captain Gleed, still ringing in his ears. It was time to nestle and breed. And hopefully to repeat his previous performance by producing strong, compliant and dependable sons, to keep him in his old age. At last his time had come! It had taken long enough – in those days almost a lifetime long.

What news of George Horton Mawer? Still an infant, not even able to speak, let alone protest at the scandalous behaviour affecting his innocent life so much. Poor little beggar! – he would have to make the best of his precious baby innocence, until his rude awakening came: that he would be stigmatised for ever more – Amen! Of one thing there would be no doubt; local people in the know would never forget the 'Horton' in his name, which he would eventually try to erase.

But 'considering his background', how would this disadvantaged child get on? This much I learnt when I listened to the whispers: he grew over six feet tall, served in a Scots guards' regiment in the 1914–18 World War, and had established a successful business in nearby Spalding. (Much later on I briefly met this man – my half-brother. He gave me an odd, cursory inspection and never said a direct word. When you learn of the embarrassment it caused him and my dire circumstances at the time – how could you blame him!)

George Horton's failure to marry both Mary Mawer and my mother (though he made an 'honest' woman of Alice) seemed in startling contrast against the uncompromising, high state of morality that he steadfastly postulated and seemed so deeply immersed within.

Setting aside the gossip, scandal, tragedy, good times and bad, what was then left to describe as normal? Noses low on the grindstone, eyes down to the ground.

With hard work being the rule of the day (every day, except the Sabbath), no wonder those independent folk were bemused when advanced machinery came along to lighten their harsh enslavement. What would they do without hard work? Book reading was branded downright time wasting; the piano was suspect; no wireless cinema, or TV existed – what would they do for entertainment? (apart from talking to each other, which they did quite a lot). They enjoyed what was available: plenty of fresh food, and whatever free delights surrounded them. No wonder the families kept on expanding, often at an alarming rate. Their surplus children drifted away in menial bondage, usually to the growing towns, along the sprawling railway network. And often they achieved success: they were accustomed to hard work and striving desperately to be independent.

'All's well that ends well!' – that was the thankful motto if some calmness came after so many desperate struggles.

8

The Clough, Cheal and Risegate fields,
Are rich and bountiful in their yields;
But if prices and demand are poor,
Over the land (so worrisome)
The crops remained unsold.

And human life to compound the plight,
Could be swamped by desolation;
In saddened times – when,
The funeral sounds of a tolling bell;
Jarred the grieving frozen minds.

That doleful warning knell,
Vibrating across the flattened fens;
Reverently disturbing, backache toiling,
Of labourers working in the fields –
Listen! the passing-bell is sorrowing.

With the marriage of George Horton to Alice Mawer in 1892, and his previously unfortunate breach in life, which increased the Mawer family with that 'unnatural' child, George Horton Mawer, in 1891, it seemed that the Mawer and Horton families were destined anyway to be inextricably linked. His sister Alice had already married Joseph Mawer, and produced yet another Alice and Fred, who also expanded the family. In those days, and back still further to the times before the railways spread across the land, courting was mainly done on foot, by couples living in nearby places, a mile or so away.

Around 1900 onwards, a strange sight began appearing on those flat Fenland roads: the tubular-framed bicycle, mounted on two wheels, pushed along by folk with the straightest backs you've ever seen – such dignity! This latest innovation moved as if by magic, without the feet touching the ground. It liberated the working class; they could now work and do their courting several miles away from home.

No wonder in the days of walking (for the common people anyway) the local families inter-married with other families round about; not quite incestuously, but getting a little near the mark, producing many *tribal* similarities: a broad forehead and a prominent nose (but not a hooked Roman one).

Since 1760 (and perhaps before that) it was the proud Horton family custom to name their first-born child, George. From that date four Georges had worn that dynastic mantle (how astonishingly brave when history shows up time and time again what happens to ruling dynasties, never mind the aspiring ones).

Now it became only too apparent – 'the sins of the fathers do descend upon the children!' How unfortunate it was that that first *Staghorn* child produced in fornication, George Horton Mawer, would be brought up in the same district. Now, a first-born 'natural' child to George and Alice (even though in every way legitimate) could never be named George – such an unfortunate duplication would be regarded as incredulous. Think of the derision, especially from the village wags, if such a thing had happened and two 'George Horton' offspring ever appeared side by side, or even apart. What comparisons would be made? More to the point, what would be said by the jocular villagers: 'Which one are you, George the 1st or George the 2nd?'

The continuity of that cherished family name would be dragged into dire disgrace. And another thing to seriously ponder: would one or both inherit that animal nickname? That abominable, beastly 'Staghorn' tag.

George would smarten up sometimes, at funerals, weddings and other essentially formal occasions. A funereal, double-breasted suit in fashionable black, of best quality heavy-duty cloth, was his defiant sartorial answer to the slightest change in fashion. His impressive coat was fastened up with black cloth-covered buttons and, further up, the generously cut sharp, pointed lapels surrounded a bold cravat (also in jet black), suspended under a stiff starched collar (which proudly held his head erect through good times and bad). Attached below the collar was a long voluminous shirt, tucked so snugly over his bodily bits and pieces – the extravagance of wearing underwear was never even considered and this same garment could double up as a warm nightshirt.

His large picture-photograph hanging proudly in 'the room' showed a captured gaze more like that of a successful squire, than an ever hopeful, struggling yeoman.

George Horton's marriage soon began to prove fruitful, as would be hoped for after proving himself on that first 'out-of-bounds' with Mary Mawer, the serving maid. 'Divide and multiply' – this urging came directly from 'the Good Book' – that's what they uprightly believed. It was probably just as well they followed those instructions in such anxious times: the death rate was so high that replacements were constantly needed.

Two healthy boys were born in quick succession. On the 14th May, 1893, Horton's near child bride Alice, was delivered of a healthy male child, William, in a normal gestation period, well within the respectable confines of marriage. This time *Staghorn* had not too hastily rutted; tampering had not taken place until the time it was right and legal so to do. Strictly speaking, this was not a honeymoon child either; honeymoon indeed – what a waste of time! Cattle never went on honeymoon (or 'treaclemoon', as Lord Byron described it). Duty bound, the groom took what came, when it did, in rightful entitlement.

John Thomas, the second child, was born on the 30th August, 1894. At this rate of progress, a working family team seemed to be assured. Thus far, these two lads provided double-indemnity insurance: two male family slaves to work on the farm for board and keep and a tiny allowance to spend on themselves (more often than not, next to nowt). But to name the child John Thomas (after the paternal grandfathers, John Horton and Thomas Mawer) blatantly parading that Victorian euphemistic name for the male penis – small wonder that he reverted to calling himself plain Thomas.

At long last, but not before time, with the promised future tenure of his land, and a healthy child-bearing wife, George Horton was on his hopeful way.

Average life expectancy for a man in those days was around 45, for a woman 51. It follows therefore that many born into this world would not even reach those optimum ages – sadly, many children were cruelly orphaned.

A tragedy upset the tranquillity of the Cheal in 1879. Human loss and sorrow was officially recorded in a Certified Copy of an Entry of Death: Branton Sansam (age 40) died, Lucy Horton's husband of only eleven precious years from the time of their brave elopement. They bolted along the London and North Eastern railway line, on their way 'up to town', where they married in Maize Hill Chapel, in the district of Greenwich in the county of Kent on the 16th July, 1868, according to the Rites and Ceremonies of the Independents. Branton was entered 29 years old, and Lucy 21; at the ages when parental legal consent would not be needed, although they had protested, so I was led to understand. In those strict days opposition to family marriages could be hard and fierce.

Four children were orphaned on that tragic day: Branton, b. 1869; Annie, b. 1871; George, b. 1873; Horton, b. 1874: my goodness that was going some – four children in five years, considered normal in those days. But how would widow, Lucy Sansam, manage? There was no comforting capital sum from the estate, or any large life insurance. With four children's mouths to feed, all under school-leaving age, what could she do? More importantly, what would she be expected to do: take in washing? remarry as soon as possible? or be lonely and disconsolate in her widow's weeds? Not Lucy! She fought gallantly to survive, even though she was stretched to near impossible limits, according to the accounts I heard.

There was no poor relief for a woman of property, no matter how lowly her circumstances. In final desperation there was always the workhouse, which she and her family managed to evade. Vegetables were plentiful; rabbits for the pot, and the odd cut from a neighbour's slaughtered pig might occasionally have been dropped at her door. Brother George helped as much as he could. I heard him mention this in later times (and no wonder, with some intensity of feeling when his own fraught time came along). He also taught farming practice to Branton, his nephew, who remained wedded to the land. Although desperately plighted, along with many others, the Sansam family valiantly struggled and managed to retain a foothold on their land. Lucy's father John's small legacy in 1889 would have been a fortune to a widow proudly battling against the kicks in life.

Branton not only took his father's forename, eventually he inherited part of the family estate comprising five acres, one rood and 15 perches, together with the family red-brick cottage in the Cheal (a structure called home, built as basically as possible, poking up from the flat countryside, depressingly forlorn, like many other crude hovels, similarly slum-like but adequately suitable for society's labouring slaves). Although he was an excellent market gardener, it's as well Branton remained single – one mouth would be more than enough to feed. No wonder his grandfather, John

Horton, had objected to his father's marriage to Lucy, his daughter: 'Bah! Why not wait until you find a man with better prospects and far more freehold acres than a miserable five.'

Many people's lives were forever being unsettled: not by having too much; from having too little and more often than not far less than that. For such was the bother of too much depression; there seemed no way out of the impasse they were up to the necks in. And sometimes from around a blind corner came the raw unexpected, when the skin of life would suddenly be shrivelled away.

During 1893, Horton's brother-in-law, Fred Mawer, aged 40 (married to his sister Alice), committed suicide by hanging at Station Cottage, Gosberton Risegate. He had loaded his entire potato crop on an open railway wagon and overnight an unexpected hard frost had destroyed the lot. He left a widow and three children of school age. (This cottage was to be my own birthplace. Often, I was frit but morbidly curious during my enquiring childhood, when the older children pointed out the hook over which Fred hung the rope to take his life.) A previous tenant, so it was rumoured, had drowned himself in the drainage cut at the front of the cottage. This place is *cursed*, was the considered village opinion: overlooking the fact that a nine-acre smallholding was at best a precarious foothold living; more likely than that, a way to disaster. In truth, despite all the honest plodding, all the hopes and teeth gritting, this smallholding was too small to be viable; especially if misfortune came, which it had with monotonous regularity. Not so friendly 'Station Cottage' better to change to 'Doomsday Holme' – a place of ruin and death!

Yes, George was always good for a few bob if times were lean or tragedy descended, which it was sure to do from time to time. Apart from assisting some of his neighbours, he helped to support both his widowed sisters and their seven school-age children (would that if ever a desperate time came on him, they would be sympathetic and helpful in return).

In 1902 Horton's wife Alice (now aged 28) was carrying their third child, after a gap of several years since the birth of their last child, John Thomas. Towards the 'end of her time' Alice became a tragic victim of a progressive medical condition that could be a certain cause of death in those days: the dreaded eclampsia. Fully recorded on the Death Certificate as 'Pregnancy Albuminata Eclampsia' – followed by the almost obligatory 'Exhaustion' which speaks volumes by itself.

In 1902, how could a country doctor, Dr Davison, cope with this potential killer? Professional ante-natal care would be non-existent (for the people isolated in the country, remote as the Cheal); except for old wives' tales, and untrained local village 'midwives' with practical experience, coping as best they could, totally incapable of dealing with child-birth risks beyond the normal – the normal ones were difficult enough. That the act of creation could bring death proved that being born could be a dicey business – never mind the risks of living.

George Horton, after some ten years of marriage, was now abruptly widowed. Sons, William aged nine, and John Thomas, aged eight, were motherless; not only cruelly robbed of their mother, the stillborn embryo was a girl so they were also robbed of a sister. Across the social barriers there was no escape from untimely death: the sudden departing, long before the end that might be reached; so often did it happen, it became an accepted part of normal living – funerals were expected and usually followed by a slap-up 'knife and fork' tea.

Now pause for one moment and consider some recent family events; of the cruelly unexpected, in this case three: Horton's brother-in-law, Branton Sansam, died in 1874 (age

41

37); brother-in-law, Joseph Mawer, tragically died in 1893 (age 40); and finally, in 1902, Alice, his wife (age 28), and stillborn daughter, both died. The average age of those adults, at 35, being well short of the then life expectancy of both male and female.

' "Things" happen in threes!' was believed by many village folk; as though it had been sacredly written: yet another layer of superstition? Or was it just a shrug of acceptance that there would always be distressful 'threes' – or 'ones' and 'twos', or whatever combination might eventually come along to explain away the unexpected?

9

The 'river' in the Risegate village extended to the east through the Risegate outfall into the river Welland and then the Wash. It was called the river 'Or' or 'Haw', or 'Hoare' – or even 'Whore' – depending on each villager's varied tone of speaking: repeating the sounds passed down by previous generations; such was the likeness of these inflections, the lot was accepted as one. But the more this question was looked into – the obvious began to look different. Our village 'river' flowed duty-bound, especially after a storm had passed. It was really a drain which had been hacked out of the earth by men with spades and wheelbarrows, outside of living memory, to relieve the surrounding fields from the constant danger of flooding.

Originally named 'ea' – from the Old English meaning 'stream' – it was later changed (by the Norman-French influence) to 'eau', but would still be pronounced 'or' instead of 'o'. On published maps it is not called the River Eau (the 'river-stream'), it is correctly printed: Risegate Eau. Throughout all my growing years in the village, no one ever corrected this common error. I always called it the 'River Or' – everyone understood, so why all the fuss, except perhaps, to pedanticise.

Now consider this further bit of frustration: why did they call the next village 'Clow', when the spelling was Clough? The dictionary pronunciation = kluf: a ravine or steep valley, usually with a torrent bed. Not exactly a true description of a drainage sewer. A clue turned up on the old maps where it was referred to as the 'Risegate Clowe': not a village at

43

that time; a sluice in the then larger village of Risegate ('Clowe' being the German word for sluice, dam or floodgate; until Anglicised to Clough (as in cloud), by the drainage engineers.) Later becoming the name of a separate village after the sluice became redundant. Further towards the Wash there was Lampton's Clowe and near Holbeach another clowe, both sluices eventually no longer needed; the latter becoming the village of Holbeach Clough.

The derivation of the 'Risegate', my birth village, presented a much wider problem – albeit an intriguing one. The spellings on the old maps varied between 'Rysgate' and its present form, suggesting that this might simply have been a case of misspelling: the interchange of 'y' with 'i', a common variation in those days.

Until the facts were further examined it might even have been suggested that the Risegate village was the first place in the world to fit a 'rising' hinge to a gatepost; to clear the gate, wide opening over a holus-bolus of cow muck, and other clogging farmyard bits and pieces, growing into an obstructive mould. But that explanation seemed out of question: the rising hinge needed securing with stout screws and the newly invented English screw did not come into use until around 1830, when it was invented. The Risegate/Rysgate names on the old map long pre-dated that.

From examination of the old plans, showing the drainage system in some detail, one interesting fact emerges: in the early days, into the first quarter of the twentieth-century (at least), all the drainage dykes surrounding the nearby fields had a 'sluice' at every discharge point into the main Eau sewer to the south and north of this watercourse. These sluices would be closed (i.e. wound down) to prevent the water flowing back into the Fen when there were very high water levels in the Risegate Eau, and opened (wound up) to enable the water in the dyke to be discharged. Local folk authorised by the water board would operate the 'sluice gates' – raising or lowering them according to the quantity of settled surface water, thus keeping the main drain and dykes in balance and from being overwhelmed (as the excess water flowed to escape). These 'gates' were fitted into the end of brick culverts under the roads on either side of the Eau sewer, and the 'gate' was moved vertically in a metal frame by a man-powered, handle-driven screwshaft.

Would it not be possible over time for those sluice gates to be named 'rise-gates'? And like 'clowe' be used as another name for a sluice. In an area with so many of them in constant use, it seems reasonable to suppose that 'risegate' would eventually be used to name the surrounding area.

In 1295, in the reign of Edward III (some 229 years after the Norman invasion) our bossy Norman masters still had not settled down, which provides a further valuable piece of information and deserved due consideration.

In that year it was recorded upon an inquisition taken at Gosberchirche that '...the sewer of Risegate had gutters which ought to be repaired and maintained by the towns of Gosberchirche and Rysgate [a good example of using both 'i' and 'y' spellings], and that it was obstructed by Ranulph de Rye towards the marsh, and likewise that it ought to be of the same breadth and depth, and that there ought to be a sluice betwixt the marsh and it of sixteen-feet wide; and that the course of that sewer, which towards the sea was called Newe Eegate had wont anciently to ran directly through the midst of the marsh in Gosberchirche, belonging to the Abbot of Peterborough, until 36 years before...'

So there it is, the difficult de Rye was unwilling to allow access to his land to enable the drainage improvements to be carried out. Clearly, two village (town) spellings are used in the above report. Was there already a 'rise-gate' privately constructed by de Rye to control the flow of excess floodwater from the gutters into the sewer? Was this sluice known as

45

Rye's-gate – eventually to become the Risegate village name, after a little adjustment in the spelling? Who knows...? Somewhere in the archives must exist the true answer.

10

During my early impressionable childhood years in the Lincolnshire Fenland community where I grew up, people seemed not so arbitrarily divided into slots of lower and middle classes. They talked in the same accent (often included dialect words), wore dungarees during their working day and were inclined to grumble a lot. All in all, they formed that range of menfolk more broadly described as 'sons of the soil'.

Apart from the wide estates owned by the powerful church, the dukes and lords of privilege had never bothered to usurp large marshland estates – not even when the Fens were better drained. Our local Norman gentry, de Cressy and de Rye, were small fry and very soon gobbled up. Unrelenting struggling was the normal way of life, forging the local toughened culture: down to earth and practical.

My mother, Elizabeth Ann Green, known as Lizzie or Liz (not so much in those days to imitate the proles, not just to be matey; not even out of a fine sense of economy to reduce the amount of lettering – much more in friendliness, often tinged with simple affection) was born on the 3rd December, 1876, in the village of Gosberton Risegate (pronounced locally 'the Rysgit', or so it sounded to me) in the house opposite Station Cottage, the dwelling said to have a curse on it, or so some local people said – destined to be my birthplace and early 'home sweet home'.

At the time of Alice Horton's death in childbirth (3rd April, 1902), Lizzie was once more living at home, after lodging with her sister Florence (Flo) then married and living in Keighley, Yorkshire, in the north, far along the railway line. Liz had been employed by a confectioner, but the intense heat in the bakehouse caused her to have severe nose bleeds. So for the time being she was in a state of *resting*, and no doubt re-considering her choice of career. She was now aged 26, living in an age when women's careers were slavishly tied to the kitchen sink and progressive bouts of childbearing.

Liz's father, Edward Green, was born in Spalding Common in 1845, and at the comparatively early age of 24 married Dorcas Hannah Sharp, aged 23 (he managed a signature, she signed with an X). He (my maternal grandfather) died in 1918, at the ripe old age of 73, of Fibroid Phthisis (not tubular). And the good doctor, E. Morris, MRCS, added clarification to the death certificate: not the usual clincher, *senile decay*, but *heart failure* – which occurs to us all sooner or later, so in this respect he was on a certain 'each-way' winner.

Edward's father, also named Edward, married Frances Noble in the parish church of Spalding on the 18th August, 1844. Both Edward and Frances signed their marks with a cross, which were suitably witnessed. It would appear from this sample of two generations, three out of four were illiterate and that schooling for the labouring poor was scarce or non-existent.

Although both Edwards were described as labourers, my grandfather also engaged in sub-contract work, usually in the winter months, when he agreed a price with the farmers for riddling the potatoes in those long straw and earth-protected potato 'graves', usually positioned in the field by the side of a handy road. In the locality, Edward was known by his nickname: 'Tattie-Green'. On his death he left some £40 (in gold sovereigns) in a tin carefully hidden away from Dorcas, his wife, now separated from him and living in her own small cottage in the same village. What a scandal that

48

would have aroused at the end of the nineteenth century: not of 'living in sin' – for wickedly coming asunder! Yet, after bringing up seven children, it must be considered a near-miracle that they had any surplus energy left to even think of escaping from each other – so deadlocked in their tried wedlock had they become.

Purely of statistical interest, but not a good scientific sample, out of the seven Green children brought up 'strictly chapel' only one retained a lifetime's enthusiasm for regular church attendance.

Of their later permanent lifetime's marital arrangements, one daughter was to be unfortunately entangled and doomed to 'live in sin', outside the bonds of formal blessing. But again, consider the mathematics: six out of seven dutifully conformed to the rites of marriage – the only state then decently to live in and die in when the time came. A very high standard indeed, but unacceptable – it was not high enough! For if morality is allowed to weaken, what then comes along as a substitution?

Once more living at home, for the health reasons previously stated, Lizzie Green was an ideal temporary choice to fill the post of housekeeper to the widower, George Horton, and become a surrogate mother to his children, William now aged 9 and Thomas aged 8, so cruelly made motherless by the convulsions of the dreaded eclampsia – inexplicable to children's understanding. Lizzie's upbringing within a large family, used to country struggling would be an asset to a widowed farmer, with all the problems associated with the land; and the empty space of wife and mother – a vacancy so difficult to try and fill.

During her working period in Yorkshire Liz had become engaged to a young man of some promise: wasn't he the son of an alderman – no less? My word, that was going some for a simple country maid. An engagement ring (a cluster of gold spaghetti, with various stones set in the strands), proudly shown and sparkling – appearing to be somewhat superior to the usual slim-line ones of poorer country girls. Many letters were kept in her drawer, lovingly tied in blue ribbon, and not only that, there were stuffed and embroidered 'sweetheart cushions', with 'I love you', or other deeply felt endearments neatly stitched thereon (in the days when *love-making* was only fostered within the purity of the mind).

It was only a question of a little more time before the final clinching wedding ring would be dutifully fitted. More time indeed... She'd already been courting and mooning for five years, at least! There was first the 'walking out' period, before the parental approval visits, leading to the couple's feet finally being accepted *under both families' tables.* Then, there was order about; certain conduct had to take place – anything less was not respectable and not true to the form of the day.

Liz's fiancé made regular romantic visits to keep up his serious intent as all true lovers would and should. But sadly, one of his visits became his last – he simply, silently, turned away – did a bunk and never came back! The pile of love letters stopped expanding, those stuffed, sweet-heart endearments began to fade and fray a little from too much fondling.

But why did he go 'off the boil'? The truth I never discovered. Many years later, Aunt Kate of Lincoln told me this story: on his last visit, Liz's betrothed took back a skep of fruit (the wicker basket kind) and he never bothered to return the empty which, as every polite country person knows, is an ill-mannered thing to do.

Lizzie Green continued in her career as housekeeper and surrogate mother, a valuable support for George Horton, the widower. Other suitors did show an interest but without success. Deep in her heart, and firmly in her mind, she expected *him* to return, with that empty skep. She now had no time to sit and moon (though melancholy must have pained). Becoming committed, she cared for those two sorrow-stricken children and fully occupied herself with all the burdensome duties that cropped up, day by day: the washing, the cooking, the cleaning, in an almost primitive way. The 'appliance' in those days was human application: the carpet beater; the scrubbing brush; the coal-fired oven; the potties under the bed, daily needing emptying; the washing, bubbling in the copper, 'podged' of dirt by a three-legged dolly; the water for every use carried in buckets from the pump. She would also feed the pigs and hens and collect the eggs. During the busy farming seasons (in her spare time) she would also lend a hand to pick the ripened fruit.

11

Within the first quarter of the twentieth century, again something happened and repeated. There were large sales of land from 1906 to 1914, and the even bigger turnover after the World War ended in 1918. The landowners for various reasons (selling at the top, the obvious one) were perhaps getting fed up with years of depressed rents and uncertainty; the tenants screaming for relief in bad times, or even worse, doing their moonlight flits! And there's nothing like boom conditions to excite throwing all previous caution to the wind. Buyers rushed in, raising the wherewithal so essential, more often in those days from an attorney, usually eager to lend from funds available, at the most advantageous rate of interest. Apart from having to be tenacious, by the very nature of their risks, farmers must be among the most tried gamblers on earth.

> The Cheal, Clough and Risegate fields,
> Are rich and plentiful in their yields;
> But if prices and demand are poor,
> The quiet land (devoid of feeling)
> Brings forth its own whirlwind.
> Land prices high, land prices low;
> Sell on top, buy when down.

Remember Mark Twain's sensible advice about buying land: '...buy ... they're ... not making any more of it'.

Yet, surprisingly, in all the years of four generations, back to 1760, the Horton family never owned any patch of land, except their purchased burial spaces – not for them the choking mortgage millstone to tightly constrict their necks.

Then, at last, it came to pass, in Gosberton Cheal, during the booming land prices in AD 1907, some 18 years after Captain Gleed's promise, 'George, I will never turn you out!', that the 'never' abruptly dropped out of that promise. And this lamentation from George would be forever repeated – perhaps too often: 'Captain Gleed promised that he would never turn me out – and he did!' But a promise is no more than hopeful intention – even when it's solemnly made and seems so firmly set (unless it is witnessed, or signed and sealed, and even then it might end up conditional; or far too vague to seek amends). The stark truth is: some promises run out of time, as this one obviously did – even the best of intentions can blur. The disbelief of Horton's plaintive questioning often rippled in my childhood mind: Why! why! why! was I so dispossessed? (For one simple reasons: land prices were high; it was time to sell and make a handsome profit.)

Although there were signs of changes creeping in, some ways seemed forever endurable, for 'the olde ways were the best!' – the trying ways that severely tested, not only the body, the very soul! But in recent times (and they can include a century or two) the past and present were slowly merging – but not without resistance. The old-timers would sniff, and snort with scorn at most of the innovations coming along; removing some of the back-breaking work that they had been accustomed to from their early days, which they probably believed was truly ordained. Before mechanisation human muscle power was described by the experts as 'labour intensive'. On the smaller farms, those traps of drudging work often enslaved the entire family for rewards of little or nowt. On the larger establishments the labouring classes were cheaply available: grateful if they could clothe their backs, have a bed to sleep on, a roof over their heads and a hope of filling their bellies. What more could they possibly want?

So off to work they would go: round and round the fields; up and down the rows; acres and acres of them – ploughing, hoeing, raking, spinning; pulling, slashing, picking. Day by day grinding away in tedious repetition, on the farm – the factory in the open country, in the fresh air and blazing sunshine, in the snow and in the rain. Some seeds were planted individually, with a dibber stick (fashioning an indentation, like a maiden's breasts). Mangolds and beans went into those exquisitely rippled impressions. Seed was also sown by broadcasting by hand from a lip seed suspended at waist level by a strap over the sower's shoulder. Scattered over rough ground (the pacing out and scattering kept to a practised tempo), the seed afterwards buried by harrows (perhaps nowadays hard to believe, I watched my Father Horton do this, in 1926). Back in the olden time corn was hand-weeded in May and June by a plentiful supply of young labour. Boys and girls (often of a tender age) were also employed scaring off the birds from the newly-sown or sprouting crops. At harvest time the wheat would be cut by a sickle or scythe by a team of harvesters; if necessary, working on into the bright moonlight. A reaping band comprising five men and women, sharing the work equally, would harvest two acres a day. As the scythes eventually took over from the sickle, they were wielded by men. Extra care was taken to 'keep the heel of the scythe down' as the blade mowed through the corn. And they would exercise special care not to slice a finger off, when they sharpened the blade's dangerous razor edge, with the stone carried in a pouch hanging from a belt. Those who made up the straw bands to secure the sheaves found it impossible to avoid the stinging nettles or those equally fearsome pricking, thistles (well do I remember this suffering, as late as 1936, when, at age 14, I started work on a labour-intensive farm).

Astonishment, even some alarm, arose from the middle of the nineteenth century. In the fields a mechanical, clattering contraption, pulled along by noble shire horses – the newfangled reaper – was disturbing the quiet rural scene. By 1871 it was estimated that a quarter of Britain's corn crop was being mechanically harvested.

For some time the stackyard still survived, along with the steam threshing engine (first puffing in from the 1840s) – but not for long. By 1946 the combine harvesters were trickling in, gobbling up the harvest fields, extracting the grain, grinding up the straw for easy ploughing, or ejecting it ready for the baler to collect. No longer was it necessary to employ nine threshing operatives producing ten tons of grain per day: the combine harvester could beat that in one hour. It was like a plough might appear to ancient man. Yet this latest costly innovation took some time to grab the lead. To be truly efficient it needed larger fields, no restrictive hedges, and dykes (if possible) to be culverted – the prairie had arrived in dear old England.

But listen! Slowly but surely, the put-putting tractor was beginning to establish itself; despite its use at first being scorned by many farmers. So the horse still appeared to remain unchallenged, but only for the time being. By 1939 the tractor number in use grew to around 55,000; with 700,000 horses still working on the land. It was in 1946 that the tractor number in use really took off, when the Ferguson TE20 arrived on the scene. It was highly successful because it was so versatile (and only fed while it was toiling). And without as much as a word of command, it would burst in action at the flick of a switch, powering its mobility and the specially designed implements, to do so many jobs previously done by horse or man. Sadly but inexorably that magnificent beast of burden, the shire horse, became a near-endangered species. Except for a few treasured teams, they would disappear from the country scene. Awaiting a gallant return? One day perhaps – who knows!

There were many more changes to come. It was enough to make some old-timers scratch their heads in disbelief. And many would be heard repeating, like a phonograph with its needle sticking: 'You cannot stop progress!' – and by golly, so it seemed!

What would Charles H. Duell, the Commissioner in the United States Office of Patents now have to say, in respect of his rather ill-timed statement in 1899? It is worth repeating, if only for a snigger: 'Everything that can be invented has been invented.'

To be fair to Commissioner Duell, he did make his confident statement in 1899. Many people before and since might be forgiven for becoming alarmed as they viewed the new inventions, widely accepted as progress but to change their settled world for ever. 'What was good enough for my grandfather and father, is good enough for me and good enough for you!'

12

The Lincolnshire Fenland Horton family, father John to son George, had rented the Gosberton Cheal 50-acre farm from around 1830; managing through good times and bad; keeping their heads above water – even to build a reserve in the bank. Theirs was the second largest farm in the hamlet and even though it was rented land, their 'master' status would be readily accepted; not only by themselves, but also by the knowingly local people.

But all that wasted rent for nigh on 80 years! Sufficient cash to buy their rented land, several times over. The beneficiary was a country Gentleman and Squire, who left the sweat and the worry with the tenant-master (though firmly holding the reins of ownership). The world seemed set in its ways, the glowing hopes of communism were yet to sparkle and burst into flames: to set the people free from exploitation; in glorious communal settlements, working happily on 'the people's' land.

In 1907 (after George had held the tenancy for 18 years), panic must have set in when Captain Gleed decided to sell his land. What on earth do you do if your farm is to be sold from under your feet at a time when opportunities for renting land were steadily decreasing and your lifetime's journey abruptly hits the buffers – clang! You could pace the floor and worry. You could even drop on your knees, but a fat lot of help that might bring.

Luckily it happened, only by sheer coincidence, that a smallholding had become vacant in the nearby village of Gosberton Risegate, about one and a half miles away. Nine acres of land, with a modest cottage and a few outbuildings, with the appropriate name of 'Station'. (The London and North Eastern passenger station was conveniently placed next door and their railway cut through the property, inconveniently isolating the far field.) Lizzie Green had now come home. 'Station Cottage' was situated opposite the house in which she was born.

With no other choice but to rent a few acres of rich flat land on which to scratch a living, this was not the place George Horton would be comfortable with. It was that *accursed* place (or so the local people said). Horton's sister (Alice) cruelly became a widow there when her husband, Joseph Mawer (aged 40), committed suicide in 1893 over the loss of his entire potato crop destroyed by frost when it was loaded overnight on an open railway wagon. And it was also remembered by the older inhabitants, that another tenant had drowned himself in the Eau flood-drain which flowed in front of the cottage, for some other sad and desperate reason.

This was not the best of omens. The boldest possible warning notice should have been displayed: BEWARE! DISASTER BECKONS.

But what a comedown in life for the proud Horton family: from 50 acres to nine. From employing workers as a 'master' now to descend to only a little above a humble cottager (a labourer, renting or owning a cottage and a field). And still Horton remained a paying tenant; at the whim of his new capitalist Squire (Harold Dods), who as well as being a landowner was a successful entrepreneur, owning many coal depots at stations along the railway line. To be absolutely fair, Squire Dods of nearby Donnington, never made Horton that 'never turn you out' promise; his security was based more on blind faith – that lightning would not strike and punish him twice. Another 'notice to quit' was inconceivable, he'd only just taken possession of his new home.

Now consider some profitable possibilities in the balance sheet of Horton's family (within which would surely now include Lizzie Green, his faithful housekeeper of five years). His two growing sons, Thomas and William, would eventually leave school and work, paying most of their earnings towards their board and keep (as was expected in those days). He had some capital in the bank (enough to cover the (likely) £20 annual rental for some years to come). And the possibility existed to rent additional fields, worked by cheap family labour to make such a gamble profitable. On the face of it, much opportunity existed for such a skilled and experienced man. So when Horton, Lizzie and the boys moved to Station Cottage, in 'the Rysgit', all was far from being lost – their life was still alive. Horton may have slipped down a few rungs in life, and far too many acres down, but the family was still far from the bottom, where much of humanity tended to pile. He had no alternative but to start again, even at the ancient age of 53, well knowing that from his background, becoming a wage-labourer would be unthinkable.

Despite all this unexpected misfortune, his sons (apart from losing their mother in childbirth, which must have remained a permanent sadness) were comparatively well off: adequately clothed and fed and brought up securely in the strict chapel tradition – of promised reward and threatened punishment. As 'natural' members of a well-known and respected local family, they were full worthy of their place in society. By no means at the top, but confidently being aware they were somewhat removed from the dreary bottom; and fully expected to retain their proud village status, as sons of a master-man.

At home, in 'the room' of Station Cottage, full of antique furniture (nowadays desirably sought after), there hung on the wall over an ancient ornate sideboard (proudly displaying past family success), a set of five framed photographs which both intrigued and caused me to wonder, when my time came along. And that was long before I could read the scripted writing, flourishing the pride of ownership, under each scene. Taken from several angles by a professional, of 'G. B. Horton's Residence' his 'Stock', 'Lands', and 'Farm'. The date underneath was 1877, and the address was stated as 'Fairfield, Michigan' (nowadays it is 4650 West Horton Road, Sand Creek MI49279). To have a fine family home is one satisfactory thing; to have a road named after the family must be the ultimate path towards final success – a proud display of the American dream. Owners of over 1,000 acres of freehold land, these descendants of Sam did not allow themselves to be in hock to a feudal landlord. More of Sam and family later on...

But when did it all start; that intense desire of the Hortons to succeed in life? Was it in their striving genes (which might also bestir my plodding mind)? It took me over 50 years to piece together many snippets of family history, and much more besides.

In the eighteenth century there was a George Horton (George, by tradition, the first male born) who died at the early age of 34 in 1781. It would be incautious to go further back. Who knows, a thief or murderer might be discovered. Described as a farmer and shopkeeper, he lived at Stickney, near Spilsby, not far from famous Boston town. He left a widow and two dependent children, and a total estate not exceeding £100. The eldest male orphan, again named George, became a successful grazier, renting his land from Richard Gleed, at a place called Offleet (near Boston, the one in England), and left around £3,000 which was a fairly useful sum, when he died in 1831 at the ripe old age of 61. He was buried by the tower of Quadring church (I found his memorial stone in 1996, now beginning to crumble, having long since served the family's grieving). Three of his older sons (out of seven children): George (again the eldest), John (my grandfather), and Samuel, took over the Cheal farm,

60

shortly before their father's death: renting 50 acres, again from Squire Gleed. William, another son, died aged 39, in 1850. His headstone stands in Wigtoft graveyard (still in good condition when I called in 1997). With twirly adornments etched thereon, he must have achieved some success in life, in order for his beneficiaries to afford the services of a stonemason.

It appears that Sam was the son who, 'suffering from a round bottom', decided to emigrate. According to the American family story: 'Two Generations of Hortons', (Sam) '...being venturesome, with a young companion (Henry Cripps, of nearby Gosberton) set out from his Cheal home when a lad of seventeen and landed at Castle Garden, New York, in 1835.' There's more of his boldness to come...

13

During the spring of 1911, a daughter of the adventuresome Sam, a second cousin of George Horton (Alice, wife of Casper Rorick, a banker of Seneca, Michigan), visited her English relations, who were still scratching away on their small dirt-farms of hedge-enclosed fertile land. And more likely than not she glowingly extolled a long list of routes to success that God's Own Country could provide.

There is no record of her impressions, but it's highly likely that Alice Rorick felt somewhat shocked at the primitive conditions the Fenland natives seemed content to wallow in. And her American forthrightness must have left a lasting impression – fancy, can you just imagine! And not for Alice to share the crude cottage conditions (not even as a welcomed guest): she stayed nearby in the town of Boston, in the comfort of the White Hart Hotel. Such grandeur and extravagance. Just you fancy that – those rich, fussy Americans! Unlike the unwashed Brits, unduly obsessed with hygiene and their creature comforts.

William and Thomas had reached the impressionable ages of 18 and 17 respectively, in 1911. No doubt, all too familiar with those pictures hanging on the wall in the 'room', showing the American Hortons' farm buildings and imposing residence (a dwelling inclined towards the English lodge-style: similar to 'Cawood Hall' in Gosberton; sporting a name so grandly resurrected). Without much doubt Alice would also have explained that it had been replaced by a fine turreted edifice, the old lodge not being sufficiently grand. The new grange, boldly showy, was more in keeping with a successful magnate rather than a country squire. But whatever name was given to this fine new structure, 'Fairfield' or 'Fruit Ridge', you can depend on it, the snobbish sort of English person would have labelled it 'Parvenu's Place', most probably out of envious disbelief that a person from such lowish beginnings could have done so well.

Without more ado, 'Americkee' was the way of bold adventure in the pursuit for equality and happiness. So this was the way the boys decided to go, to emigrate to a land where 'Jack' could equal, and often outstrip, the master. The possibilities seemed endless, so the opportunity must not be missed. Alice even suggested that their father should also emigrate, but quite apart from a looming expectation, George Horton would never have left his beloved Fens.

Any problems over the cost of their passage were soon resolved. In an agreement (at the going rate of interest) Alice arranged a loan from her husband's bank, which they subsequently paid back as soon as they possibly could. To be in debt was almost a crime; they were brought up to feel like that.

Much curiosity and excitement must have spread around the Risegate village. Some folk would be bound to ask that dampening question: when you get to 'Americkee' how on earth will you manage a living? And any answer would have to avoid any personal misgivings. And then, after a polite pause, would come a measured reply: Fancy that! Followed by a nod and another pause: just fancy that – I never did! But inwardly they might think, but be too restrained to say: The field across the way always looks greener (distance blends the mingling weeds). So mark my words – they'll wish they were back before long...

But it must have been a saddish day when they left behind loving smiles and brave waves (trying hard to disguise the misery, pretending it was not disturbing). Usually it would be a lifetime's parting, in the days when the expense of a return visit was beyond the reach of most people. So when they went they 'burnt their boats' with that hopeful one-way ticket, on their long journey across the wide Atlantic gap, brimming with a tempestuous ocean (the same stretch that nearly drowned great-uncle Sam when he was nearly blown to death, in 1835, crossing under sail). It was duly recorded in a copy of the passenger list, kept at the Public Record Office in Kew, London. The following is from entry, BT27 No. 707:

> SS *Laurentic* of the steamship line White Star Dominion (official ship no. 127959) departed 10th June 1911, from Liverpool bound for Montreal. Master: J. Mathias. Registered tonnage 9255. 1160 Statute Adults on board for a journey of 21 days. (In shipping terms, 'Adults' were those over the age of 12.)
> Contract: 66732 Mr J. T. & Mr Wm Horton. Occupation: Labourers
> Class 2nd (single unaccompanied adults, English).

(Although the ships had plenty of third-class accommodation, they travelled second. And can you blame them for avoiding the poor steerage conditions that existed down in the bowels of transatlantic passenger ships of those times?)

Postcards and letters arrived, full of excitement about the journey, and the many sights they'd seen. (After I started to walk, but before I could read (around 1926), I discovered several postcards picturing a steamship, with scrawly writing on. All stowed neatly in Horton's private chest of drawers, next to piles of cheque stubs which must have covered many years of banking. In addition, I found a photograph of two youths dressed up in their Sunday best, old enough to wear long trousers: they were complete strangers to me – shrouded and missing!

But why had these boys passed like ships in the night,

leaving hardly a ripple? If they were related (in any way), why were Lizzie and Horton so secretive? Might there have arisen future questioning? If their name was Horton, why am I called Green? What a frustration. Can you imagine? Just fancy that! Of all probable secrets, this seemed most intriguing; enough to cause much later questioning – you can easily fancy that!

Affixed with a penny stamp, one particular postcard shows the anxiety Lizzie had for their welfare, after that final goodbye. It was kept a lifetime by Tom, along with other old-country mementoes, including a book prize for regularly attending the Risegate Methodists' Sunday School.

To: Mr T. Horton,   From: Station Cottage
c/o Mr C. Rorick,   Risegate
Seneca, Michigan.
America   11th July, 1911

Dear Tom,
Thanks for letters which we have received and the cards. We were so glad to know you have landed safely and are all right. They all keep asking about you both. Mother got her card and others as well. We are all right and well, hoping you are the same. Writing letter tonight.
Goodbye with love from Lizzie. Write soon.

So wrote the housekeeper, the surrogate mother of eight years, who was so obviously concerned and fond of them. Father Horton is somewhat obliquely mentioned under the plural 'we' – you'd have thought he would at least have added, 'And lots of love from Dad', or at least something of feeling or encouragement, even if less emotional (although they were out of sight, just to prove they still lived in his mind).

Back at home (presumably as yet unknown to those innocent, adventuresome boys) something was kicking and stirring. After eight years, without any doubt, familiarity between the master and his faithful housekeeper had become too carelessly close. Whether or not she was suitably rewarded is somewhat wide of the point: Lizzie's life would soon become woefully isolated, and somewhat beyond the pale. My God! – of all things to happen! The housekeeper and surrogate mother was now sinfully in the pudding-club. Sown, seeded, and soon to sprout! My word, just fancy that happening in 1911, in a back-of-beyond village of some 60 readily offended people of puritanical disposition.

Lizzie must have been blazing mad. At the age of 36 (of a life previously unblemished) she had become pregnant by an old man of 57. 'Staghorn' – that disgustingly, over-sexed monster, had again extended his swollen pusher to recklessly ooze his seed. The letters and postcards stopped coming. Declaring a silent condemnation? What else would you expect those upright boys to do? Brought up within the acquired moral constraints of 1911, decisively to distinguish between right and wrong; the simple moralism of all decent village folk – especially of their father, a firm believer that uprightness should be the earnest aim of everyone, and so it was in his case – rigid and stiffened!

Did Alice Rorick, flexing her New-World female assertiveness (after being told of this sordid situation), become determined to rescue these innocent boys from a fast-looming scandal? For although their leaving may appear to be adventuresome, in truth it was probably opportune – saving those poor lads from a deep disgrace. One thing remains puzzling: although Lizzie was now seven months 'gone', didn't they guess the bulging reason? Being unacquainted with such fleshly evil or, more to the point, blinkered in their virtuous innocence, small wonder when the bitter truth became known to them, the condemnation then set in.

Yet another maiden pregnant and no marriage in sight. In those days the honourable course for the man was to marry the girl and put their lives to rights – then the sniggers and the winks would soon fade away. 'Staghorn' had struck again (as had happened with poor Mary Mawer when she also became sinfully pregnant), and he was blatantly continuing in the unmarried state, having trespassed yet again on another female servant. *You must get married for the sake of the child!* Up spoke the local people, their hands and voices raised in horror, as indeed you would expect (more especially as three more bundles of sin were to follow, making a total of four). Unlike poor Mary, Lizzie remained living in the *Horton House of Sin.* After all, she had brought up his motherless children so it only seemed fair that he should now assist in the upbringing of her own growing brood, though, without much doubt, Lizzie Green must have been blazing mad. No wonder she was to hide the physical fathering bit, as though it had never happened; which in any age would be difficult to accept – in fact quite remarkable, but not wholly exceptional – it had happened before so was this forthcoming birth to be another virgin miracle?

After the first bastard child, Oscar, was born in September 1911, Tom and Will must have felt cheated, disgusted and soiled. Their own family respectability, hitherto proudly upheld, was now tainted by unavoidable association. And all this on account of their father's fleshly sin, which would reflect like a mirror over the coming generations; fulfilling that awesome warning: that some sins are not only punishable, they descend over time. (It's as well the boys escaped from the Fenlander's scorn by leaving their disgraced home in June.)

Never at a loss for a brandishing quotation, the good villagers would respond with a suitable biblical admonishment: *The sins of the fathers shall descend upon the children to the third and fourth generation.*

Although Tom and Will had left the scene, with certainty, there was no escape for the Green children, created in and out of sin, along with the rest of the human bastards. What a burden to be landed with. Waiting for those *sins* to descend; just because of a wayward father. But why must such fear loom so large? Often do we not discover that *the biggest fear is slavish acceptance* – the untreated cause of some states of anxiety and much intense festering.

All that consternation, all that worry (for far – far too long!), until I chanced to read the full Commandment again – the text in the Modern Version (which shows how much delay there'd been). It's the one about not making 'carved image' (and the rest), as it goes on: 'You shall not bow down to them or worship them; for I the Lord Your God, am a jealous god. I punish the children for the sins of the fathers to the third and fourth generation *of those who hate me*. But I keep faith *with those who love me* and keep my commandments.'

So never mind a few words quoted out of context; they were borrowed for the greater good: the threat that punishment on earth for a father's sinful behaviour will descend to blemish future generations. But beware of shortened quotations and simplified brain-washing slogans – they can wake up the very sleeping devil.

My word! The relief at finding such a simple explanation: that bastards, so it appears in this particular instance, are not specifically singled out and punished by God. Yes, what a relief that was after many years of divine cringing, that I would not suffer from sins descending.

With simplicity, Lucretius, the Roman philosopher, managed to convey a helpful thought in nine words (although 'relieved' instead of 'happy' would have been my choice of word): 'Happy the man who knows the causes of things.'

But alas! alack! The punishment had to fit the sins. Already Horton had recklessly lost his first-born son, George Horton

Mawer (now being brought up by his grandparents, as a marriage had not taken place). He had also lost his wife, Alice, and stillborn daughter. Now, to cap it all, he had 'lost' his sons, as they sped away to escape from their father's latest careless caper – fast germinating, and soon to show: an undesirable human bastard, conceived of heated copulation outside the bond of marriage.

There was more punishment to come. In a six-month period ending in October/November of 1918, an estimated figure of 20,000,000 or more people world-wide died not from the rifle bullet, gas or bomb: they were victims of an influenza pandemic which mainly attacked the younger age groups, from ages 21 to 29; especially striking those in close proximity. During this vulnerable period in question, William (now aged 25) was suddenly smitten and died. He was serving in the United States Army, awaiting his posting for overseas duty. The irony of it all: a soldier trained for battle – to be killed by a bug!

Apart from the shock of the tragic news of Will's death reaching home, just consider the mental jolt to Tom. To have lost his mother and stillborn sister in childbirth; now to lose his only brother; to be forever estranged from his father; now far away from his roots in the Fenlands; separated from his relations and lifetime friends of his early impressionable world. It would be understandable if some brooding troubled his path, as he strode to seek an understanding – not always easily possible, when angry passions open up and blaming begins.

In 1911, after they arrived in the USA, how did the brothers get on, still clinging to the memory of the life they'd left behind? In a land so vast and flourishing, anything seemed possible; yes, anything! Even happiness could be pursued! Such seemed the hopeful chance for those two impecunious labourers from a smallholding in Lincolnshire; not exceeding nine acres, on rental from a landlord. Contrast this with the 'new' Horton wealth: the ownership of several manufactories, producing tons of cheese; and freeholders of over 1,000 acres of land – not on a temporary lease: fully enclosed property backed up by title deeds, long since taken by force from the roving, heathen Indians. Both Will and Tom started out as hired hands of strangers, at rock-bottom, where the only way is upwards, raised by one's own bootstraps, in the land where the possible need not be just a sleeping dream.

From all accounts it appears that no 'family' help came the boys' way from the wealthy American Hortons. This new proud family (two became State Senators) might have been put off by their tainted baggage – their father George's fleshly misbehaviour. They, being ever mindful that 'the sins of the father...' etc, might embarrass and 'descend upon' them, all the way across the Atlantic Ocean. But that is by way of pure speculation.

But supposing Alice had not arranged the passage loan (for whatever reason). Would the boys have stayed at home, somewhere in the Fens, deep within the dirt of their roots? And by so doing, braved the storm of their father's latest scandal (the impregnation of Lizzie Green)? And would that scornful 'Staghorn' nickname have been embarrassingly passed on to them? The shame there would have been from that dreadful stigmatic branding. But that again is purely speculative; sometimes a bruising push can set afire all kinds of ambition. Tedious questions are often followed by tedious answers – if only this; if only that ... and so on. But listen, can't you hear that wondering 'fancy!' once again? And feel the groping and the grinding to sharpen up the wit of wondering if another life could possibly exist beyond the boundary of their village.

During 1922, the year of my birth (the last of the four bastard Green children) the prodigal son, Tom, returned home for a brief family visit, staying in the Cheal with his aunt Lucy and other relations. Not for him the biblical welcome, the father was the one estranged. After some years of silent brooding, a blaming now took place, which threw away any hope of reconciliation; so deep was Tom's disgust at his father's erring ways. After eleven years away from home there was no change in his reflective thinking.

In this sad case would the wise Lucretius have amended his saying to: 'Unhappy are men who continuously brood about the cause of things.'

Tom returned to America, purchased a smallholding of some 20 acres, married and raised a family: Brandon and Thomas, thus ignoring the Horton family tradition of naming the first-born George; now blatantly remindful of family sin. Grandpa George was to remain buried alive in a sin bin. He was 'the cause of things' – the depth of anger and disgust which simply would not go away.

(For a time I would have had much sympathy with Tom as I did battle with my own cause of things. Until I accepted, once I stopped being surprised, that on this frail earth human life can often lack perfection; in which case, condemnatory feeling can be raised to bursting. But, thankfully, usually not for ever once the cooling time comes and both cause and effect no longer sting.)

14

From September 1911, at Station Cottage, human life was multiplying and continued to do so until 1922. During this peculiar period four *irregular* children were born in that flat Fenland 'Risegate' village, some 15 miles south-west of what appears to be a giant tooth gap, breaking up the coastline between Norfolk and Lincolnshire. Aptly named 'The Wash', its treacherous mud and sand banks are cleansed daily by the tide, leaving narrow channels for shipping; the main one into Boston, for many years a thriving port.

But people may well enquire: why was this such a peculiar period? For one simple reason: although Lizzie Green remained George Horton's housekeeper, she slept in her own private bedroom, remained single, and became our *Mam!* Horton remained the 'master', and slept in the master's bedroom, and we children called him *Horton*, which (for a time anyway) gave us the impression that children might be produced without the seed from the male. So Mam it was and Horton it was, but when my arrival came, Mam was 46 and Horton was 68 – making me a *last chance kid!* But there's no need to gasp. Compared with the ages of the ancient biblical procreators, Mam and Horton were just starting out in life. And I can truly confess, it never made an earth-trembling difference: life was so full of excitement and adventure on our isolated smallholding we never in childhood had much time for refined considerations. And later on in life we became past-masters of affectation: the annoyed grimace at *such goings on* – in other people's lives, of course! At the very least, it was essential to exhibit a painfulness, to show disdain for those who allowed their sinfulness to overcome their virtuousness and fall away from the expected ideal.

After watching the ritual of seed sowing, year after year, then watching the growth, I began to wonder where on earth had my own seed originally come from – surely not from a bag, or packet? Might it have been possible that some of my prehistoric ancestors walked down from the far frozen north to escape from a previous ice age? Perhaps they boated along the river Humber and its flooded appendages, crossing or disembarking at its narrowest and safest point, then trekking south down the Jurassic Way, eventually branching off to Mareham Lane. Then probably wandering towards the sunrise in the general direction of Boston which, apart from the tall, *stump*, church tower, would most likely have been splashing about in the sea tides of The Wash, had the town then existed. One thing we can be sure about: with a bit of luck and a lot of courage; often *frit* our of their wits by deep-rooted superstition – they finally arrived.

To add further confusion, Fenland folk, are called *yellow bellies*. There are several derivations: where we lived it came from the frog with the yellow belly whose habitat is hereabouts. So be careful if you pay a visit to Lincolnshire – the natives are very particular. They'll expect you to correctly sort their 'bellies' out; white, pink, sunburnt or yellow – or any other future shades to come.

During village gossip time, which happened most of the time (by the blazing fires of winter, and the warming sun in summer time), the latest scandals were extracted and fed upon to full satisfaction, especially those involving hidden fleshly bits. Every pregnancy, well, nearly every pregnancy, was known about; coming marriages were discussed at great length (including dark hints of gussets let in to enlarge a maiden's frock). New village arrivals had to be learnt about, dissected, and put in their true ordered place: 'They are as

73

good as, but not better than,' in our marking and defining world.

There would also be growing excitement about the coming Chapel annual outing to the nearby holiday resort of Skegness (Skegg's-Nest, as some of the locals often called the place). The children's excitement reached fever pitch as the great day approached. A *free* visit to the seaside; a cold paddle in the sea; rides in the funfair; iced-cream (which it was in those days: a yellowish concoction kept cool with ice blocks), leaving a powdery aftertaste. Candyfloss was licked, after it had first become stuck all over hands and face. And the inevitable would happen; some children became sick, especially on the swinging fun rides, to be finally finished off in the ghost train, often with shrieks of real fear, rather than delight. And we'd be sure to take a few sticks of rock home, after watching the manufacturer roll it out on a long board, after inserting the 'Skegness' letters deep within. A few cheeky picture postcards were also sent, with: 'Wish you were here – I'm in the pink!' After all, for some, this excursion was to their annual holiday.

We also spent far too much money on the penny gambling machines, and even watched the fluttering postcard pictures in the movie machine showing *What the Butler Saw* and many other flickering postcard shows. How very, very naughty, on a Chapel outing – such furtive, sinful ways. So 'fancy' this and 'fancy' that – would you believe – what next!

Seldom did anything slip by unheeded: current village news was updated, revised, digested, regurgitated and carefully distributed, morsel by morsel; wise heads shook and nodded (sometimes accompanied by silent lip reading, if children were present). Usually, by the end of the day the especially juicy bits would be gossiped all over the place; in fact, if the story was an early starter, by teatime you just might hear it twice, now dangling and flowing in several variations

– well I never, just you fancy that! On many days there would be a good deal of tut-tutting, for it was a sin to think about sinning – never mind the actual act itself! Although secretly enjoyed, all those youthful, overflowing dreams – how awful! As for any other pleasant, titillative frigging, shameful! The wasting of the very seeds of life! Folk lived in constant earthly fear of the Devil's punishment, reminded by the white hot sparks flying madly from the village blacksmith's forge. No wonder, even in a time of mass unemployment, the parsons were still fully employed.

But what of the four children, delivered of Lizzie, the housekeeper, and spaced out over eleven years? Something was suspiciously wrong and completely out of keeping: to have an average birth spacing of two and three-quarters years, when the normal gap was often a year, or even less – and by no means unusual at that. For it was commonly held by many men folk that *gifting* babies in regular succession, not only showed their own prowess, it also kept the womenfolk busy. And, furthermore, it was a good cure for the *pains under their pinnies*, which might cause their thoughts to stray. Yes, something was decidedly wrong; this birth spacing smacked of irregular behaviour and the men wouldn't fancy that.

But just consider Lizzie's living-in problem: of thwarting the employer's randy need of access – most probably by locking her own bedroom door to escape from his panting advances. That is until she eventually calmed down again, and once more Horton increased the population – truly deserving of his 'Staghorn' nickname; for it was widely known that a standing-prick has no conscience.

It is just possible that without knowing it, Lizzie was following the advice of the 'wise' Revd T.R. Malthus, who had advocated sexual restraint as a method to prevent the population exploding beyond the means of subsistence. That trendy Reverend fellow wasn't such a crackpot after all!

Consider how families were more often spaced: George Horton (my great-great-grandfather, the grazier) in the early nineteenth century had produced eight children in nine years. And later on, my aunt, Lucy Horton (married to Branton Sansam) had been gifted with four children in five years – though only two examples, they were typical in those days – resulting from the *honouring and obeying* in the expected submissive way; turning women into incubators just like breeding farmyard animals.

In regular succession, Mam carefully selected our callable names. Some folk might say she was getting way above herself: there was Oscar Ewart, Winifred Olwen, Stanley Vincent and myself, Gerald Clifford. There were no Toms, Dicks, or Harrys; and most certainly not another George – the name which over the centuries had been regularly used for the first-born of each Horton family (perhaps influenced by all those royal Georges; becoming quite dynastic).

Personally, I would have preferred a simple common name instead of the posh Gerald – even though it comes from the Germanic name made of the elements of 'spear and rule', by way of the Norman-French. There was, however, a consolation prize: most folk called me Gerry or Ged – both simple and easy to spell (and in any case, for goodness' sake, you can always change your name).

Did Mam arm us with those distinctive forenames, suggesting a bit of style, perhaps mindful of the possibility that one of her expanding brood might achieve some fame in life. Why not? Didn't our eldest brother, Oscar, years later exclaim: 'Considering our poor start in life, we all did well in the end'. Well, relatively well – considering. Much later on, my understanding came to this reasoned conclusion: that whatever the circumstances of our birth (natural or unnatural), Mam would have named us exactly the same. It was her style, truly it was, if it was taken as posh – too bad!

You could tell by the way Mam pinned on her large black hat, trimmed with red roses, that she aimed for the best effect: a little to the left, then to the right, up and down a little – how exasperating when you're desperate to catch the local train. Yes, without much doubt, Mam should have strode on life's wider stage (she even mock-poshed up her accent when we mixed among strangers in Ayscoughee Gardens, or on the local passenger train. It tickled me enormously that life could be play-acted in this way, Although I never had the nerve to attempt it myself.

But when all said and done, and that amounted to a questionable lot; being gifted with a 'funny' forename and being landed with an irregular family name, caused me far less pain than a brushing nettle sting, compared with the upheavals destined to come: above my head a noose was hovering.

15

In the winter time, without fail, the Risegate Eau froze over, weight-bearing thick; safe enough to make long slides, use our ancient skates, and the home-made sledges (sometimes made from chitting boxes). Horton always gave us his annual warning: not to trust the ice under the shelter of the bridges, and especially to take care when the thaw commenced. As usual, he used a rhyme to highlight his caution:

> If it bears it's safe;
> But when it starts to bend,
> It soon begins to crack,
> And when it cracks it breaks.

Fixing the skates to our shoes (by inserting their spikes into the heel, through a hole bored out by a gimlet), we balanced our bodies with outstretched arms as we sped to the Clough School in great style, soon to feel as warm as toast, our frozen feet relieved by hot aches.

Come the spring time, the whips and tops would come out. The whip handle (a foot or so long) would be cut from a tree, unless we bought a penny one. The leather thong, obtained from the saddler (Mr Hutchinson), for 'little or nowt' would be secured to the handle by a short length of waxed string, usually thrown in free by way of encouragement. At the end of the thong we tied another piece of string, to allow the top to be 'wound up' and to do the lashing. We sped our tops along the smooth macadamised roads, without fear of traffic: mainly slow horses and carts, motorised vehicles were still few and far between.

It was also time to buy a few marbles, and perhaps an odd 'dinkie' or two, those shining glass ones with strips of colour inside. We used them to subdue the marbles. Alternatively (especially by the kids on the poverty line), pop bottle necks were broken off – the ones with a small glass ball inside – somewhat frosty looking but often used as a dinkie.

Conkers were baked in the oven, then pierced and dangled on the end of a piece of string. Thus began the whacking time, to decimate your opponent's conker in so many goes, which were carefully counted to enhance the conquering one. All that excitement and it didn't cost a penny!

Cigarette cards, found in discarded packets or begged from the smoker as he fumbled with his packet, usually came in sets of fifty. Motor cars, film stars, footballers, cricketers, flowers and many others. We used to barter for missing ones until we got a set, then stick them in an album. With the others we would play a competitive game. Lean one or two against the wall, flick a card in your hand, vying with your opponent, until the target card or cards fell down, leaving the ones already on the floor for the winning player. With skill and determination it was possible to gain a large pack; over time I became quite adept.

On Guy Fawkes morning we knocked on all the cottage doors as we ran to school, and recited this begging jingle:

Remember, remember the 5th of November, the poor old guy.
A hole in my stocking, a hole in my shoe –
Please can you spare me a copper or two.

Sometimes the family dog was set yapping about our heels, but usually folk paid up and looked pleasant – perhaps a halfpenny, or a penny, and it soon mounted up. Although we wore guy masks, the giver would often demand to know: 'Whose boy are you?' So we had to oblige and remove the mask to satisfy their curiosity. Many other activities happened in regular turn. Everything seemed so simple, yet often there was great excitement in our everyday living (I speak of the time before the yo-yo craze came in; those humming, sometimes wobbly things, costing all of thruppence).

Bubbles, the weekly penny comic, was avidly read from cover to cover. Long before I could read the ballooned words blown from the characters' mouths, I loved to 'read' the pictures – such excitement!

The 'cats whisker' wireless set was achieving a wide distribution: for most people it simply was not affordable in the 1920s. A write-up appeared in the local *Spalding Free Press*, of the 6th November, 1934, extolling the latest 'portable' wireless. It comprehensively detailed the new HMV 'Superhet Portable Fluid – Light Six', which was rather futuristically referred to as a 'radio instrument'. It could be used in more rooms than one, without troubling to erect an aerial or earth attachment (and moved about in the same way as a standard lamp).

The price of this new, wonderful HMV portable, which could bring music and voice in any room was 16 guineas (for those not acquainted with Victorian times: £16 16s (16 pounds 16 shillings). This might seem a reasonable price to pay for the latest state of the art wireless set; until you compare this sum against a labourer's wage of those times, of usually less than £2 a week. Without any doubt, a wireless set then was simply not affordable by the struggling masses. No wonder Horton somewhat vaguely replied, when we children asked if we could have one: 'Yes, that's a good idea – we need less wire.' Followed by: 'Bah! – What a useless contraption.'

The *Daily Mirror* was delivered, to widen our narrow

view of the world. I always enjoyed the cartoon, of Pip, Squeak and Wilfred, who battled so hard with the Russian spy named Popsie, who was always ready to set off a football-size bomb. There was also news of a possible workers' revolution which ticked and smouldered away, threatening to carve up all the land and redistribute it to the down-trodden classes, bringing such equality that the privileged high and the wretchedly low would quickly disappear. 'They must be sloomy (stupid), to talk such balderdash,' Horton would touchily say. 'Who will then do the labouring? Who will give the daily orders? Jack never was, and never will be, as good as his master.' And that was that! Such confidence...

We had one 'proper' book in the home (one between hardback covers). You could tell it was outdated. It was illustrated in black and white, outlining simple farming methods, still used by the subsistence farmer: how to dig, sow and mow, and all the other time-consuming activities (by hand, of course); of glorious, wonderful work, as nature truly intended, or so it seemed. With a twinkle in his eyes (he could still read with both of them), and perhaps displaying the faintest hint of being superior, Horton taught me words that I would remember all my days.

Allowing a suitable hesitation between holding the book and opening it up, he would turn to the CONTENTS page, then, making sure of our rapt attention (every blessed time), he would start to proclaim some words with an actor's flourish. Apparently (so he methodically explained), 'contents' meant more than it seemed: the heading letters of the words were also a code. Go forwards and they could indicate as follows: **C**ows **O**ught **N**ot **T**o **E**at **N**asty **T**urnip **S**eeds. Now, believe it or not, the code also works backwards: **S**am **T**akes **N**ell **E**very **T**uesday **N**ight **O**ut **C**ourting. Truly, my young ears were all agog. Shouldn't wonder that this masterpiece had passed down the generations from the time Caxton began to use the first printing press proving that wisdom and development are closely twinned.

Apart from his constant moral strictures (of which he had collected so many), Horton also passed on useful tips: 'Fire is a good servant but a bad master', was one (so we avoided the careless use of matches, especially near the stackyard on blazing Bonfire Night). 'Do not place a rake against the wall with its tines outwards', was another, 'otherwise, you'll get a whack on the head from the handle if you tread on them'. There were many other bits of advice. For instance: a lamb is a sheep, but a sheep is not a lamb; truly, it went on and on – sometimes mildly, sometimes fervidly. After all, now over 70, he had a lifetime's experience to draw on, and he seemed anxiously keen to share it. So a lot of talking went on.

As I grew older and looked around throughout the changing seasons, I would sometimes feel a mental shudder when I glanced across the bleak, flattened fields in the winter time. At other times the endless covering of green, yellow and gold, made me feel despondent (reminding me of the slaving work of the labourers in those fields, of which I would soon be one). Not in the Fenlands the gentle flow of sweeping pastures like the distant rolling Lincolnshire wolds, stretching out the view, suggesting a possible freedom. The daily view of flatness requires appreciation of a very different kind.

In the outhouse (between the washhouse and the coalhouse) were stored the Brambly apples, awaiting a better winter price; the sacks of corn after the threshing; the maize for the chickens; the 'cake' for the cows; skeps and chitting boxes and much else. But the sight that most impressed me, hung or stood along one wall, there, stowed in the neatest order, were rows of all the hand tools, clean and shining and smeared with engine oil to preserve their working surfaces, after being sharpened on the whetstone. There were forks (of varying tines and angles); several rakes for fine tilling and collecting (including a wide wooden one, *religiously* used at harvest time for gleaning); so also hung spades, hoes and shovels – lined up like soldiers before a battle. One two-wheeled hand-drill stood erect and ready, as proudly did various dibbers.

A scythe (with its dangerous cutting blade wrapped around with hessian sacking) hung safely high, near the sickle and the hook; all out of bounds to children – all treated with respect. There was an assortment of riddles in various gauges (but not a wool one to be seen); a rope line to guide the garden trench digging, carefully set out between two stakes, and moved backwards spit by spit, leaving the trench so straight, the intention may not have been but it all seemed so time-consuming. There was a chopper (so vicious looking) to cleave the mangoles into slices for cattle feed (supplemented by the rough cattle 'cake', which I once tried and had to spit out). Next door, in the coalhouse, we had a huge hammer for splitting the large lumps; a heavy-duty axe for splitting logs for winter fuel; and a useful crowbar to prise apart or loosen. There were many other implements, long since forgotten. My favourite tool of all (hand-made by the village blacksmith, Mr Billy Edgoose), was the highly useful 'spud' – nothing to do with a potato, used mainly for cutting the roots of weeds; and easy for a child to use, by holding halfway down its handle. Of course we had a wheelbarrow. How else would we have managed without the muscle-powered conveyor of the farmyard?

Like some people say they have seen a vision; it soon occurred to me that these tools had one thing in common: they never operated unless they were moved by human hands. We never owned a horse, but occasionally borrowed one from Billy Branton, a nearby smallholder in Gosberton Westhorpe; yet another extended relation. Even our trolley (a flat truck on four wheels) was occasionally pushed and pulled by the family, with Horton holding up the shafts where a work-horse should have been.

Armed only with his hand-tools, Horton seemed so proud of slaving away – day after day, in the summer time up to and past the setting sun. I once heard him snort out, as he viewed with unconcealed contempt some lighthearted people, laughing and chattering, after they had returned from a day trip to the seaside. 'Bah!' he exploded, 'That's all they think of these days – pleasuring!' So scorning did this word sound that for years after that I deeply held a belief that pleasuring was truly a deadly sin. No wonder Horton was fit and active right into his old age unlike farming folk today, who ride the fields on tractors, put on weight which can bring about a deadly heart condition.

'Hard work never hurt anyone!' Horton used to say, with such relish that his words used to make me shiver – fully aware that his contagious influence was beginning to touch its feel on me. Hard work, indeed! Yes, row after row of it, acre after acre, field after field: and when it seemed finished, it started all over again – all that boring repetition. The picking, plucking, cutting, slashing, lifting, riddling, hoeing, spading away. Noble work (extolled from the pulpit), exhausting the serfs, keeping them out of mischief and on their knees – humbled and suitably grateful. Maybe hard work never hurt anyone, but wasn't it so time-consuming? Keeping the nose to the grindstone, which can be painfully felt if carelessly rubbed against.

Horton had another regular saying: 'There'll be so many bad years, followed by the good ones.' After the losses would come the winnings – the faith he had! That the longest losing sequence would end before the dwindling stake in the bank is exhausted. Isn't this the eternal optimism of the gambling classes? Of which farmers must be included (though nobly so) – so often are they bitten by a losing state.

It's bad enough if you have no capital left to buy new seed; but just as deep is the desperation if your produce cannot be sold. The helpless feeling that can come along, far too often; testing the very sinews of any fervent optimism. And as I grew older (to 1928, when I was six), I heard some words from Horton which I thought was yet another repetitive lament. I never directly connected them with my apparently trouble-free life. Yet he spoke them many times – those ominous warning words – the words which I should have feared. '*Nowt makes little or nowt!*'

As time went by my clothing became more than a little shabby; second-hand (third, or even more), and often not the best of fits. That never had bothered me. One poor labourer's son had the soles of his worn shoes covered with one-inch thick pieces of a discarded motor tyre – such displayed wretchedness! Perversely, I derived some comfort from that. My holey soles were covered with cut-out, inserted cardboard; soon soggy on wet days, but proudly invisible. Between times, we had a lot of fun – simple fun; the kind of fun that costs nowt on a farm, so life happily carried on. Many times had storms happened in the past, so why should we worry about the gathering of yet another – even thundering passes!

If we ever felt sorry for ourselves in our somewhat lowly position, and Horton overheard us chuntering, his eyes would sharpen like an eagle's, and he would pierce them at us and say: 'What are yah grumbling about? Yar've got a good bed to lie on, plenty of food in yar stomach, and clothes on yah back. What was good enough for my father, is good enough for me, and is good enough for you. What more do yah want!'

These words, so often did I hear them, spoken by a proud old man: conveying his persistent belief to be suffered to a point of martyrdom. An utterance of almost holy feeling to convey his excessive respect for tradition handed down the ages. And what is more, slavishly to be accepted. An attack on the discontented; the defeat of the rebel's disrespect for custom – instilling the discipline to bear hardship's pain – with a stoical acceptance and without the slightest questioning.

16

Farm land to rent was becoming scarce, no wonder the ensnaring noose was hanging low and tightening. In the brief period between 1919–21 (before I was born in 1922) there was an even bigger turnover of land sales than in the earlier period, 1906–14, when Horton's beloved Cheal farm was sold and he was dispossessed of land farmed by his family since the early 1800s; mistakenly believing that a new lease would always be granted.

To take advantage of the boom in land value, Mr Harold Dods, Horton's landlord, decided to sell and they say lightning never strikes twice: first in the Cheal and now at Station Cottage. It must have been a sudden decision. No prior notice of intent was issued, not even a letter of thanks for being a good tenant (which, undoubtedly, he was). As the law stood there simply was no redress, ownership was all powerful – the landowner was king! One day, a day which turned out to cause alarm and panic, a neighbour (Mr Richardson) informed Horton: 'George, there's an auctioneer's notice pinned on your gate.' Printed thereon in the usual jargon, it briefly stated: A smallholding, known as Station Cottage, comprising 9 acres of land, outbuildings and a cottage to be sold by auction (on a date thereon specified).

The landlord was taking his profit, as would be expected of a successful businessman. And farming conditions, which followed a few years later, would most probably cause him to think, thank goodness I did!

(Quite contrary to the advice of Mark Twain: 'Buy land ... they're not making any more of it.') Many were selling and moving away from land they considered too risky – especially when deflation came, which seemed too often and lasted by far too long.

Now had descended fear and panic, sleepless nights and carpet pacing, from the fireside to the outside door, and back again. Not only was Horton wearing his boots out with ever pressing mental torment; he would also trot out his current lament: 'Lord help us and save us!' His religious fervour came crying through; so much so that his faith shone like a lighthouse beam, flashing the hope of a possible miracle. A temporary one did come;, but not from a divine source: he would buy Station Cottage, out of sheer desperation. Yet another yeoman forced to risk his lot (and that of his family) with a hefty mortgage. Horton attended the sale. There was no mercy for the proud sitting tenant. In such a mad boom what happened could have been anticipated. The bidding went through the roof, broke the tiles and shot skywards to a height where giddiness intoxicated the mind.

This was another bubbly period: happy days were back again; good times were here to stay. The band was playing a winning tune: the dangerous 'millstone around the neck' had ceased to be. Optimism, like the rising warmth of the summer sun, rose to greet yet another day; why think of winter when you're basking in the warming sun and pleasantness is all you feel? In short Horton became the landowner of his precious holding – at too long last becoming such with all the attendant worry and risk.

And with that wild auction bidding, came the future mountain of debt. The final price for those rich, nine Fenland acres was a little over £1,000 (secured with a loan of £1,000 at 5%, and a small balance from Horton's precious, depleting capital). The annual interest payment of £50 now towered above the previous rent. And that was only the interest. Fat chance of reducing the capital loan, unless the boom continued and produce sold at ever increasing prices.

Yes, a simple remedy was required: a few years of raging inflation, of both produce and land. (In some circumstances, inflation can prove to be a good thing – despite what politicians preach. If you're buying land on a hangover loan, rising values can be a blessing in disguise.)

Then tougher times arrived once again. The mounting unemployed were suffering privation, unable to buy nutritious food. Yet some fields would be left fallow and crops would remain unsold. Our Bramley cooking apples were piled up in the barn. Before they rotted, we ate some ourselves in pies (gave some away to our struggling neighbours, and eventually fed the rest to our pigs). But you know what happens when you devour your own stock – the trading income comes to a halt. No wonder when I reached the age of seven, in 1929, Horton's lament was dramatically changing. Instead of the previous 'nowt makes little or nowt', he cut out the words, 'little or'.

So now it became 'nowt makes nowt!' Those words rang out. And still brother Stan and I grinned at each other. We were not disturbed by the tone of his 'wolf' cry, now becoming more persistent. Poor old Horton, now past his mid-seventies, was destined to outlive the bulk of the struggling population of those times. And then he began to speak in trembling tones, like a chapel preacher praying for all sinners: 'Lord help us!' became his despairing cry.

But did I hear him incorrectly – was he really saying: 'Lloyds help us!'? That would have made more sense. Lloyds was a bank. But that was not possible, we banked with the old National Westminster, no doubt long since refusing to guarantee his account dipped in bright red ink.

Cocooned in an innocence, excited by each new day, I never even considered that life would be other than much of the same. We village children played the usual games and pranks. Apart from working in the fields (which I unashamedly shrank from), our games became more daring as we grew older and bolder: climbing high trees; attempting to 'swim' across the Risegate Eau; and dangerously burrowing right through a corn or haystack, risking a fatal collapse. On Saturday Mam always gave me a penny, which I usually spent on a 'penny-packer' (a wafer biscuit, thinly introduced to a thinnish chocolate liquid). This smeared chocolate fix was far from satisfactory, so I spent my penny on toffees instead, after much consideration.

Then, many wild birds still nested all over the place, in the hedges, trees, scrub and even in the grass. A few grass snakes existed and the pits beside the railway approaches to the bridges contained a wide variety of life among the reeds. Gone were the wild geese and the herons. We had a stuffed heron in a glass display case. The number of times I pulled its beak to witness it violently shake, as though protesting at its grotesque state in death – on full display, now speechless. Any living creature that ran on four legs, flew on the wing, had meat on it, or could be stuffed, was shot, trapped or poisoned. No wonder silence came; except for the put-putting tractors. But wait a moment, just take a look, you must admit there's efficiency now in acres of neat rows – the onward unstoppable march of progress. New generations of farmers will not think much about this. What you've never known, you can hardly be expected to miss.

'Bastard' cropped up in conversation – bastard this! and bastard that! It seemed an essential part of many conversations, and by all accounts so it would remain. 'You're one of them!' said Fred (a knowledgeable lad) fixing me with both his eyes, to make sure of the direction of his enlightenment. I ignored him, frightened of answering back and showing up my ignorance. So he looked at me straight again, and with the faintest sign of a cunning grin, he repeated that revealing message – the tone was much higher the second time round. 'You're one of them,' again he said. And still I just ignored him.

There were trips to the nearby Spalding market town, nearly five miles along the railway track. What a thrill to see the locomotive swaying and steaming away, advancing from the distance. Although the drivers used to give a friendly wave the noise was frightening, so I used to run to the wall by the ticket office for safety, until the hissing steam abated. Although we lived next to the station, more often than not we would scramble on board in a panic – late again! Why did Mam take so much time to arrange that huge black hat, fashionably trimmed with red roses? The hatpin would be pushed in and out, until the angle was correct – after what seemed eternity. 'Oh, come on Mam, we'll miss the train!' She'd look out of the window and explain, 'No we won't, the signal is still at "go", it's got to change to "stop".'

After wandering around Spalding town, and completing several essential purchases (including kippers – for little or nowt), we made our way across the Welland Bridge, built of stone in 1838, for the growing horse-drawn vehicles. Then, showing all the signs of beginning to be beset with motorised traffic problems. Once safely over the river, which always seemed in full flow, sometimes violently so, we turned right past Ye Olde White Horse, which had been built some 600 years ago. A few minutes along Church Gate we began the most exciting part of our trip. A regular visit to Ayscoughee Hall gardens.

How we loved to wander and stare in amazement at the shaped yew hedges, providing archways into the next bit of exploration. We walked politely along the garden paths, never daring to disobey the many signs: 'Keep off the grass'. I enjoyed studying the stone statuary, even though some limbs were then missing and rusting iron bars showed through. Were they victorious Romans, or Greeks? I never did find out.

We also walked by the side of the ornamental pool and

caught sight of the fish, but never dare dangle a net or line: that would have been a banning crime. At the end of the pool the impressive war memorial came into full view; occupying, as it rightly did, a bold position. I used to pause and look at the many listed names of that slaughtered generation. The *war to end all wars* was but a few years old. I stood there in silence, feeling assured in my mind that when I grew up I would never be called upon to take part in such barbarity.

And then came the real excitement, the anxious purpose of our visit: we walked through the rear gate across Love Lane into a playground area, where there were swings, slides, roundabouts and the usual see-saw – all free! And as many goes as you like. From the gardens Mam pointed out the spire of Spalding Parish Church (nearly 650 years old – a most impressive building). We never visited that great symbol of Christian faith. Mam, being a simple Primitive Methodist, would have been overwhelmed – apart from that she was somewhat in a lapsed condition.

Before we left the gardens, we ate our sausage rolls (and perhaps a cream bun or fancy cake, if funds were flush). We usually snacked in one of the alcoves (then, along the inner wall next to Church Gate). As usual Mam would never believe the time of day. In her experience all clocks were wrong. So we often bolted towards the railway station, to ride in style the journey home in a comfortable third-class carriage. But we'd only just be on time. The porter would be waiting to slam the carriage door shut, before the guard whistled and waved his flag.

17

With nowt making nowt,
And nowt to make nowt with
(Produce rotting or unsold),
A grim time had come.

Back on the farm, Horton's constant pacing of the carpet continued. Still those 'wolf' cries rang out – we had long since become used to them. Mam, being much more practical in her desperation, sent for a lucky Cornish charm, advertised in the local press. She also kept repeating her own brand of protestation: 'They are robbing us – ends and sides up! Of hundreds and thousands!' Such mornful ambiguity. Yet I also believed that 'they' existed. The number of years it took before I began to ask a searching question: who, what or how are 'they'? The basic cause of all our threatened trouble.

Then Horton changed his tune, after 1928, when rock-bottom was looming, killing the boom; like a puffed-up bubble bursts on a thorn. 'We shall be ruined and end up in the workhouse!' he now exclaimed, going on and on. Sometimes throwing in his, 'Lord Bless us and Save us!' bit as a hopeful measure. Desperately seeking a worldly-solace he puffed and sucked on his penny clay-pipe, burning steadily on 'Noxall' twist-tobacco; producing clouds of smoke like a London smog. Well do I remember how my eyes smarted when I sat on his knee and he made a regular 'pup!' noise when he exhaled and puffed out the foul smoke, to foggily surround both of us (perhaps this is why I never became a smoker).

'Noxall' twist-tobacco in those days, at eight pence an ounce, was not easily affordable. Obtained from Mary Pointon's village shop, where our *tick* had long since been exhausted. The soothing nicotine worked, for a time; but so hooked had he become, deep craving had set in. Every week, several ounces were needed to cope with his desperate need. Luckily, Mam came up with her own ingenious solution. She hit upon the idea of mixing the costly tobacco-twist with decaying rose petals, which we had in plenty. Instead of allowing them to die, the petal corpses would henceforth be cremated in a pipe. It was great fun collecting them and storing them in boxes under the stairs. With some satisfaction we watched Horton puffing away without any suspicion. Sucking away during his drugged journeys of escape – at a lower cost of burning. By way of further economy, when Horton's clay pipe broke, we used the discarded bowl to blow soapy bubbles. Yuk! the things you do when you're poverty stricken, and you've been brought up to 'waste not, want not'.

But that word, 'workhouse'? Whatever did Horton mean – 'end up in the workhouse'? My mind did not comprehend so I ignored his desperation.

Then came a new mournful cry. 'I wish I was dead!' cried Horton, as if he was in terrible pain. Now 77 what a happy release that would have been. Especially from a fatal touch of the blessed pneumonia; the old people's friend. Sometimes he added a tidy touch, as you would expect from a proud Fen farmer – a cry that contained the fuller version: 'I wish I was dead *and buried!*'

Buried indeed! A job well done and tidied up. Out of sight is out of the way; nothing unsightly left lying about. That is the way he worked his land: all rubbish removed or burned and constant war waged against the smothering twitch-grass.

Looking back, I would recall with some relief: thank

94

goodness he never died (not then anyway). I needed him alive, suffering though he was, to keep some security about my young head. Was his cry truly inviting death? The way some old folk try to seek comfort; by acting out to speed life's journey, by far felt too miserably prolonged. When life suddenly becomes beyond them, and the memories of the days-of-yore are paraded as the best. Would that be unfair, was it truly that? His state pension of ten shillings (50p) a week would provide us with our basic groceries – at our low level of living. No indeed, Horton was needed alive – his death must not come yet, we couldn't manage without his pension and no other state assistance was then available (except that workhouse place he had so fearfully mentioned).

But why was Mam wasting so much time, fussing and fuming over the Station Cottage property? No will had been made, making her the sole beneficiary (or even part beneficiary, for that matter). The *accursed* place was strangled by that interest debt. Horton was now elderly so any beneficial life assurance was unaffordable, though he did have a 'burial' policy, the few pence premiums collected by the Pearl Insurance agent. If Mam was vulnerable, so also were her children – no wonder she hated the enemy *they* – who were crawling like lice and jumping like fleas, all over the place; which, to say the least, was mightily irritating.

Should Lizzie Green now turn to the *master*, Mr Horton, who had first employed her as a housekeeper, and make this desperate plea: If you die what will become of us? Where will our livelihood then come from? There'd be no farm income and even your pension would cease!

And what could Horton say in reply, except what he usually did: 'I've got no money – not a penny piece to my name!' What else could you now expect of an old man deeply in a dejected state and also inclined to loss of memory, and up to his eyes in dreaded debt. There simply was no money, not even hidden in a mattress, or secreted in a biscuit tin. No money; no seed to sow; no income – just misery! Bankruptcies and evictions were fast growing. His costly rich earth remained unemotional, in its usual indifferent peace; after all, this had happened before and would most likely happen again.

Mam was not a *common-law* wife – there was no such legal entity (except in misled minds). Ask a solicitor, the pension trustees, or a life-assurance claims manager, if there's still any doubt. Mam and Horton were co-habitees, living together purely by habit; not even pretending to be man and wife, and *partners* had not become fashionable. So in that grave olde worlde they would be branded as sinful; there was no alternative description – certainly not a respectable one.

The legacy descending from Horton's grandfather, George (the wealthy grazier of Offleet, near Boston); and that passed on by his father, John (comfortable but not wealthy); as well as his own capital, amassed in 'the Cheal', was now gone. Predictably – *gone in three!* Not through gambling, high living or womanising (although some might point their finger at that). The plain truth was glaringly simple; born in 1854, Horton had lived too long. If he had died at the age of 70 (when I was but two years old) he would have left this earth with his pride intact and his confidence unbeaten. Now the meaning of the word 'viability' had descended upon the place, and although we were existing we only did so by ignoring the interest debt still accruing. Without much doubt, our nine-acre, mixed organic farm was simply uneconomic. Yet Horton had battled so hard – such was the pride he had!

It would be unthinkable that he would cover his precious land with glass; producing early inedible flowers (even if he'd made a profit). To build a giant glass-covered factory? He'd say, 'Bah!' to that. Sadly, but it's the truth, he would

96

have been no worse off if he had drilled unsuccessfully for oil or gold, in the last years on his land. And even if he had used the finest fertilisers soon to come on stream; he would still have failed. Supply towered over poor demand and the gathering depression had now become a frightening slump: no wonder people were desperate and bewildered – never mind their troubling sins.

But all that apart, there was the good side (for me anyway); the side I would always remember, in gratitude; the simple life on a small farm, where life in its various phases could be observed and experienced. My word! – how we were conditioned to grit our teeth in the face of the latest storm; to remember the former blessings, in the hope that they would return – in humble thanks to be received.

Mam continued to cry her protestations, as she had done for most of my childhood, or so it seemed, especially in the quiet of the bedroom when she was making the beds. 'We've been here for over 20 years, My Lord,' (she was conducting her case in the higher court). 'This is our rightful home! They're robbing us ends and sides up, of hundreds and thousands!' And so it would go on. Thus, I remembered (would I ever forget) that accusing *they* word!

Our ancient mattresses, stuffed with goose feathers, covered with heavy blankets and gaudy home-made quilts, were quite a challenge for Mam. She sprinkled Keating's to kill the fleas and some were caught by hand. I tried to hit them with the back of a hairbrush, shaped like a bat. (It's difficult to hit a flea which can jump 300 times its own length, using its own hind-leg power pack of a super-elastic substance, which, if gifted to man, would enable a jump higher than the Empire State Building in New York.) The few I caught I dropped in the po and watched them wriggle in the pee, until they finally stopped their struggling. Proving beyond doubt that children can be downright sadistic, given half the chance.

Notebooks at length were filled with evidence for the High Court judge (the very top one!). Mam would have her day in court, *they* would be demolished, *they* would learn a thing or two. It seemed that as our problems grew she became more excited. She couldn't wait for her day of battle to prove rightful ownership. After all, we still were in full possession and that, so we are told, is nine points of the law. But that might not be the case, so who on earth thinks up all those wise statements? Suitable, so it seems, for covering many of life's hopes and problems, which so often end in pain or dismay.

Mam, O Mam! – you're in a jam,
Confused and cluttered up.
Do listen to the warning bells,
The tranquil peals are missing
– but still you batter on!

18

'Hard work never hurt anyone!' was another one of Horton's binds. Maybe, but so monotonous: all that chopping, raking, picking, digging, sowing (and the blessed rest!) – round and round, row after row; entrapped in tedious bouts of unthinking routine. Such work may have rewarded the stoics, indifferent to pleasure or pain, but my own answer to this problem came along quite soon. For although this menial slavery might be considered praiseworthy, it was something I determined to escape from.

Now fast approaching ancient 80 (far beyond the average mortality age of those times), yet another Horton refrain began recurring: 'My memory is not what it used to be!' Had the comforting curtain of forgetfulness begun to draw across his troubled mind? To blind out the shafts of cruel light, beginning to pierce him through and through, as the mirror of his life shone back his past and he fretted where it had gone to.

Mysteriously, to add to our punishment, brother Stan suddenly developed a 'wasting disease' in his right upper arm (a then common description for the sudden, permanent loss of muscular movement). He was sent away by the authorities; far away to a hospital in Nottingham. The treatment was electrical and a prognosis was duly made: as he gets older he'll grow out of it. At the time this explanation seemed quite reasonable and provided much relief. Regular letters were received from Stan who seemed to be coping with his new experience. I missed him. He was cleverer and four years older than me. Didn't he teach me to add up huge sums by placing many tens on top of each other and adding up the ones? Brilliance is catching, for a time I felt quite enhanced: the benefits of knowledge are truly liberating.

Inescapably, time was moving towards the late 1920s and neither blessed nor fortunate relief was in sight. Mam now resorted to reading tea leaves in all our empty cups; after twirling them around her head three times – no more and no less! The faiths people grasp, more especially when delusion sets in. Things taken for granted started to go missing. The pig sty was now mucked-out and empty. The last grunting, occupants had been sold for much needed cash and not replaced by piglets. The last calf was sold to a local butcher, who collected it in his trap, pulled by a frisky pony. Its legs were tied to prevent it jumping to freedom and running back to its mother. Saddened, I watched it ride away, with a forlorn look in its pleading eyes. The calf's mother also disappeared. Whether to become butcher's meat, or it died a sudden death and ended up in the knacker's yard, I cannot recall. In any case, by now the old cow was probably fed up with the hot-blooded, wham-bam penetrations by the visiting stud-bull; for which its owner was duly paid a handsome fee. Much gaping interest did I take when its attendant (dressed in a cow-gown and sporting a bowler hat) guided the bull's ghastly expandable, in rod-like condition (swollen in its thudging-grip), by directing the coming penetration with the curved handle of his walking stick. All that pushing and shoving seemed somewhat alarming to me – aren't animals disgusting, when they copulate in bare skin!

Our faithful cats never left us. So long as they are fed cats remain loyal: there was no market value in their meat or skins. They were half-wild anyway and could easily survive on mice, wild birds and even the odd ferocious rat. As a special treat on Sunday they would fight over the empty sock-eye salmon can (sixpence from Woolworth's, if funds were flush) – sometimes getting a head trapped inside, needing a tug to pull it out. We always had plenty of vegetable and fresh salad in season. Tomatoes (considered a fruit) were purchased, cut in slices and dipped in sugar and vinegar, which I find delicious. We had a regular supply of free-range eggs from our family of hens, found after a daily search along a hedge bottom, in spaces where they made their nests. Occasionally, when one became a little scraggy (and before it died on us), Horton would wring its neck out of kindness, and Mam would dress it, before it went into the cooking pot. The cow's moo and the pig's grunt no longer greeted us. Apart from those squawky chickens and the meows of the cats, there was an empty silence about the place; except a few wild birds still sang for us. During dusk, waves of bats would swoosh low over our heads, busily feeding on the wing. Their darting and diving frit me to death.

We still sold the odd skep of fruit for cash, when we could. By a desperate arrangement our arable land was shared 'in halves' with a local farmer, Mr Charlton, who did his best to provide some support. All this time the interest debt kept growing. We children worked in neighbouring fields during the school holidays. I remember this experience from the age of five – no wonder I detested labouring work. Mam and Horton still lamented, as would be expected under such dire circumstances. The slump was ravaging. So cash-poor did we become, our clothing became tatty and we stopped attending chapel; better to hide away and keep what little pride we had left, than embarrass others with our conspicuous destitution.

I also remember in 1926 (or was it '27?) Mark Bates, the local threshing ('thrashing') contractor arriving for the last time. What a thrill that was to see him proudly manoeuvring his equipment into our stackyard. This was the only time Horton would allow 'strong drink' on the premises (no doubt remembering his mother's fatal tippling).

It was customary to supply the eight or nine crew with beer in large stone jars. I sipped some and it made me cringe. The large drive-wheel of the steam engine was connected to the threshing drum by a long belt. 'That belt,' said one man, 'would slice you in half if it came off and hit you.' I ran off in a panic retreat, 'frit to death' I can tell you; my vivid imagination forming images to escape from.

Around the same time I gaped in wonderment one day on seeing a steam-plough at work in a next-door field, belonging to Henry Smith, the then occupant of Creccy Hall. Horton was with me. We both watched spellbound as the two powerful steam engines pulled a six-furrow, interchangeable plough by a cable, winding each way on the drums underneath the 'bellies' of the machines. Horton watched with a quizzical expression on his face, and after some little serious thought he called over the dividing dyke between the two properties: 'Don't get too near the bank, it might collapse and you'll fall in!' Whether or not the engineer laughed to himself over the fear of a nosy old man, nevertheless, Horton did make a valid point, under pressure those banks could give. I never saw another steam cultivator at work, so fast was life on the farms changing.

The same Mr Henry Smith was reputed to be a fearsome character – why else would they nickname him 'Rawpelt'? He was, of necessity, tough minded and got things done (as you would expect of a striving yeoman, with a fine Hall to support). Any employee who badly crossed him was invited to leave – forthwith! Although, to be fair, some stayed loyal for years. He was progressive in his methods, trying out the 'cultivator' and using tractors to plough his fields all night long, guided by artificial light. My word! that would challenge all the received thinking; especially if he worked his fields on the Sabbath, the Seventh Day, reserved for both rest and worship. Without much doubt, to the timid, Rawpelt's reputation could instil fear and trembling – even at a distance!

As if ignoring all the trauma settling about him (which was not the case), Horton, like a highly-disciplined warrant officer applied a set of unbending regulations. It seemed at times he had rules for everything, which is only to be expected if one survives beyond three-score and ten. There were many customs he set great store upon; in addition to all his moral certitudes, which seemed to imprison him like a ball and chain: can't, mustn't – not even think! And not least, that especially irritating one – you must!

We mustn't poke a stick up the pig's bum to make it squeal; chase the chickens around the place, in case they dropped dead or cracked their eggs; all those hand tools must be replaced, after polishing them bright with an oily rag; fruit on the bushes and trees must not be 'stolen', only the fallens might be eaten. (When I was but four years of age, Horton told me off for this transgression, and I went bawling and complaining to Mam.) The pump came in for special attention: we were told in forthright terms, not to pee anywhere near it, to avoid polluting the well. During a drought, odd bits and pieces did come up from its lower depth. There was always a glass jam jar to drink out of. We waited until the nasty bits sank to the bottom, drank the water down to a level just above them and then poured away the polluted rest; in normal course the water was sparkling clear.

'Always keep a piece of string and a pocket knife handy', was a piece of sound advice for one good reason alone; to use as a belt in case your braces broke down. 'Waste not, want not', was yet another catchy slogan – not that we had much to waste, too many things were wanting.

We collected the stray ears of corn during the biblical annual gleaning. Annually we bespattered the family's excreted waste from the earth-vault lavatory (the 'petty'), all over the kitchen garden, to grow the finest organic vegetables you've ever tasted. 'Waste not, want not', indeed! 'You've got to eat a peck of dirt before you die' – that's also what he said, so many times.

If we broke any of his many rules (it seemed impossible not to), he'd speak another set of words, beginning with: 'My eye on you!' And he would pierce us through with both eyes, not one! Stan would sometimes return some 'chelp' and run away until Horton cooled down. 'He needs dressing down!' would be his angry retort. But calm would prevail after a few puffs and piffs of the noxious 'Noxall' twist-tobacco. Although many times he must have felt a much required need, Horton always chastised us with his voice, never with his belt – especially the cruel buckle end, which some strict fathers were then reputed to use, although I never came across any actual evidence of that. One thing I do know for certain: that that kind of brutality never came our family's way. We were and would be traumatised enough, without being thrashed with any weapon of torture.

19

Horton's pacing to and fro over the carpet was wearing it out and that's about all it was doing. His 'bless us and save us' prayerful pleading, and not even Mam's Cornish charm with its fixed expression or her interpretation of the tea-leaves in the cup, after swirling them around her head (strictly three times – no more, no less!) seemed to bring us any benefit. On top of the mortgage debt still piling up, we also owed the 'on trust' account with Mary Pointon's village store. What a blow that was to Horton's pride to have that valuable trust removed. What a depth to have sunk, now that his former pride in solvency could no longer be sustained.

During the freezing winter of 1930–31 we sat huddled around a few embers for a fire. The logs were all used up so why didn't we chop down the giant oak by the stack yard? Horton would rather freeze to death than do that. Coal was out of the question, we couldn't afford such a luxury. Enterprising as ever, during the pitch darkness Mam went foraging for coal along the rail-line; entering through the crossing-gate to our far field, safely out of sight. The locomotive firemen used to discard partially burnt coal to relieve the steam pressure when they were waiting to pick up a line of trucks from the goods-yard siding, and this she searched out. Horton never went on those 'gleaning' expeditions, looking for fuel. He'd rather freeze to death than become a thief; remembering no doubt the strict moral training instilled into his mind. And fully conscious of the fact that we now lived next door to our newly installed village policeman, PC Brown.

Came such relief from this stolen warmth which provided us with comfort during that interminable bitter winter, when the frost formed over the bedroom windows, both inside and out, in crazy ice-etched patterns. Hating to get up I struggled under the blankets and cuddled our warm contented cat. Now here's a bit of interesting tattle to engage a curious mind: during all my early village living (up to the age of nine), I always slept in the 'husband's' half of Mam's bed, as indeed the latest offspring always had. To remind Horton of his sinfulness? Or to flash a clear signal: Keep out – I've had enough! My innocence never cottoned on to the reason for this contriving.

During all our desperation, no reckless wagering was ever attempted. Not for us the hopes of winning horses, or the expectancy of a football pools' win. Gambling was considered sinful: except for the striving kind which we had so long been engaged in – plod-honest farming! In such continuing desperation no wonder Mam sometimes exclaimed: 'I'm all of a lab-dab-sweat!'

We children were no longer attending chapel, because of our scarecrow style of clothing – such false pride! Instead, Mam took us for Sunday walks, in the quietness of the afternoon, hoping we'd not be seen. Sometimes we went with Horton to 'walk the fields' and listened to his excitement about the burgeoning shoots. In due season he would lift a clump of potatoes or carrots to note their progress. That is, in the days when we had growing produce to inspect; and when even the tough times still seemed hopeful of ending.

On our slow Sunday walks with Mam we had time to notice things. There was so much of interest – both wild and tame, and any newcomers to the village would have to be stared at.

The Fens may be flat, but if you know where to look and listen, they are never dull; at least not in my young day. Outsiders used to call us 'swedes' or 'turnips' – far

106

better than some calling-names. And as I grew older I would often wonder:

> Where have all those pits since gone?
> Filled with rubbish, now covered in.
> We used to look for workable toys,
> And sound wheels to build trolleys,
>
> Many artefacts await inspection,
> Old bottles – quite a collection!
> Now valued at a pound or two –
> Worth a dig, I'm telling you.

I also remembered the rhyme about our local churches, more especially as we passed by Gosberton Church:

> Gosberton Church is very high,
> (Much higher than a chapel.)
> Surfleet Church is all awry,
> Pinchbeck Church is in a hole,
> And Spalding Church is fit to foal.

The experience of one particular walk bothered me: we went to view the traffic on the main ramper-road. The smell and the din startled me. All those newfangled two-wheeled motorcycles, many with sidecars attached, carrying a single passenger, or mum with two children. Battling against the speeding motor cars they were often dangerously competing for their precious slice of the highway.

After the quiet of our village, this was a scene of scrambling madness. No wonder a local vicar was heard to remark in high dudgeon (at all this Sunday pleasuring): 'They are not having babies any more; they're having baby motor cars!'

Along the road towards the Westhorpe we passed by Paling's Farm. They could afford a wireless set: was this because they grew acres of flowers, in and out of glasshouses? So that was it: flowers paid – spuds, wheat and cabbages then lost money! And what now would Horton add to his usual, 'Bah!': 'You can't eat flowers! These newfangled ways will bring their ruination – you'll see!'

Appearing to be somewhat disturbed one day, Mam drew me aside and into her confidence. 'I'll show them!' she said (in a mood to do battle). 'I'll let them see I've got friends. I'll post a letter to myself.' Selecting a white oblong envelope she then put inside a plain piece of cardboard and addressed it to herself – would you believe! Then to give the plot some credibility, off we travelled by train to Spalding and I posted the envelope into the mouth of a red pillar box; an old one marked 'Victoria Regina'. What an excitement, to post a letter knowing it would cause the postman to call at our home, in full view of everyone – the very next morning!

So on the morrow, along with Mam (with such confidence!), we strode out of our drive to the lane; in view of all the neighbours (especially those peeping behind their curtains), and any possible passer-by who might chance to pass along. Mam saw the postman approaching, and with confidence that springs from foreknowing, she raised her arm to poise her out-stretched hand, as the postman busied in his bag to sort out our letter from the rest of the mail. Mam bid 'good morning' and accepted the letter, the one I posted in that white envelope, still feeling cardboard stiff. Much speculation would go the rounds (Mam was sure of that!). She lifted the envelope and gazed upon it. A puzzled expression captured her face (Mam should have been an actress on the stage). She appeared concerned about the name and address; after all it had come all the way from Spalding Town, as the franking of the stamp so boldly expressed. Man did not open the envelope, not in the lane nor along our driveway. She read the address several times, appearing to be deeply concerned (my word! How she extended that part of the

108

act). Then, with purposeful strides she walked back home. Such drama, such useless fuss! Just how hopelessly daft can some people get? Never mind, it pleased her. From somewhere, somehow, someone had remembered to write a letter to isolated Lizzie Green. My God! How poverty-stricken can friendlessness sometimes feel? Every week as regular as the sun rises, it was customary for farming folk to attend the local Spalding Market. It provided a social occasion, as well as an opportunity to discuss, grumble, and show their concerns over the dismal market prices. Like clockwork, Horton always attended and usually brought back some salted kippers 'off the stones' which we had for tea. Additionally, and this not only pleased me but never ceased to surprise, he handed me a penny's worth of peppermints in a white triangular bag. For such a frugal man to waste his money on peppermints required a deeper explanation other than a normal show of kindness, which undoubtedly it was.

Without using words, by this simple act, was this his silent way of communicating a poorly hidden fact? That: I am your father, this is more than a pennyworth of peppermints – it's a gift of my true feelings.

20

Bartering and borrowing helped many small farmers to exist. It saved a lot of bookkeeping and reduced their income tax liability; not that many ever paid a penny-piece on their 'losses' stashed away in tins or mattresses. One of many instances springs to mind, of working alongside sister Win and brother Stan, around the age of six, picking potatoes by the thousands, grown by the millions; the roots the Fens produce so well.

Occasionally, Horton borrowed Billy Branton's horse, a nag well past its prime, known by the name of 'Farmer' and liable to peculiar moods. Now had come the time for settlement of this simple lease-lend arrangement. No money ever changed hands, not even a penny-piece came our way. It was as though ready money had never existed. Such appeared to be the meanly outlook that sometimes deadened us.

So destitute had we become that our tatty clothes had now reached the state of being suitable for cutting into strips to make a peg rug. But that wasn't the worst that might happen – not by a long chalk! For protection, by way of caution, no 'evil-eye' peacock feathers were allowed in the house; mirrors were always covered during a thunderstorm, to stop the lightning reflecting, and striking us stone dead! And breaking a mirror automatically sentenced the offender to seven years' bad luck. One day Stan broke a long wardrobe mirror. Our breaths were held as we wondered low long it would be before the punishment began. From that time onwards, even the slightest mishap affecting Stan now had a cause to happen. Already he had been stricken by that wasting disease and we all knew that things happen in threes. So widespread was the state of village poverty that it seemed quite normal to me. And it was most certainly nothing to do with broken mirrors or the loss of their silent reflection.

Surprisingly, Stan and I experienced a piece of good fortune one day. In the loft over the washhouse, whilst ferreting around, we found a row of black shoes, with such posh uppers we couldn't believe our eyes. The sight astounded us, they looked like a display in a town shoe shop. In almost a whisper, in keeping with such an awesome occasion, Stan (once more) explained the reason for this hidden mystery: 'These shoes,' he said, 'once belonged to Will and Tom, Horton's children now in America.' A problem existed which was soon overcome. The soles had holes in them, scuffed and bored completely through. So one might ask the question: Why weren't they repaired? I never did find out but, presumably, in the days of Tom and Will, money was more plentiful.

Now approaching twelve years old, Stan ingeniously solved the worn-out shoe problem: he marked out cardboard soles with a pencil, cut them out and inserted them into the holey shoes. I also stuffed paper up into the toes, as the shoes were at least half-an-inch too long for me, and slipped about too much. On dry days the cardboard was scruffed away, especially after walking a mile and a half to school; on wet days it became a soggy mess. But what did that matter when such posh uppers afforded us so much pride.

'Get me a seedy* pencil,' spoke up Horton one day; as though struck by a violent impulse, caused by a sudden gush of blood to the brain, 'I'll write to Tom in Amerikee and ask him for help.'

---

* A pencil with an outer cedar wood casing (a recent innovation during his lifetime) was pronounced 'seedy' on this occasion.

That he wrote a letter remains in doubt. Tom was now his long-lost son. Some five years before, in 1925, he had returned for a family visit (three years after I was scandalously born). Tom's natural father, then 71, was surrounded by four young children, all by his mistress-housekeeper, all sinfully produced out of wedlock. In the strict moral climate of those times, the prodigal son required no forgiveness – the boot was on the other foot! It was the father who had so recklessly wandered. During that unhappy visit, Tom never came to the house; never said hello to his half-brothers and sister – but what would you expect? In such a small locality, think of the disgrace that had descended on a previously well respected family. Furthermore, it was only too obvious, there'd be no legacy for Tom. All Horton's capital from his successful days farming in the Cheal, had by now dripped away, in demanding bits and requested pieces. From what I subsequently gathered, there had been a fearsome row between son and dad. In a cutting act of purgation, Tom's parent was dropped dead! Not for him any hopeful understanding that might lead to a reconciliation. But why not:

Heed your Mother,   Consider their mixed Blessings,
And your Father –   Weigh their transgressions;
As Earthly as you can.   Humanly – if you can?

It might be considered that Tom had the rawest deal of all Horton's mixed brood – and he was the legitimate one! Which goes to show how unfair life can be. He lost his mother and sister in childbirth, at the age of eight, in 1902. His brother Will died in the 1918 influenza pandemic. Now his fornicating father was banished forever, after besmirching the Horton good name – with at least two known women (Mary Mawer and Elizabeth Green), bastardising five times over: producing George Horton Mawer and the four offspring of that brazen hussy, all known by the name of Green. His roots were severed, but memories must have remained; most probably, mixed up ones at that. And did bitterness impinge? Wouldn't that be expected? After all, now aged 31, hadn't Tom's life been sinfully ruined for evermore and a day, bogged down by unrelenting blame?

During his earlier life, especially in his more prosperous Cheal days, Horton had often assisted struggling members of his family. Without question, he was both helpful and an easy touch. He gave financial assistance to his sister Alice in 1893, after her husband, Joseph Mawer, aged 40, committed suicide over the entire loss of his potato crop; frozen when left overnight in a station wagon at the local station siding. Alice was left a penniless widow – utterly destitute in that very accursed Station Cottage, in which we now perilously lived. A meat hook was often pointed out to me; one of several in an outhouse, where Joseph desperately secured the rope.

George Horton Mawer, his first bastard, fleshly incarnated with the unlucky Mary Mawer, successfully tapped him for £100 to set up a retail confectioner's business in New Road, Spalding. He must have made his Horton father's conscience prick with words of inescapable truth when making his request: 'After all, you are my father!' Thus proving without much doubt, that blood can be thicker than the clarity of water.

When Branton Sansam died in 1874 (aged 37); cut short by the dreaded pneumonia, Horton not only assisted his widowed sister, Lucy, and her four school-age children, he later instructed his nephew Branton (the eldest child) in the skills of farming. Others he helped, too. George Horton was known to be good for a few bob in times of difficulty; which seemed, one way or another to occur with regular monotony. So no wonder, when his own desperate times befell, he felt that he was owing. But the whole community was now poverty-stricken; money was so tight the mint must have been on permanent strike.

113

So look at the basic facts again. Land bought during the 1919–21 boom, at the peak of the market, with a £1,000 loan at 5 per cent, producing a £50 annual debt, was now cripplingly unaffordable. By way of comparison also consider this: in 1992 a story appeared in the *Lincolnshire Life*, that a farmer starting out in 1931 rented a farm of seventy acres at £1 per acre (in fact, some fields were rented for less and many more were left fallow. I remember seeing them). Horton's position was dire: he was legally committed to £50 annual interest for 9 acres, which now could be rented for £9, on a yearly term. This left a stark realisation: hard times were going to annihilate many struggling yeomen. And once the dominoes started tumbling – when were they going to stop? No wonder they referred to a mortgage as a 'millstone around the neck!'

It certainly wasn't the best time for even the bravest farmer to gamble; yet some did, and held on: often grumbling; sometimes battered, living in the hope that good times would return. The faith they had! Horton could no longer afford to buy seed for sowing. The cows and pigs were never replaced, once they went missing, sold for whatever price that could be obtained. The chickens still clucked and strutted about and favoured us with large fresh eggs. The faithful cats remained, and the wild birds still nested in our well attended hedges. On odd occasions, we had visits from a harmless grass snake, which hastily glided away when it sensed us; anxious to escape the human predator, always eager to kill. Bees still buzzed and wasps droned and stung; especially if aroused by village lads pouring water into their nest; as I recall only too painfully well! The wild rabbits rutted and romped, until they were caught and cooked in a pot, and the hares suffered a similar fate.

Such was our simple country living. It was as well it cost little or nowt, for there was little or nowt coming in.

114

21

Are some folk mistakenly comforted by an illusory mirage, expecting it to be their oasis? Such faith some people have that something will always turn up in the end, sufficient enough to see them through; that good times will follow bad in some preordained succession.

Horton was now desperately requesting a timely cash injection, from family members, and even from George Horton Mawer, his first bastard son, whom he had gifted £100, now prospering in his confectioner's shop. His pleas were also extended to neighbours, especially those who *owed him* for past favours. The answers were all the same: though full of sympathy and understanding their refusal reflected their own desperation – nowt was making nowt! But to get back to the problem, even in good times (never mind the present frightening mess) who on earth in their right senses would pour good money after bad: to rescue an old-age-pensioner, up to his eyes in debt, and with four bastard children and a concubine housekeeper to support?

Horton's final hope centred on his nephew, Brant, the one whom he had helped and tutored after his father died so young. Brant had slaved all his life on five acres of rich Fen soil, plus, latterly, some three acres which he rented next to our Station Cottage. It was part of a field sliced and isolated from Cressy Hall, when the railway line was pushed through the village. The railway company built a bridge over the Eau to connect this odd piece of land to the main Gosberton road, next to the village station. On the Eau bank, a few yards on our property, Horton had given Brant permission to erect a timber hut, used to store his hand tools and to shelter in during inclement weather.

Apart from his main cash crops, on his total eight acres, Brant specialised in cauliflower and asparagus for the hotel trade. With some leaning towards the entrepreneurial, he also experimented with a few rare bulbs (said to be directly purchased from Holland). And, following a growing trend he grew tomatoes and plants *under glass.*

Apart from his other worldly goods, I know for certain he owned a bicycle; a sporting gun; a faithful dog named Spot, and a cottage slum. He rode his bicycle, as most Fen men do over those flat roads, with head erect and shoulders held back – just like a guardsman. Although he was a proud independent cottager, if all the sums were truly worked out, he would probably have been little better off than a day labourer. The pride they had, those workmen-owners, their status enhanced by a doubtful freedom: to be the master of their own confinement.

Around the middle of the 1920s there appeared a picture of Brant in the local press, dressed up in his Sunday best, his head protected by one of those wide caps (looking like a risen pancake with a peak), which in those days was the height of fashion. He should have posed with his sporting gun, as he appears to be in an overgrown jungle. The caption under the photograph proudly states the following:

'A corner of Mr B. Sansam's Garden at Gosberton Cheal, showing some roots of King Edward and Majestic Potatoes grown on a Special Manure. The tallest root is almost 9ft in height, and all are supported by canes. Every root had a remarkable number of potatoes, the heaviest being 81, and the weight being 16lbs. The heaviest potato of this root weighed $2^{3}/_{4}$lb.'

Go easy on the nudging, the knowing smiles, or the

decrying of this brave experiment. After all it was a partial success. But the use of cane supports would have caused a costly problem, especially when the uninterrupted winds swept across the open fields. Brant's progressive idea seems not to have caught on; no further news appeared. Even so, he deserves due credit for trying; not forgetting 'Dod's Special Potato Manure' supplied in a sack, also proudly displayed in the picture.

Horton's life was again jolted by the saddened event of his sister Lucy's bereavement on the 18th November, 1927, aged 77 (a remarkable age for the times she lived in, especially considering her life of hardship). The same Lucy who had romantically eloped with Brant's father to the City of London to get married. Both being sticklers for conventional correctness. No hanky-panky from either of them – no certificate, no cohabitation! No wonder she deplored her brother's sinful condition and disowned his unnatural additions to her proud family line.

From the time he was able, Brant, the eldest son, had supported his mother during all the years of her widowhood, as a dutiful son or daughter was expected to do: in the days long before Beveridge and any adequate form of widows' benefit. Before that, too many poverty-stricken widows had no option but to take in washing, or scrub for the better-off, for a few desperately needed pence. Or they would remarry (often a widower, and collect another family) and most likely produce another new child or two, of their very own. Perhaps far from ideal, but at least respectable, which is what most people strove to be.

It was during 1928, after arranging a fine memorial to his mother (Lucy Sansam), still proudly standing by the entrance to Gosberton cemetery, on the left side, that Brant, quite understandably, decided to *escape* from the Cheal and to sell his five-acre freehold field, which he had finally inherited. At 60 years of age he decided to journey to a

117

different kind of *freedom.* Away from the enslaving soil on which he had so long struggled. And, no doubt, to his utter relief, escaping from the shame of village gossip, tediously reminded him that his randy old uncle, George Horton, had produced yet another brat to feed, on his miserable income and the old age pension. And their remarks would be varied and plentiful; more in amazement than spitefully led, with the usual jocular touch: *I see your uncle George has still got plenty of lead in his pencil.*

My word, the humiliation that would have inflicted on a bachelor of tight-knotted virtue – such gnashing of teeth with no relief. Not once – four times over twelve years his disgraceful uncle's proneness had showed; sinfully adding to the family's pile of shame.

The interplay between uncle and nephew was not one-sided, after all, didn't Brant on one occasion help us to get a good price for our potato crop? Oscar and Win often worked in his field for nothing, so he also must have been owing. Didn't he buy all our manure for £5? 'Leaving none for our own fields,' grumbled brother Oscar. Perceiving this to be an injustice: that this money should have been a family gift, for past services rendered. And so it went on and on ... how easy it seems to foster resentment – and to forget that £5 was then three-and-a-third-times a labourer's weekly wage.

No one had offered to lend us money. The last chance was Brant who was still considering Horton's request which it was hoped would be dutifully met, once his nephew's land was sold. But minds were getting desperate, soon Brant would be gone. 'They say he has taken a job in a shoe warehouse, because he's tall and can reach the high shelves,' said Mam, always well up on the news. She seemed quite impressed that Brant was removing his life from Gosberton Cheal. Escaping the dreary drudgery, the common lot of the struggling cottagers: set, pull, pick, slash, hoe, dig, sow and

118

mow, on the lower rungs of survival, imbued with honest pride, a hopeful disposition and last, but not least: a deep and respectful fear of God.

After Brant had sold his land and just before he'd left the Cheal behind for good, Horton, in a tight-spring anxious state, was still awaiting his nephew's answer to his request for cash, to help him to clear the pile of debt growing huge on our land.

On a day I would remember well; there was a flurry of agitation existing between Horton and Mam. Brant was visiting his shed in our garden at the rail station end, to collect his tools for the very last time. Without any explanation Horton went to a cupboard and lifted a sporting gun cartridge off a shelf. It was probably an odd one he had found in a field and carefully stored away. 'Take this to Brant,' he said, handing me the deadly missile, which caused within me a feeling of alarm – these things could blow your head off! I'd seen dead animals riddled with shotgun lead, so I held the cartridge gingerly – not for me the fate they'd had. I knocked on the timber door and Brant opened it. 'Horton sent you this,' I said. He didn't seem pleased or grateful. It was such a relief when he took it. His glance didn't linger, he didn't say 'thank you', but acknowledged my gift with a grunt. At least that was something. He was a man with a spare style of prose – *in dialect it is called being clunch = sullen, stiff, of few words.*

Looking back it seemed obvious; Horton's true message delivered by me was something distressingly simple: *Surely by now you've made up your mind to offer help to your old uncle, who helped you and your mother so much in the past. I'm in a state of distress – please, do not abandon me, your own flesh and blood!*

'What did he say?' asked Horton, when I returned home. 'Nothing,' I said, not mentioning the grunt. In an instant I noticed Horton's facial expression change to a wounded

119

look of desperation. And Mam, who had anxiously listened, showed a look of disbelief that this possible lifeline had been so chillsomely severed. This beleaguered couple were now on a roller-coaster journey which was moving them fast downhill. And depressingly worse than that – a safety brake could not be found.

'If you help people, they turn on you!' Horton said, with such an intensity of feeling that those words would forever be etched on my mind.

After he had spoken, I sensed that his cry of despair had been dredged from the very bowels of his being. And I saw for the very first time his true resignation. That failure had passed and defeat was staring from an ever-closing distance.

His 'God Bless Us and Save Us', pleading was now over and done. Mam, undefeated as ever, continued to write down her pleadings for the consideration of a High Court judge.

Nephew Brant quietly disappeared, somewhere towards the East Midlands, his Cheal family's trying ties falling clean away. He had shaken off in one deft move the scandalous gossip from which he had so long suffered – your randy Staghorn uncle has spurted out again!

Sadly, at the age of 78 in 1947, Brant met his death on the highway (knocked from his bicycle and fatally injured). Yet another death to add to the roads carnage figure then still swelling.

When this sad news reached Gosberton Cheal, no doubt there would have been much head nodding and sympathy expressed in the wake of this tragic event. And most probably at least one person (possibly more) would be bound to make that well-worn remark: *If only!* If only Brant had stayed among us, he'd still be alive today.

[The £50 interest debt earlier referred to may have contained both interest and capital repayment elements. However it was made up, by the time the world slump came along it became impossible to meet this annual obligation.]

120

22

In 1879 a feeling of anxiety must have spread over many aspirant farmers: those getting too big for their ploughs and cows. Lord Burghley, of Brownlow-Henry-George, family inheritable name, MP for North Northamptonshire, Deputy Lieutenant for Lincoln, major in the Northampton & Rutland militia, late captain of the Grenadier Guards, etc, a proud Establishment figure, made an astonishing statement: that farmers' wives and daughters should give up the piano and French lessons and put their shoulders to the wheel. It was further satirically suggested in the *Saturday Review* that the appointed royal commission on agricultural depression should have in their statistics a section comparing the yields on farms, with or without a piano.

We possessed a fine piano, passed down from George Horton (the successful grazier, late of Offleet). And not only that we had a harmonium, left to Mam by Granny Green. To my knowledge I never heard a French word spoken in the home (except those now absorbed from the Normans). Horton never played a single note; Mam tinkled her own sombre compositions: Oscar was tuneless; Win would rattle off by ear all the popular tunes; Stan plunked 'God Save the King' with one finger, and I just banged away in frustration, wondering where the tune was hiding. Unquestionably, Lord Burghley's warning was not for us. It was obviously for those farmers of burgeoning acres – the new master class; upsetting the former settled order, of people no longer keeping in their place.

Nowt makes nowt, no longer applied; we now had *nowt*

121

to make nowt with, which was more alarming. And no longer did Horton exclaim: 'I eat well, sleep well and ail nowt!' His carpet pacing increased, and unanswered pleas to the Other Place were continued. Mam still exploded within the fierceness of her true belief: 'They can't turn us out – this is our rightful home!'

The world slump was worsening. Horton had not paid any interest on his mortgage debt and the amount outstanding kept accruing. Pressing reminders came, couched in words that were intended to cause alarm, which obviously they did. Who likes to be in threatening debt?

'I've no money, we're ruined!' Horton said again one day to Mam. And he burst out: 'I haven't got any money, not a penny piece to my name!' And then he hastily got up from his Windsor chair, and left by the outer door. But not before making a remark that, had I been more worldly-wise, would have chilled me to the bone. 'I'll cut my throat and end it all – out of the way!' is what he said.

[*In the early 1990s a study carried out by psychiatrists aimed to find out why farmers are twice as likely as others to kill themselves. People forget that a country-living can produce similar levels of stress as those found in inner-cities, including central London.*]

Some time elapsed with Horton still missing. Perhaps recalling the hanging suicide of Joseph Mawer, aged 40 in 1893 (the brother-in-law of Horton) in this 'accursed' place, and the story of the drowning of an earlier tenant in the Eau at the bottom of the garden, Mam anxiously turned to me and requested: 'Go and see where Horton is.' I looked across the field by the house, moved into sight of the stackyard, on to the crewyard – there was no trace. Next into the barn where all the tools and animal feed was kept. Everything seemed in place. (Had I then known of the suicide tendency of farmers, I would have first checked that all ropes and cutting tools were firmly in their place.) Under the barn roof was an open loft. Quietly I climbed the steps. A sound became louder as I poked my head above this upper floor. The sight I got was not alarming. There was Horton deep-throat snoring fast asleep on some bales of sacks. Quietly I reversed my steps, and reported back to Mam. She seemed relieved and so life went on. *But supposing it had happened: I had found a lifeless corpse – hanging or bleeding! What a jolt to my young life, that would have been. My God! How desperate must life get to be, before THE END IS NIGH!*

Horton faced his misery, stone-cold sober, strong drink was never allowed in the home. So he drugged himself with Noxall twist tobacco, when funds were available. When that temporary calming wore off, it was back to: *God bless us, and keep us from the Workhouse.* And now had come that threat, *to cut my throat and end it all!* Yes, his constant pacing of the carpet, in the grip of deep distress, wore down both the carpet and the household but nothing else.

By 1930 we were fast moving away from the overdue demands, but not by reason of clearing off the arrears – nor for that matter, of suddenly finding some treasure or valuable mineral on our land. By now eight years old, vividly do I remember the solicitor's clerk calling to obtain Horton's signature on a Private Treaty Sale document. Someone, so it appears, was ready to risk his shirt on a farming venture. Another smallholder full of optimism and eager to follow a flower growing venture, as would be seen quite soon. Horton signed over a stamp, almost, so it seemed, in a condition of thanks-giving.

Off went the solicitor's clerk, leaving behind a frazzled feeling that our desperate time was chiming. So this was the representative of *they* – the enemy who were *robbing us of hundreds and thousands by tricking us out of our rightful home!*

Mam was seething in her brain (but in truth she had no

rightful standing, being merely a mistress, without as much as a tuppenny interest). And Horton still with four teeth remaining in his head; with the lens in his glasses becoming unfocused; and his mental capabilities turning remotest, did what many hopeful seekers do when a fearful calamity suddenly strikes. Ever an optimist, he whirled out a spinning statement quite common in those times: *Worse things happen at sea!* And then, as though this wasn't enough, he sang a few words of that hopeful song: *When My Ship Comes In!*

Some irritation seemed to be gathering against our family's flouting of the buyer's lawful expectations. Holding out, ignoring the notices to quit, we never stirred from our cottage home. Mam laid down her own law: what are bits of paper when you're confidently in possession, which as most people know, is nine-points of the law.

We never experienced *rough justice* like lynching; saving a tedious trial. Our treatment conformed strictly in accordance with the law. By correct legal process we had now become squatters of a certain kind: we hadn't illegally moved in – *we had lived here for over 20 years – this is our rightful home!* That's what Mam kept on saying, in a true belief that she was right.

At the time, the thing that impressed me most about this young clerk's visit, was the sudden realisation that some lucky folk went to work in their Sunday best. There and then I made myself a solemn vow: I'd be one of those fortunates. Overalls of coarse cloth worn by working farmers, and usually plastered in muck and mud, were not for me. So I made a childhood decision: to smarten up and only work in Sunday best.

It was like a film, or so it seemed, not a flickery black and white one; in vivid colour and three-dimensional. One day, a few months after that fateful legal signing, a stranger turned up. He drove a large shire-horse pulling a cart through the main gate, and he never spoke a single word. Unloading

124

a plough and yoking a nag, he then furrow-sliced our vegetable garden where we grew our household's food and some over for sale. Round and round he plodded, as casual as you please; through the existing vegetable patch, the privet hedge along the path, and all the flowerbeds. But by far his worst act was to plough straight through our asparagus bed, cultivated over many years. Horton went out to have a pleading word, but he indifferently carried on.

At one point the horse's head came within an inch of our window, as the plough turned about. There was no mistaking the message: he was asserting his right and taking possession. It was not an act of vandalism, although I wondered later on when our fine oak tree was felled to the ground, as well as the walnut tree, and every fruit tree about the place.

Mam was so upset that she began to tremble and roundly made her protestations; not to the man, to some invisible attorney: 'He can't do that, I'll have the law on him!' But he could, he would and he did! *They* had at last turned up in determined bodily form. Possession was urgently required, so exercising had begun. The 'nine points of law' were changing hands. The tenth seemed determined to follow.

23

The years were disappearing – it was now 1931. Early summer to be exact; before the school summer holiday. Those six weeks of freedom were spent by many children working in the fields; usually picking potatoes, earning money desperately needed to supplement the family budget, especially to replace clothes outgrown or worn.

My years on earth would soon amount to nine. I had long since overcome my early shyness at the Clough and Risegate elementary school. In reception I covered my eyes when the redoubtable headteacher, Donald Hector Gordon Ross, came into the classroom. I had also stopped hating the tolling of the school bell, reminding me that I would be separated from home and Mam, all day long. Long since had I passed the infant stage, of fraying bits of cloth, learning to tie bows with shoelaces, cutting out patterns in coloured glossy paper, and singing simple infant songs (long since forgotten) from a tiered row of desks. Miss Bruton was in charge and told us she could see backwards in her glasses as she wrote on the blackboard. Even so, some of the children didn't believe her and misbehaved. 'Hands on heads!' she would bark out and, after a suitable cooling-off period, 'Hands down!' There was none of the free-style wandering about in her classroom. Miss B. taught by chalk-and-board, combined with instruction, ding-donging into our heads some rudimentary essentials, to later help us cope with our simple country life.

One day during that summer in '31, the exact day I cannot remember, the representatives of *they* came; in short, the disturbing sheriff's men. Those unexpected visitors, forcing their way they swept inside armed with full authority to execute a simple order – *throw them out, into the road!* PC Brown was on duty to oversee the workings of the law, in the fairest way possible. Not only was he a kindly man, he was also our next-door neighbour.

Our furniture, and all the private bits and precious pieces of our lives (including my few toys) that had accumulated in our time and from the several lives of our recent ancestors, were all piled up like a heap of old junk, outside our main gate, which was now closed and barred our way. We were herded out like cattle, which was harsh, but it was lawful. The new owners needed possession and their patience had at last been exhausted. The hand tools were left behind, as were the cats and the chickens, the latter probably ending their days in a hungry stomach. Also victims, some might say; suffering because they had shaky owners.

Brother Stan and I had gone to school that day before the sheriff's men arrived. But use your own imagination: a sudden crash at the door, a scuffle, cries of anguish, then 'OUT'. That summer morning we carried on as normal, writing, reading, adding sums and singing songs throughout the day; until four o'clock and a wild mad dash down the long-way home, hungry for our tea and the usual childish chat about the day – we were a talkative lot, yarning in those days was a form of entertainment.

Approaching and nearly home, about to pass the village policeman Brown's house, then to enter our own driveway, we were stopped by Mrs Brown who invited us for tea. With a few words of explanation she told us that our family had been *turned out*. Turned inside-out would have been a better description. Outside seeing is one thing, inside feeling is something completely different. In, out, roundabout; here we go again! Before I went into the Browns' house for tea, I looked towards our farm gate. Brother Oscar and Horton were frantically loading the furniture onto a borrowed horse and cart, to take to our new home.

In no uncertain way we had received the red-hot poker that day – the music stopped and the silence was frightening and I felt a quiver of alarm. We were out; chucked out! – down and out! I had never experienced anything like this in my eight years of living. From that day and all my tomorrows, I would always experience some doubt if life appeared untroubled. Henceforth, I would always retain an acute awareness of the possible and the probable.

But we'll have to see what happens tomorrow, take one day at a time, that's the sensible and less worrying way: *Take no thought of tomorrow, tomorrow will take care of itself.* Who made that absurd statement? We had done that for some time, ignoring tomorrow and look where it had got us! Not up the proverbial creek – some ten minutes' walk, west along the Risegate Eau; the local drainage stream; into a country cottage, as bad as any city slum – that was our tomorrow!

Clearly, we were destined to live by the Risegate Eau. Now the stream was a few yards away and we had no grand pathway leading down from a front door. This was a tiny two up and two down, with no rear entrance; a real comedown, with only a little bulgy-bit at the back for a kitchen space. This home-sweet-home was probably designed on the back of an envelope, on site, by a local jobbing builder. All the walls went straight up and down. We shared a dirt, vault toilet at the end of a narrow strip of neglected garden and a pump outside the front door, with our semi-detached neighbour.

You can imagine that we needed a shoehorn to squeeze five of us into such a confining space. Of the two bedrooms one was so small the bed almost covered the entire floor and one window was so tiny we had to take out the fixed pane of glass to allow fresh air in. Needless to say there was no washroom. We managed as usual with an enamelled bowl on the table. The stairway was an almost vertical ladder which Horton could not climb, so he slept fully clothed in his Windsor chair.

For the first time in my life I became aware of class distinction – we were now in the pits, at the very bottom. Poor old Horton had at last been humbled and I along with him.

Apart from the hovel we were now living in, our standard of living remained at the same lowly level. We were still to be pestered by the usual lice, fleas, flies, cockroaches and ants. And now the river rats came to greet us, right up to the door, looking for scraps of discarded food.

We continued to be hard pressed for ready cash, but at least that frightening mortgage had ceased to exist. So now we could live without the constant threat of the workhouse and 'God Save Us and Bless Us' was not so pressing. But intuitively I knew that I wanted a better life than the one I was getting. Not to be greedy, just to be freed from this wearisome – come-day, go-day, God-send-Sunday, hand-to-mouth existence. But perhaps that was expecting too much – take no thought of tomorrow, indeed!

Mam continued to be deeply incensed with this violent intrusion in our lives, and her net for *they* became ever wider. *They* had turned us out; *they* were all against us; *they had robbed us ends and sides up, of hundred and thousands!* 'And don't forget it', she would add, to give extra measure.

Horton was puffed contentedly on his smoky twist-tobacco and seemed overcome by a sense of resignation in his 77th year. Yet, underflowing in all that apparent new-found calmness, there still bubbled a boil of anxious steam. In short, his mind started wandering and moving his anxious legs.

One sunny afternoon, after returning from school I found Mam concerned. Horton was missing; he had vanished a little time too long. Where? Would I go back to the farm to try and find him. His mind often wandered over his long past (it's as well the future wasn't visioned). Perhaps he had gone back to repossess his land – that would be worth a gossip! I could see the old man fighting off the bailiff's men with a two-tined fork. He was plucky but not quite as fierce as Mam – she might have peppered their bottoms with a sporting gun. It's as well we didn't own such a lethal weapon. Was he now trespassing? Notices were all around: 'Trespassers will be Prosecuted'. That wasn't too worrisome, even I knew that trespassers cannot be prosecuted unless they did damage. What damage could an old man do? He loved the farm. Never mind about that, find him! So I had better get a move on. (He might even have gone back to his birthplace in Gosberton Cheal.)

Along the Siltside road, towards the rail station end of the village I walked a reluctant step, fearful in case someone should ask me about this embarrassing journey and I would have to think up a story, we kids called a ligger.

Beyond Jimmy Edgoose's smithy and Pointon's bridge; past Burrell's chicken depot and Paulie Goodyear's cottage on the left; finally to do a sneaky walk alongside the policeman's house. Thank goodness he appeared to be out on duty catching bad men, not concerned with arresting a broken old man for trespassing – surely not! Then, through the private drive up to the main gate, which surprisingly wasn't locked or bolted. No sign of the usurpers yet, the enemy who had thrown us out – this was too easy. Why not take over again – become squatters in our old home! Towards the farm building, I saw our old chickens, still clucking away (a kind neighbour was feeding them and collecting the eggs). But no sign of the cats – never mind about them, with all the juicy rats and mice about, their life by comparison was heaven. Just think how crazy it would be, to be envious of our old farm cats!

130

Suddenly, I saw him. The sight was both alarming and perplexing, and I felt an instant rush of despair; for the old man and for my dear old home. Horton was there – at *our* farm, *their* farm, and I couldn't believe my eyes! There he was, perched on top of a step-ladder, cleaning out the low guttering on the back of the pantry extension, the cool, deeper room where we used to keep the milk, cheese and butter – before the last cow ended up as butcher's meat. The cottage had been made uninhabitable, the back-door sagged and some windows were broken. Had *they* done that to stop us returning? Surely I was experiencing a dream. But that couldn't be; this was happening in the early evening. Furthermore, I was hungry, I hadn't had my tea! And for certainty I now knew that this place was owned by strangers. Moreover, it was silently depressing like an old graveyard.

'What are you doing, Horton?' I asked. A daft question surely because it was obvious what he was up to. (Perhaps I should have said: 'This is crazy, we shall be the laughing stock of this village if folk find out what you are up to.' But that might have upset his precarious balancing act on the stepladder.) He gave me a daft answer to my daft question, with not a little exasperation in his voice. Intently he peered at me as he answered: 'Doing,' he replied, wearily scratching his head and adjusting the awful mildew-tainted hat he always wore; before he continued with an equally daft answer: 'I'm cleaning out the guttering, it's all stopped up!' This made good sense, the rain water ran off the roof through the guttering and down pipes into our well to supply water for the weekly wash. He continued the task as this unblocking job seemed most essential. Some panic started to trouble me. My orders from Mam were explicit: 'Find him and bring him back!' That was a firm instruction, but would he comply without a fuss? He could be pig-headed and he towered over me. A giant of a man with his Viking beard, and poor me only eight years tall. What was I to

131

do? Would he make a scene? Luckily he was not and had never been a violent man. All he needed was bringing down to earth, with as much skill as possible; and that is not always so simple – certainly not for a child.

He seemed completely lost and it was obvious to me that his mind now lacked the clarity it once had. This was perhaps a progression of the 'my memory is not what it used to be' complaint he had recently been making, now showing with the loss of his bearings. 'Come home, Horton,' I requested. 'We've been turned out and it's teatime, this is not our home any more – come home with me.' I remember well his vague, defeated expression as he turned to me and for a moment appeared to be grappling with the stark horror of his true situation. He still hesitated on top of the ladder. The last handful of dead moss and accumulated dirt was collected and violently thrown to the ground. I put words to that and kept silent for a moment as a sign of respect. Slowly he stepped down the ladder and gazed at me with frightening intensity. Yes, at me his youngest bastard child, the last of his clan (ironically, without his name). A child who could do absolutely nothing to help him – gazing like an inquisitive bystander, a useless appendage to his many problems. 'I'm ruined,' he then said, appearing to talk to himself and reinforce a dreaded conclusion.

In a sudden swing of the mind, jolted by cold realisation, he made to accompany me, back along the Siltside Road to our rat-infested hovel, leaving behind his long life's dreams and his fearsome struggles with the land. Ruined, down and out – it surely wasn't planned that way – but then, with any sense, it never is!

During that homeward trudge under the widespread Lincolnshire sky, falling low across the flat horizon, I noticed the heavens were glowing with 'shepherd's delight'. Good, I thought, red sky at night. That means tomorrow will be a fine day; for playing football, hide and seek or climbing trees. Meanwhile, it was teatime and I was feeling hungry.

Mam was now in a state of dejection, brought on by this new low condition of our lives. Even I knew that we had slipped many pegs downwards in life. It was that obvious and it hurt more than a little – my pride of place was lost. Were we children also receiving the wrath? Divine punishment for our parents' sins? That was often what the preacher in our chapel ranted on about. It must be true, it was happening to the family so we must all be sinners, otherwise why were we being made to suffer so.

24

So there we were, in a hand-tied-up situation living in romantic vision of a simple country life. We children still attended school, worked and played. It didn't seem possible that another disaster could arise. Horton had been forcibly moved twice: from his farm in the Cheal and from his Risegate smallholding. But was this now the time to remember that time-honoured warning: Things usually happen in threes...?

The tied cottage laws were still in force in 1931. Over 40 years later (in 1974) some statistics were produced in a survey of tied cottages, in which were listed the main reasons for tied-cottage eviction. There was estimated to be approximately 300 population evictions during that year. Some 19 per cent of farmers who have ever had tied cottages have sometime had experience of taking action against an employee, so even at this later date evictions were regularly carried out. Any eviction is frightening enough: a lifetime's service could end up in homelessness. In 1931 another category should have been added to the reasons for eviction: failure of the labourer to turn up to work, after accepting a tenancy.

The reason for this seemed obvious. Mam had been at it again! So steeped in resentment had she become, that out of a fit of pique, she had forbidden Oscar to work for Henry Smith, the man locally nicknamed *Rawpelt*, our feudal landlord of Cressy Hall. Most of my life I was to ponder this mystery: why on earth did she rock such a fragile boat? There's no doubt, this was akin to playing Russian roulette with all the chambers fully loaded. But Mam was Mam and in her fighting mood she liked to give the buggers hell! All throughout that busy summer, Henry Smith waited patiently for brother Oscar, his tied labourer, to turn up, to fulfil the obligations and keep the bargain he'd made with the landlord when in such desperation at the recent eviction he had pleaded for the cottage tenancy.

> Mam! Mam! Oh Mam!
> Of all the windmills to tilt,
> Why did you charge this one?

Before we were ousted from our *rightful home*, Horton had accidentally pierced his foot with a fork. The wound grew into an angry 'place', red and raw and suppurative. Mam bathed the foot in the family washbowl. And although she applied lashings of Germoline (strictly applied by the second finger of the left hand, the one most hygienically safe according to village lore), yet still the throbbing wound would not heal. To be fair to that miraculous salve, a deep infection had long set in. We all used to gather round and gape at the raw, angry wound. Mam would bind it up with bandage strips torn from a discarded bedsheet. She seemed to enjoy this medical challenge, obliviously in a state of honest ignorance that a gangrenous condition could possibly result in a leg amputation. A kindly neighbour came by and after due inspection of the raw cavity, supplied an odd soft slipper, which Mam sliced open to enable Horton more comfortably to hobble. What else could be done? We couldn't afford home visits from a doctor, not at half a crown (12$\frac{1}{2}$p) a visit.

But what a family, still living by the riverside, still existing in a defiant state, ignoring stark reality in a come-day, go-day, God send Sunday and Monday, right round to Saturday again. We had reached a state of resignation, drearily repeating. But that contractual obligation to provide labour to the landlord (which we openly were ignoring), as part of the bargain made when we desperately begged for possession of his pig-sty slum – what of that?

Another normal school day arrived. Who on this earth decides what is normal? Life's course can often be changed by complete strangers in an oblique, professional way. Within bounds they usually do their best, those stoical administrators, strictly guided by the Regulations, to try and fit awkward pegs into confining cubby-holes. But might it not be the case that they cannot always stomach the unpleasant reality of what is going on?

At the beginning of one particular day, the exact day I cannot remember, brother Stan and I set out for the Clough school as usual with all the urgency we could muster, which usually meant jogging the entire one-and-a-half-mile way. Stan egged me on so I had to stick it out, not without a painful stitch. It was all right for him, being much older and more practised, he could run for miles and miles without as much as a noticeable puff. On that early morning run to school, sometimes I hated him!

School never bothered me; money never bothered me: my ragged clothes never bothered me – in fact nothing of any consequence bothered me, except to be delivered to those flat potato fields and have slavishly to work hard all day, picking 'taters' by the thousands into those wicker baskets, which became heavily clogged with the rich soil and made the task so back-breaking – not only for children, even for the adults.

> Potato picking in wicker baskets,
> Clogged and heavy with sticking soil;
> Picking them by the score –
> Baskets full, and thousands more,
> Until I'm exhausted and sore.

136

How much more of this achy toil?
Up the row, down the row,
Round and round the spinners go –
Inflaming my blood to boil!

The precious money earned from child labour was desperately needed, to buy food and clothes. This kind of work from early childhood was unexceptional in those hard times. In fact, if you didn't play your part to provide extra money for the family income, village folk would not be amused. Much to the point, they would consider the possibility that your entire future life might be spent in idleness, if you didn't turn in a much needed hand. So get your head out of that book; reading books will not get you a living. Work! Work! Work! – that's the thing, and the harder the better; for about it seemed a sense of salvation.

Mr Henry Smith of Cressy Hall (our landlord), who had been waiting several months for his new labourer to turn up during the busy period of the year, must have been scratching his head in more than slight exasperation. They didn't call him *Rawpelt* for nothing.

Farms in those days were labour-intensive, many labouring hands were needed. And tied cottages played an important part in their day. It was the system that had evolved out of necessity and was widely used. It wasn't all bad, except if you were tangled up in it against your will, to the point of feeling imprisoned.

So what would Mr Henry Smith be reasonably expected to do in those harsh times? He had waited patiently for his new tied labourer to turn up. His labour had been desperately needed throughout the harvesting season. There seems no doubt about it, after a fair period of waiting and warning, his only recourse would be to obtain the services of the essential eviction man, to get rid of his reluctant labourer and obtain the services of one who would be suitably

137

compliant, and show gratitude: for being given a humble roof over his head and that of his family.

It did not seem humanly possible that there could be yet another act of misery and more bewilderment hovering above our place of home. Once again, we were about to succumb. And once more, I didn't know it!

As usual, during the autumn term (sometime in late October), Stan and I attended school, and Oscar went to work, still in the wrong direction and still cocking a snook at the tied landlord. Later that very day a man arrived and consulted confidentially for a few minutes with the headmaster, Mr Ross. I was sent for and this put a stop to my beavering away contentedly in a lower class. Brother Stan was already waiting by the head's desk. We were introduced to this strange gentleman who bade us follow him. An alarm bell started ringing in the back of my head – something was wrong! As we all walked to his car he briefly explained that we were being *turned out* of the cottage and would be going into the institution. Institution? He didn't fool me with that fancy title. This was really the Spalding Workhouse. It had only recently been renamed The Poor Law Institution, in 1931 (when we became inmates). Whatever grand title they had tagged it with, a workhouse it had been and a workhouse it remained – a grim purpose-built building for destitute folk. Mam always called it 'that place!' And many might say: it's too good for them; nothing to pay, three good meals a day, adequate clothing and a bed to idle on. Horton had forewarned me: Union, Workhouse, Institution. All those titles he had mentioned, in fearful tones of respect. But why on earth was this happening to us? The answer I accepted never made true sense. So why Mam, why did you risk the landlord's wrath? You must have known the consequences...

The smart-suited official turned out to be the relieving officer, the man who delivered the few allocated means-tested shillings to the feckless, undeserving poor. It wasn't much of a relief to me when he took charge of us for a short time to deliver us back to our cottage in his tiny Austin Seven car. We were not going to receive any money relief – only to be relieved of our family life – and this had to be done with the least fuss or feeling. Very few words were exchanged between the three of us on the fateful journey from the Clough School to the Risegate village. About a mile, but still an anxious distance away, we passed by the Black Horse public house, where a few folk had gathered to stare, bitten by curiosity – and no wonder!

For the second time in six months, piled up by the roadside were all our family possessions. It was almost as if they piled up by themselves, this ghastly routine was becoming so regular. We were again suffering degradation and the law or society was firmly not on our side. 'The sins of the fathers descend upon the children to the third and fourth generation' – to quote that well-worn truncated biblical saying once again; in which I also divinely believed and spoke for many years to come: those words of condemnation, widely wielded like a cleansing sword.

It was only too obvious, all was not well and I knew it. Stan knew it too, but what can you do when the rawness of life hits you, and you tumble into the frightening unexpected? An ambulance stood by; after all we did seem accident-prone and somewhat broken and bent. But was it more the grip of infliction as it tightened around our feckless necks?

By now I knew the difference between shivering and shaking. Man was violently shaking – from head to foot! It was as if she had just witnessed the massacre of her entire family by a giant Viking sword of our recent ancestors. Horton was in a state of bemusement: most likely his blessed touch of senility helped to smooth for him the utter rawness of his final plight. His injured foot was still in a fearful

139

condition (another reason for our need to be rescued). The gangrenous-looking wound would not go away; even with all those lashings of miracle ointment, many bathings, and yards of torn-sheet bandages. This was a big disappointment to Mam, she fancied her skills at 'doctoring' and disliked being defeated.

Brother Oscar had been called from nearby Charlton's farm, where he was busily at work. Now aged 20, our older brother gave Stan and me a grin, not in amusement, more in encouragement, no doubt trying his best to comfort us. He knew full well what was happening and the fateful reason why: that his tied contract of service to the landlord had remained unfulfilled. But Oscar's grin, perhaps more likely forced by the stark realisation that this was yet another bout of retribution – brought on by wanton fecklessness as once more the hands of *they* were striking hard upon us.

The stolid eviction men continued to earn their day's wages by busily piling up all the furniture on the Marjorum Public Hall side of the road. It was quite a heap. Luckily the grass verge was wide enough to take it. Again, all our family goods, the material outward bits and pieces of our lives and the antique quality furniture which had been lovingly collected and cherished by the Horton family over many years of hopeful struggles was now to be forcibly abandoned. Feeling a growing sense of unease, I took a last glance to live on in my memory before the men covered the heap with a large tarpaulin sheet, kindly offered by a watching neighbour.

Our outward pieces had gone, our inward pieces remained, awaiting to be reassembled; like the ragged bits of a faded jig-saw puzzle. What next? That was now the more burning question. My curiosity became overtaken by uneasiness, as I felt my mind beginning to bob about far more than usual.

'Worse things happen at sea,' suddenly said one of the

more jovial busy eviction men, exercising the British priceless sense of humour, which must always be used to the full in times of extreme adversity. Yes, the jovial man was quite right, you can drown at sea. Here on the relatively safety of land, we had managed to drown in a different way. Whether this was the hand of retribution, or the timely assistance of hopeful intervention, was much more than I could possibly reason. (One thing I firmly decided there and then, that whatever job I took in life – however desperate I became – I would never be able to exercise the essential coolness of a sheriff's eviction man.)

Another dosage of childhood trauma was fast approaching, like our local steam train, and the feeding-spoon was poised – full and ready! Home had not prepared me, school had not prepared me, no one had prepared me, except that sudden confrontation with the unrelieving, official 'relieving' man. But surely no one was purposely picking on poor me. This was the normal way of things: *Children should be seen and not heard!* How could caring grown-ups cope if a child's raw feelings rocked the official boat? Was it ever thus? Countless lonely children, scared and often wrecked a lifetime long, left to silently brood and question (how grateful I would grow to be for my first few years of quiet, secure existence).

So listen for a change, some of you assured officials (wrapped up professionally in your various titles); you may think you are coping with hopeless kids – in fact the kids are often trying to cope with you.

The kindly uniformed ambulance man came towards us: 'Will you get into the ambulance, Duck?' he requested, first of Mam. She'll never do it, I speculated inwardly, but she did. Mam was temporarily defeated. We all got on board. This ambulance was to be the tumbrel of my young life; transporting me to a world I had vaguely heard of but never hoped to experience. But I was young and spirited,

141

and eager to learn. And last, but not least, I possessed a latent sense of humour which I would desperately need to develop.

Instead of a feeling of trepidation, perhaps my thoughts should have been: if this is what is to be – come on, let's get on with it! Steadily the ambulance moved off on its short journey to Spalding. We could see out of the blue-glass windows, but thankfully for us no one could see within. Even in such low desperation it is of utmost importance to keep within oneself what little pride there is left. Our release from the landlord's servitude had ceased, as also had our precarious toehold in the Fens. Yet once again we were stricken and now there was no doubt about it – we were truly DOWN and OUT!

Where is the child's escape route – sometimes in pleasant daydreams, or disturbing nightmares. Is there no reasoned escape? Pre-knowledge of a devastating event would produce only a lot of wasteful worrying. A plunge into an icy cold bath can sometimes be very invigorating and stimulate a move which might turn beneficial. It can also take your very breath away. For the weak-of-heart it can sometimes be fatal. That's about the size of it. So get your breath back, take a fresh deep one and go into the next challenge, instead of wallowing forever in a patch of swampy ground. To learn from varied experiences. To get on with life, be grateful for tiny bits and pieces of satisfaction and only meagre bouts of happiness in this world we have to strive in. And if that sounds a little harsh, what else would you expect when faced with insoluble problems experienced by others, which also batter you?

> Admiration of the Fearless,
> And those of High Esteem,
> Scorn for the Feckless,
> May those who vent be brief.

142

Encourage all the Strivers,
They might yet succeed.
To the Devil the Sinners!
Arouse the abject Meek.

25

We arrived at last at the sombre Victorian prison-home planned to house the slothful and unfortunate poor for their own good, in order to limit the depth of their degradation and to set an example by frightening to death any thoughts of idleness in others. After alighting from the ambulance we waited patiently in the great reception hall. There a large wall clock loudly ticked the time away, bonging every quarter hour; reminding us, at least, that we were still in the land of the living.

Horton remained in the ambulance to be taken to join the elderly and sick in the infirmary wing, at the rear of the workhouse buildings. At the age of 77 he had been given total security at last: Nothing to worry about, a good bed to lie on, food for his stomach, an ounce of tobacco every week to puff away in a penny clay pipe. (Poor man, ancient enough to be my great-great-grandfather, yet he had somehow managed to seed my cloudy life.)

After some 26 years of striving together, he was abruptly parted from his concubine-housekeeper and the last four of his guilt-touched children, to be stowed away for his own good, awaiting his time for the deliverance of death: to the final comfort of a pauper's grave.

The bones of the conversation that passed between us have long since been forgotten, as we stood there waiting for the next manipulator to rearrange our hapless lives. To me Mam whispered: 'We left in such a hurry, I didn't have time to put my knickers on.' She had managed to put on her Sunday-best hat, trimmed with red roses, but not with

144

the care she usually took. I remember looking at her up and down and deciding that the knicker problem wasn't visible. In such fraught times, why do people often dwell on silly things?

From a side door, on the right of the hall, suddenly appeared a man in a smart dark uniform, with 'Porter' written across the band of the front part of his projecting peaked cap (glowing with pride in bold golden colouring). His name was Stone (Porter Stone to be exact), whose many menial duties included checking visitors at the main entrance gate. With such a name, in such a place, one might wonder if he suffered from being stonily clad. Outwardly he looked like Friar Tuck as he displayed his rotund belly, and a dutiful face that could have smiled a pleasant smile, outside this dismal building. (It seemed to me as time went on that the title, Porter, was the renamed twentieth-century Beadle.)

Next to appear was the Labour Master (in a similar dark uniform, also with the regulation job-description headband). He was accompanied by one sombre male inmate, dressed from head to foot in depressing, funereal black (as befits permanent mourning in such a purgatorial place). The Labour Master was in charge of the male inmate population and allocated the daily work (a sharp reminder to everyone, that this House demanded a state of toil). Included under his supervision were also the many tramps who queued every evening outside the porter's main gate, patiently awaiting admittance for one night's kip, a bath, bread and butter, or whatever else was sparingly offered, to be paid for by a short spell of work the very next morning before they tramped their lonely ways, begging and looking for a spell of temporary work (many having walked away from their poverty-stricken homes, rather than be a burden to the families).

Then, most likely following a procedure long since laid down, from a door on the left-hand side of the hall came a

145

toothless crone (probably not more than 50 years of age, but wearied out to the look of 80), who never smiled, perhaps keeping 'a stiff upper lip' to cover the empty space where her teeth should have been. She wore the regulation female, workhouse dress: light blue from head to toe, excited only by thin vertical white lines about an inch apart. Her head was uncovered, she didn't need a hat in this place as strolling beyond the porter's gate was strictly forbidden – especially for women, for reasons only too well known by men.

Now was the time for the grand entrance of the matron, a most dignified figure of portly dimension and as staid as one would expect her to be. She marched from her office accoutred in a resplendent dark blue uniform, with starched white cuffs some six inches long, the whole set off by a crown-like headband. And by way of serious decoration there dangled a small watch from her ample breast (with a second hand to check pulses with, which seemed very reassuring). To overview the lot of us she had clipped a pair of pince-nez to her ample nose which moved about as she solemnly surveyed us, with all the self-confidence that another human being can muster, when they are in charge of many lost lives. There seemed not the slightest doubt about it: in this world she not only knew her appointed place, most probably she expected to stand a good chance in the next. Matron was to be our earthly Saint Peter. We had passed through the porter's entrance gate; now was the judgement time, before the time for relocation. By comparison with our only other homeless option; this was to be our refuge of distress, which we were now well and truly feeling.

But, to be scrupulously fair, what else would you expect of a professional person in charge of buildings and staff, and a keen budget to run them on? The Matron wasn't responsible for the world depression. Her job was the smooth running of the workhouse and she appeared to be highly skilled in that respect (emotional problems were not of her concern). After all, the workhouse costs were borne by a form of taxation: begrudgingly paid for by the people and keenly supervised by the Guardians of the Poor. So there could be nothing slip-shod about that; every penny piece had to be accounted for, as you would rightly expect. Indeed, the workhouse was efficiently run by a skeleton staff, ill paid maybe, but pleased to have a regular job in the depth of a world depression. Under their close supervision the inmates did the main work themselves and why not? Within the workhouse walls there were inmates of all trades and skills: carpenters, seamstresses, cobblers, hairdressers, clerks, gardeners, cooks and many others – all carrying out their assigned duties. In this gloomy accommodation not far removed from a punitive prison, society (as would be expected) exacted work in lieu of payment for free board and lodgings.

Time never stands still – moreover, it never moves backwards – so seemed to remind that large wall clock, dignified with black Roman numerals, ponderously ticking away my last minutes of precious freedom, before I was swallowed up into the grip of institutionalised living. So subdued had I become that the tick-tock sounds began to soothe my brain. But why didn't that damn clock tock-tick backwards and free us from this cold-scrubbed place?

The assembled staff and inmates now went into sudden action. Matron, with the minimum of practised official words, explained that we would be taken to our various quarters, whatever that meant. There was now a slight interruption as the noisy clock bonged out its next quarter. Then their actions became simultaneous and fast moving. Accordingly, Mam disappeared through the door to the left of the hall, accompanied by the toothless crone; Oscar went through the right-hand door, escorted by the sombre inmate in black, supervised by the labour master and, as if a puppet on a string, the porter (with a thin smile creeping about his face),

147

made a finger-ticking gesture towards Stan and me. We followed him from the great hall out through the main entrance door to the children's quarters, which appeared from my first cursory inspection, to be miserably bleak and bare. A feeling of desolateness invaded my young human soul – a pain stabbed within my chest and I gulped a choke for the first time – and most certainly not for the last.

I had seen sheep follow each other in a field, often in a nervy state. Was this now happening to me? Running away was out of the question. Both anxiety and curiosity began to distort me. Porter Stone never uttered a word of comfort during the short distance he was in charge of our lives – his job was to deliver, not to commiserate. I tried my best to reason. Perhaps the Matron had not fully explained: we were only being taken to a school in this place, to attend classes. No need to fear; no need to shed tears, surely here they've got family accommodation and we'll all meet up again at teatime. It would all turn out right in the end. My childish imagination had resolved the problem: at teatime we would all meet again, and chat about our latest adventure. Goodness me! The workhouse with its shocks and surprises might yet turn out to be a place of promise.

But ignoring all the family folly, the mistakes and the committed sins, just consider the cost to the public purse. Instead of helping a family to keep a toe-hold in the struggling world, we, all four of us, had ended up in a costly paupers' hotel.

To contain our family in working environment, a few shillings of weekly relief would have sufficed, until the children reached the age of 14, subject always to means testing. Relief indeed! And many folk would add: start with one and you'll find millions with an excuse to hold out their begging bowl. And many, equally worthy, those proudly struggling to remain independent, and not any better off than the poor relief recipients, might be forgiven if they felt somewhat resentful; of what appears to be encouragement for the feckless, to their own disadvantage. Now can you imagine what some parsons might bray from their pulpits? This profligate use of public money will encourage idle folk to live a slothful life of sin!

Without a shadow of doubt, the workhouse had several uses: not only did it shelter the destitute and homeless; it replaced previous poor law relief which now was unobtainable. Thus the saving on wider outside relief was expected to outweigh the workhouse costs. And people were so fearful of ending their days in 'that place' they seldom, if ever, volunteered. Some even committed suicide, rather than face such a disgrace. In my very own village, before I was born, senile Nellie Cox drowned herself in the Eau stream, rather than let the officials forcibly put her away. They pulled her out of the water with a garden rake. 'Poor thing!' Mam used to say.

Porter Stone, with a fine economy of introduction, passed Stan and me on to the next keeper and shaper of our lives. This was to be the final one. Her name was Purdam – Nurse Purdam to be exact. (*With so much agitation besetting me I failed to work out that the nurse's name began with the first three letters of purgatory, and the last three started damnation.*) Scottish and tightly disciplined in a strict Presbyterian mould, she was without any question the Lord and Master of the workhouse children, whom she often viewed with disdain over the top of her tightly-wrapped bosom. Nevertheless, apart from my own impression, she had a job to do: to control a group of pauperised children in the most effective way possible. Sometimes, to press home her authority, she angrily called us imbeciles. But I wasn't so stupid to believe that I was an idiot, just because someone branded me so.

149

Now, with the minimum of preliminary patter, she took us into the bathroom (a huge place, with at least eight washbasins and two baths). Next came her orders: off with all your (disgusting bits and pieces of) clothes. We placed them in a sack with our names on, to be fumigated first, then stowed away ready to wear when we left this place (and that was a sign of hope). Never before in my life had I bathed in a white enamelled bath, huge enough to wallow in (for that matter I had seldom, if ever, used a tin bath, so this was another short, sharp shock, not only to my skin, to my entire system). Having quickly sized us up, several suits were ready to try on, until we found the one that fitted (later on we'd be issued with a Sunday suit, exclusively for the Sabbath). And would you believe it (I was most impressed), apart from a matching suit, socks, braces, a shirt and tie, they issued me with a fine pair of black shoes – without any holes in the soles? Our name tags would be placed above a peg from which hung a flannel and small cloth bag, containing a toothbrush (the first I had ever seen, let alone used) and a round tin of solid toothpaste. We now seemed well and truly in place.

The efficiency in this workhouse place went on at a cracking pace. So fast I hadn't time to daydream or speculate what next. 'You'll not be attending school for a few days,' said the nurse. Then she told us to sit in the dining-come-living room, which was less exciting than a railway station waiting room. But that's unfair, they have pictures of far-away places, suggesting excitement and adventure – unlike this dreary confining place.

After a few minutes, quietly sitting on best behaviour, our curiosity got the better of us. We braced ourselves to look out of the window, rather timidly at first. We viewed again the yard we had crossed; it was extensive and covered with cinders. To keep it secure, at the furthest end, it was surrounded by a high wall at least eight feet tall (built during the First World War to imprison the aliens within). Facing the front of our quarters, next to the Pinchbeck Road, were a series of tall windows. We could hear the traffic pass by but we couldn't see out. All the windows facing the public side of the building were completely frosted out. This had a two-fold advantage: it kept us out of sight of normal people and reduced our distractions to the very minimum.

At about a quarter past four some twenty children (their school day having finished) burst in upon us. They all appeared well-dressed and fed and quietly mannered, if not somewhat subdued. My word what a shock that was, that first meeting with my large new family. They gazed at me and I studied them. Before long the questions and answers began, all in a friendly mood.

In this place the received training appeared to be: children must be passively grateful. But children are children, so amongst ourselves there was and would be much relating, to find out more about life outside the boundary walls and the frosted windows of this gaunt Victorian edifice, the place I would call house but never call home.

26

Although I tried desperately to continue believing that I would not be parted from Mam, by early evening I had most reluctantly accepted that my young goose was well and truly cooked – from now on here was my life and my strange new family. My growing desolation would not be assuaged. My feelings were fast slipping out of tune; far worse than my early days at infant school – I knew then that I would return home every afternoon. Even slaving in those flat unresponsive fields, nor wearing those tatty clothes, were of any consequence compared to this sudden upheaval; this dispiriting redirection of my life.

So fast had my life changed. In the morning I had walked to the village school, surrounded by all the familiar bricks, clanging bells and village people; full of striving in my learning efforts – happily innocent! Yet here I was, in the evening of the same day tramping sadly up those cold, grey-stone stairs to the communal workhouse dormitory and nobody had attempted an adequate explanation. An animal about to enter the abattoir can smell the blood and hear the screams. That is sufficient explanation for what turns out to be a short-lived, violent trauma; my position was similar but different, it was not to be short-lived. After the shock would come the realisation and after that the compromise – the essential need in life's adjustment, to offset the bubbling anger within.

The dormitory lights were switched off by the nurse who took a cursory glance to make sure that we were all snugly tucked in. A chorus of 'Good night, sweet dreams' floated across the room from one child to another. Sweet dreams? – yes that's possible, what a wonderful escape! In the darkness I hid my head under the white linen sheets to blot out the intense black despair I now felt over this sudden violent wrenching of my life. Apart from brother Stan in the next white-sheeted bed (and thank goodness he was there; four years older and at least another ten years worldly-wiser) my real family had disappeared. Mam was no longer Mam – the nurse was 'Mam', and a fat lot of comfort that gave me.

> During your childhood did you experience,
> One bleak moment of utter desolation;
> A chilling separation from your only family?
> The door closes in a strange place –
> The light goes out, the blackness strikes!
> And you experience abandonment;
> With your thoughts gripped in turmoil,
> Choked in the frozen grief of mourning,
> A victim of someone else's misfortune,
> Which, without prior invitation,
> Has now become your own low state.

The rules of the workhouse were steadily absorbed by jerks and jolts. There was no alternative but to obey. From this imposed experience came many surprises: flowing hot water in baths and basins; the issue of presentable clothing; meals that appeared like clockwork; the suddenness of communal living and much more besides. One particular introduction both excited and amazed me. Nurse Purdom showed me how to work the newfangled water closets, two of which stood outside by the back door and one upstairs on the landing. The latter for poo only, we had potties under the bed for peeing in.

I'd never in all my scant experience come across this

type of 'petty' before, having lived all my short life in a village, back of beyond, still without piped water. What a fascinating piece of equipment it was. I pulled the chain once and it worked. Down went my poo into an outlet pipe; not into a hole beneath to pong and ferment like grapes before becoming wine. Yes, my turds actually disappeared; often with some wriggling, depending on their size and shape. Then, with time laying heavily upon me and nothing useful to do, I pulled the cistern chain without any pee or poo to dispose of, to gain more experience of this strange contraption. I awaited with curiosity and a little excitement, then pulled the chain again – it always worked! With fascination, I watched the bubbling, sparkling cascade – and that to me was a wonderful sight. Then getting bolder, I made little boats from bits of paper hanging there, pulled the chain again and watched them fighting the storm before being overwhelmed in the raging torrent. Truly, this new water toilet was one of the wonders of our brave new world and my growing knowledge was enhanced by its introduction. But no hole underneath. Where did all the refuse go? They could not kid me; somewhere out there, in a nearby field, there must be a big storage hole – there just had to be! I forgot to ask; there were other more pressing questions to which I needed urgent answers.

Nervously slipping through the gate of the walled exercise yard, Stan and I made several tentative excursions along the service road which led from the porter's lodge past the main entrance of the workhouse. During those first few days we surprisingly came across Mam. She was with two other female inmates (all dressed in the distinctive blue, workhouse uniform). This sudden encounter somewhat perplexed me. They were busily cleaning the paint frames of some ground-floor windows, suitably equipped, with scrubbing brushes, carbolic soap, mopping-up cloths, a bucket of hot water and a stepladder. Mam smiled at us and we were pleased and

154

excited to see her. We even managed a few words; the wrong ones, of course, but what can you say when others are also listening in? After a few short minutes Mam had to move off with the cleaning gang. We managed to smile an anxious goodbye. Well, that was better than blubbering about something now beyond our control? One thing I particularly noticed: my mother's hair, previously raven-dark, now had odd lines of grey appearing, and this contrast made me think: Mam is growing old! For that matter so was I, from a little too much damaged in the recent passage of time.

During those first few days of aimlessness, boredom set in (a condition I had never known before). We had walked from our exercise yard through a small gate several times. Getting bolder every time, we had explored the service road to the left and found it ended in a fence topped with barbed wire. Previously we had not dared to walk too far along the service road leading to the main gate. Imbued with a spirit of adventure, Stan suddenly said to me: 'Let's walk out of the gate into Spalding. It's only a short way along the Pinchbeck Road.' I followed him, as indeed I usually did, but not without a queasy feeling. We reached the bend where the road turned right to pass by the porter's lodge and through the main gates of this baffling place. What an adventure! We'd walk into Spalding, look at the shops, perhaps visit Ayscoughee gardens and the children's playground, just like old times with Mam. Never mind if we hadn't even a penny piece to spend.

Porter Stone was standing by his lodge giving directions to a delivery man. He spied us with his custodial eye. Appearing put out somewhat to see us, he then said: 'Don't leave your yard, there's good lads. You're not allowed outside.' *Outside!* I picked up that word with a sickening thud. The opposite to outside is inside. That's where we well and truly were – hopelessly imprisoned, in a place with no set sentence (unlike the lucky criminals), where we'd stay until rescued, or however long it took to escape. And that realisation was a sobering thought for a child of nine (or, for that matter, of any age) to have to come to terms with.

Further anxious questioning continued to disturb my mind: Why me? Quickly followed by, what next? And further still, my probing now besetting and in a whirling state, who are these strangers, who seem to be so disconnected, except when they enforce their rigid rules, to prove they are now in charge of my life?

Perhaps while trying desperately to seek a measure of comfort. I asked brother Stan a searching question (the answer to which had already begun to dawn on me): 'When are we going home?' 'We're not going home,' he said. 'We haven't got a home – this is our home from now on.' His stark answer pierced my mind and pained my chest. The homes I once knew would become but a memory, often desperately recalled, but slowly fading. Resignation had to set in. Grumbling is of no avail when your life thuds down to the very bottom, and your chances appear to be excessively thin – when you sink like the sun without any hope of rising again.

On that first workhouse day, after four o'clock when those strange children suddenly returned from school, began our initial integration. They seemed to be very friendly and quickly occupied our minds with questions and answers anxiously needed. Where are you from? was their main request, followed by many questions about *the outside world.* Some of them seemed so naive and out of touch with life outside they puzzled me, until an intuitive flash of thought provided the answer: some of these kids were life institutionalised – from birth! They'd never known a real home (not even a slum cottage, never mind a cottage farm) or the irksome experience of toiling in the fields. I had

156

various memories of another life, memories I could draw on. In this respect they were truly poverty-stricken. And do you know, this knowledge made me feel smugly superior – adding some advantage to my own lowly life? In the workhouse pecking order some are plucked and stripped away.

Most of all I missed the previously taken-for-granted freedom to come and go. Here we were bathed, fed, watered, washed and put away in a compound like animals at the zoo. Titbits seldom came our way (except if we were lucky on visitors' day). But surely that was preferable by far than my previous option: to live in the open with no roof over my head.

I would always remember the first teatime, followed by other meals in unrelieved routine. Two senior boys went off to the main kitchen in the next block to fetch the tea, in a giant urn. The bread and marge was already prepared in advance of feeding time. I'd never before in my whole life seen so many slices of bread and spread in one place, pile after pile of the stuff. But I must report that these kids looked extremely healthy, so somebody had got the diet right (there were no signs of obesity). Various other older children also busied about as if by magic; the coloured chequered tablecloths were removed, to be expertly replaced by snowy-white ones. And with some clattering, crockery and cutlery was laid out according to the set positions and ages of the children. One higher table for the older ones and a lower table for the babies of five and six years old. I looked on, especially at these tiny tots, some two and three years my junior, and I felt a sudden pang for them (surely, if some of the mums and dads of Spalding, with love and affection to spare, had witnessed this poignant scene they would have arrived knocking hard on the workhouse door demanding to cuddle and love these lonely, often unwanted, baby paupers). But to be fair, in those distinguishing

157

days, who would dare to confess a yearning to love workhouse brats? Most of the kids were long-termers, but wait a minute, for that matter so was I! Nobody, except officials, called, not even the curate and certainly not the parson. Destitution had segregated us pauper children from normal society: not on racial lines, another kind of apartheid.

Uneasiness again swept over me as I silently watched the next action unfold, only too aware that some of these children were secretly watching me for signs of tears and other childish weaknesses, in the face of this institutional initiation. In manners they were trained automatons. Grace came first: 'For what we are about to receive, may the Lord make us truly grateful.' I looked furtively for the next event to take place (now feeling a swelling lump in my throat; not the usual kind of sore throat in winter, this was much lumpier). 'Thank you!' one child said, after taking a piece of marge-spread bread, then another, and another, back and forth along the table. Joined also by the squeaky tones of the babies, 'thank you', they blessedly said. On and on it went, without let up, so I joined in. Good manners and gratitude were rubbed into workhouse children. This repeated 'thank you' was not unlike the religious responses we performed in the local church, which I would learn to parrot so well. At least in a church I could pretend to take part. Here we had to perform loud with feeling, otherwise Nurse Purdom would lash us with her tongue and that was an experience to be avoided: so we thankfully grovelled for our daily bread – one piece at a time!

The lump in my throat would not go away. I swallowed the crusty edges of the bread down my windpipe with a forcible gulp. Tears were not far from falling down my cheeks, but not in front of this lot – never! A swig of tea helped a lot and moved the congested food over the painful lump. I suppressed my tears, but only just. Only babies cry and I was not going to be a baby at the big table. How could I possibly live down such a display of weakness? At this table children do not weep and crying out in agony was unthinkable – only the total suppression of my deepest feelings would do in this God-forsaken *House*; a disturbance of mind must never be allowed to show.

In no time I found the 'thank you' routine was catching and being a bit of a mimic I soon caught on to their ways, strange to me though they were. Becoming bolder at the table, 'THANK YOU', I said in a clear loud voice – it sounded so intense even the nurse was impressed. A tormented torrent flowed within my mind. Using my scant knowledge of cuss-words, why didn't I cry out loud – thank you! damn you! blast you! – I'm not going to cry, I'm damn-well not going to cry! For certainty, not into pieces of bread and margarine. After due regard for indigestion and good manners, as each child separately finished their meal but before they left the table, they suitably mouthed their personal gratitude. With eyes shut tight each spoke the concluding grace: 'Thank the Lord for our good food, please may I leave the table?' Routinely, I copied them. The Lord never answered, nor did Nurse Purdom, so I left the table anyway, to help with the clearing up.

I had had nine precious years of family life to establish my personal character (unlike some of the loved-starved babies in this impersonal place). My ancestors had passed on to me the usual mixture of genes, widely sown from many tribal connections. But the best gift I could possibly have would be a sense of humour, to enable me, some of the time, to be cheerfully light-hearted. In many ways, I should have considered myself fortunate, and a permanent state of grumbling would not in the least be helpful. Now had come a violently growing-up time, by shocks, spurts and leaps. Reasoning started, positions were taken, often to be changed later after better understanding. People in my life were now far more closely examined and innocent trust

159

among other things became more difficult to be freely given – realism and cynicism interlocked for a time. But young children are capable of wide assimilation and, thankfully for me, I proved to be no exception. There are many steps in life, many more if you start from rock bottom where I was stowed away for the time being. So it seemed far better to concentrate on clambering and save any sympathy for people far worse off than myself. After all, wouldn't I be repeatedly told: The Lord helps those who help themselves. The cynics would readily guffaw and add, but some get helped to a greedy lot!

27

During the first few days of my initiation into the workhouse ways of conforming, my new family was most helpful. We would be attending Spalding Westlode Street school, they informed me: about ten minutes' walk away, along the public road outside the gates (and that would prove to be a valuable bit of freedom). Apparently the teachers administer the 'stick' at this school, so my new family friends told me. Rather physical punishment which at least can be quickly forgotten, than dragged-out mental punishment with no adequate explanation. In any case, there was an option completely under my own control; to behave, get on with my studies and the stick would keep away. Why should I be disruptive? I needed the school far more than the school needed me.

Education, at whatever level obtainable, was one of the basic essentials of my life. Workhouse children were never allowed to sit the grammar school entrance examination. Such a frill wasn't affordable, or considered necessary (as indeed it wasn't for many deprived children outside the workhouse gates). Only our elementary needs would be catered for – no Latin or French for the likes of us – useless anyway for lowly people. There'd be no fine imitation parchment rolls, with our precious names emblazoned thereon. Poor deprived lad! I'd simply have to learn another way, the best way I could; building brick by brick, only too aware that the roof would never be completed, nor expected to be.

Learning was of utmost importance, it would add flesh to my human spirit. How can you purposefully direct your spirit without knowledge. Knowledge I needed, experience I was getting. Now I badly required some brightness to show. So I set out to cope with every arriving tomorrow. Tomorrow can bring a new challenge, including another bother to overcome. As each minute ticks by, the past raw experiences should become less and less wrenching as I immersed myself in repeated efforts to contend. So for now, nightly go to sleep and dream, until life awakens at dawn. That seems to be the more positive way (from the view I then had of the world, it certainly seemed the sanest way).

What an escape the state school provided from the humdrum existence in the workhouse, where children existed cheek by jowl, within a large family not of their own choosing. Teachers in those days stood no nonsense and used much chalk upon the blackboard to supplement their talking. I readily listened and watched each one. These were 'outside' people, in secure work, respected and smartly suited (not beyond feeling some envy, I also imagined that they all had secure homes to return to). Maybe one day I might join them and wear a suit to work, instead of a pair of dirty dungarees. Such were the simple thoughts that passed through my hopeful, searching mind. At that particular time, so it would seem, security was the only climax I ever wanted to achieve; along with my eventual escape from submissive resignation.

Other experiences would impinge on my life – my mind sometimes pondulated – what's this? Why that! Regardless of any previously bestowed denomination (except for Roman Catholics who claimed their own), all the workhouse children had no option but to attend the parish church on Sunday. In this House of Worship with its awesome stained-glass windows, which I gazed at in wonderment, I soon came to conclude that although the shafts of colour were strikingly beautiful, they provided cold comfort, even in the summer time. And the words and form of worship seemed distant to me. We lowly lot sat at the very back next to the tall steeple, where we could observe the higher, faithful people. In the afternoon we attended the church school opposite, where we duly received our religious instruction. (I swear the teacher was especially kind to me and loaded her biblical questions in my direction. How else could I have won the weekly prize of a bar of chocolate? – so many times!) We dashed back, for Sunday afternoon was visiting time, when we saw our family or other kind visitors, if any turned up and that was a privilege to look forward to and a measure of comfort: for one hour we were allowed to be together again.

My new family also advised that there were other treats in store: on Saturday afternoon we'd do a crocodile walk and visit the Gaumont movie-picture house. Some films had captions still, so I was pleased that I could read. Laurel and Hardy, Mickey Mouse, Tom Mix the cowboy with his famous horse, Helen Twelvetrees, Lillian Harvey, Herbert Marshall, Ronald Coleman and many other exciting players flickered about (how I loved to imitate their talking and walking ways). It was a wonderful escapist dream, until the lights switched on reality again. Before the programme started a magnificent, lit-up, melodious organ rose up from somewhere underground. It was played by a very active man who swayed from side to side and up and down. And we sang with intense enjoyment the popular songs displayed on the large silver screen. Together with *Pathe Pictorial News* this entirely new experience opened up a valuable chink for me to view the world outside.

Perhaps the most enjoyable event of the year would be the annual one-day church trip to the seaside – usually, so my new family said, in voices reaching excitement pitch, to nearby Skegness. Oh! I nearly forgot. At Christmas we'd have presents and a big dinner 'blow-out' in the grown-ups' dining hall, where we would sit with our families – what a treat to look forward to! Birthdays were never celebrated; birthdays are only markers of the passage of time and who, in this place, wanted to be reminded of their passing isolation?

Now fast rising ten, with an elderly father of 78 years, continuously moving in a senile direction, a mother of some 54 summers and winters, erratically sliding into a black-hole, mental breakdown, how did we all cope? More to the point how did I cope with this life I had been given to live – this most precious gift of God? It wasn't so much the humbling of my life (saints are humble people), it was the frustration of it all: the awareness dawning that I would be entrapped in this place, at least until I was 14 years old – five long years away!

As time rolled on and passed by, devoid of much human stimulation (except from the teachers, the clergy, and sometimes the oddest people), which human models did I try to imitate?

There appeared a simple answer: I imitated in little bits! Bit by bit I grew into my new life and the problems arising from my unavoidable contact with it. From little bits at a time I adapted and adopted. It was like being on the stage appearing in a play, except it was now a non-stop performance – and I hated the part I was playing. Well, not all the time. There occurred some compensations: happy bits, even funny bits. But my gnawing frustrations would not be appeased. So I continued to observe the good bits and the bad bits, especially the bad bits, for how on earth can we get the good bits right if we cannot sort good from bad? Especially did I need one bit to answer my anxious beseeching – quickly and in some visible form – please! A cottage was required – PRONTO! And that was only the first on the list. That nothing happened would often cause me to ponder. He works in mysterious ways, that's what I had been told;

which is not comforting if you are patiently waiting somewhere in an endless queue.

My tactics changed when I discovered that instant relief was not available from the Heavenly source. So I confined my many bits of need to simpler requests, and finally settled for less demanding results in a much more restrained way – pecking away, instead of trying to gulp the lot!

My parents had been knocked out of life's ring, leaving me to collect my own bits of life's experience as best I could – the faster the better! I was a keen observer and a desperately hungry learner, building up my own stock of experiences to guide my future struggles; for most likely the best person I had to rely on was myself, as I gingerly attempted the climb of adjustment. For, surely, with little bits you can build a complete picture, though sometimes a bitty jig-saw one; for the scene now depicted could be broken up, reassembled and improved. But on the other hand, it might show a scene far worse.

From my large workhouse family I gleamed many useful bits; I adopted a bit of each school teacher I came into contact with; I observed bits of the matron – the professional bits; bits of the nurses I learned to be defensive of; bits of Ronald Colman and many other film stars, of their speaking and acting; bits of people's mannerisms; hopes and bits of ambition; in fact I adopted bits here and there of nearly every person I occasioned to meet. And I constantly revised and changed those bits in search of some belonging. No one was safe from my anxious thievish ways. My father figure around this time could be an actor, teacher or some perfect stranger, or bits of each adapted to suit my needs of the time. Bit players in my play might lead me on to better parts; somewhere upwards on the steps of life's long ladder. It's surely not a mortal sin to want something better!

* * *

165

Spalding Workhouse, which had officially become The Poor Law Institution on the 31st March, 1930, was still referred to by its old workhouse title by most people – and forever by me! The weekly visiting hours were between 3.00 p.m. to 4.00 p.m., after Sunday school. The families all met in the grown-ups' communal dining hall, which was scrubbed as clean as a new pin, by the duty inmates, at the direction of the Labour Master. The walls were painted in the usual standard workhouse colours, about one-third drab brown, about two-thirds drab green, separated by a bold black horizontal line some one and a half inches deep – thus preventing the colours from flowing into each other and causing confusion to the inartistic eye. Each workhouse family group sat around the spotless, oil-cloth covered tables. All talk appeared to be in subdued tones; as indeed you would expect of folk, down, out and feeling punished.

Slowly, over a grinding period, I noticed my mother's condition change. There arose peculiar mood swings, some of which I found quite frightening. She began to rebel against her prison state, even refusing to accept the instruction to work (which in a workhouse would be regarded as a deadly sin). And not only that, she began to declaim, in a loud impassioned way, the protestation she had so often voiced way back on the smallholding: 'We've been robbed ends and sides up – of hundreds and thousands – and don't you forget it!' Her tones got louder and louder. God only knows who would have listened to her in that imprisoned state. 'My hair has lost its nature,' she also quietly told us. After this she plastered it firmly down with carbolic soap, and this became a frightening spectacle: an outward display of eccentric beginnings? – to say the very least.

Her early cries eventually expanded to: 'I want my clothes! I want to go back to my *rightful home*, where I belong!' The workhouse place had now become her dreaded prison – realisation had cruelly set in. She was uniformed, locked up and mentally rotting away in ever-growing delusion. As an unmarried mother she'd never get out, unless she took her bastards with her. It was the rule: all inside, or all outside. At that dismal time it seemed that any going-away clothes would be a simple shroud to wrap her body in.

Some of the time she was benign, then suddenly tempestuously loud (all the inmates and visitors were regularly treated to her demented cries). I soon caught on to her changing moods. If her head seemed loosely turning, she would incline to be relaxed; if her head was held stiff I knew the worst would happen. There would be ranting and raving all the family visiting hour. On those days of precious time together, I often spent most of the time fighting back my tears. When Porter Stone called, 'Time, please', I was relieved to walk back to my own quarters, to my new life and adopted family.

It hardly seemed possible but my mother's mind further began to widen its net. As well as *they* who had *robbed us of hundreds and thousands*, she began to aim her frustrations at the head jailer – no less than the august Matron in charge of the place. Now *they* were poisoning her! She regularly found traces of white powder under the meat on her plate. So she especially made a display of scraping it off. 'Matron went as white as a shittin' clout when she realised she'd been found out,' she told us. Now around eleven years of age, I was worldly wise enough to know that my mother was acting in a funny manner. As there was nothing I could do, I just listened, accepted this uneasy situation and got on with my life as best I could, trying to ignore what I could, but deeply affected all the same.

Of almost certainty, trauma can be visited upon us from the next split-second to the end of life away. No respecter of birth, station or condition in life, it seldom fails to pay a visit – at least once, but often several times when it is least expected. It can call with a sudden raw, unexplained savagery; or just as relentlessly with creeping stealth, without invitation or encouragement. It leaves its afflicted prisoner trying to maintain a foothold balance in a maze of depressing debris, aimlessly staggering along a dark frozen tunnel of utter despair and isolation; until one day other people begin to seem normal again.

That description may seem exaggerated but from my grandstand seat my mother's agony certainly felt like that – no wonder my mind often froze.

Encouraged by the matron, brother Oscar had moved back to our village of Gosberton Risegate. There he had obtained lowly employment as a labourer with a market gardener, paying £1 a week for board and lodgings from his meagre earnings of 35 shillings a week: £1.75 (less stoppages). He had no room for extravagant living. Every week, without fail, he cycled the five miles or so to see us during the one-hour family visiting time on Sunday afternoon. He always gave me a bag of sweets and a penny or two to spend, which, I can tell you, was most gratefully received. Our Mother began to make a special request: to bring packets of fizzy-drink tablets, so that she could place one under her tongue every time she tasted the poison they were so craftily administering – especially that hidden under the meat!

There appeared many false dawns, when hopes were raised, dimmed, and disappeared down another black hole. One visiting father told his son that he had been promised a house and the lad in his excitement told his inmate pals. 'Johnny's father has got an 'ouse,' said one of the boys at teatime to the formidable Miss Bristow (who was on duty on Nurse Purdam's day off). 'Yes, about like yours, made of cardboard,' was her cutting reply. And I immediately thought: yes, about like mine, too. And that remark about a cardboard house, confirmed what I already knew: for me, a home outside this place was well nigh an impossible dream.

An inmate father (deserted by his wife or widowed? I never found out. We children seldom if ever talked about such personal matters) once gave sudden hope to his four children. 'I've discovered a betting system for horse racing,' he told them, and they got quite excited as he unfolded the promise of better times to come. How he would find the stake money? How he would beat the fatal LLS (longest losing sequence) that often ruinous punting problem, remained unexplained. Whether I was developing wisdom, or just being canny, in order to avoid embarrassment, I kept my own private hopes and feelings tightly under lock and key. No one was going to quote me! No one was going to sneer at my dark-secret dreams – my props of hopeful comfort.

My Sunday bag of sweets would soon disappear when I returned to the children's ward. Some of the youngsters, usually those without visitors of their own, would gather round and focus their wide eyes with desire on my now bulging pocket. After some hesitation, second and third thoughts, out would come the bag of sweets to be handed round and swiftly disappear, one by one, much to my chagrin – children are not necessarily by nature all sweet and generous and I was no exception. By way of compensation I kept the pennies hidden from view and made my purchase of goodies (we could spend a farthing in those days, four to a penny) at the tuck shop in Westlode Street, next door to our school. I munched every sweet, gobstopper, blackjack; sucked the tingling sherbet out of a bag, and gorged on many other teeth-rotting, cagmag treats.

Small wonder then that the confined inmates sank into a permanent state of total eclipse and vegetated daily in their dreary lives. But of what did they think, which presumably they could and did?

One sniff of feeling is given in one of the last workhouse poems to survive; found under a chapel reading desk:

169

God made the bees, and bees make honey,
The paupers do the work,
And the Guardians get the money.
Now I am compelled to sit and hear,
What the parson says while standing here.
He tells us we are miserable sinners –
He'd be the same on workhouse dinners.
But he is fat like well-fed pork,
He eats and drinks, but does no work.
We hear him promise that when we die:
There'll be great helpings
Of pie in the sky.
Then he shuts his book.
And slings his hook.

                                    Amen.

With all the experiences I had been fast gathering, my own remarks would have demonstrated that I had learnt to beseech independently of the church, without the aid of the local vicar:

Beyond my pauper's woes,
(entrapped, extending);
I seek through You,
Some blessed relief –
Occasionally (not too much!).
PLEASE, and THANK YOU!
– if you can, now and then.
If you can't, Amen!

28

Various records detailing the workings of the early workhouses indicates their other grim purpose; apart from housing the homeless and destitute, was to remind the inmates that they were society's outcasts. Many workhouses put their unmarried mothers into a distinctive yellow uniform, the colour of the ships' plague flag. The wearers being named the 'canary wards' until the practice was banned in 1839. A Doctor Meridew reported that one consequence of keeping children in under a strict regime was that they became institutionalised. In 1874, one boy who died at the age of 14 had never set foot outside the workhouse. Another, when asked what he would like to do when he grew up, replied: 'Move over to the men's side, where I can do and please as I like.' Independence had never crossed his mind. Other children, invited out to a family for a visit, begged to be allowed to see the dinner being cooked, as they had never witnessed this before.

On a lighter note it was also reported that some old ladies (far more than men) lived to a ripe old age. But then many old ladies lived to a ripe old age, without it being attributed to living in a workhouse.

By the time I passed through the porter's gate in 1931, many improvements had been made, but a nineteenth-century description was still largely the same as my own stark impression – of a gaunt building and an imposed drab routine, that deadened any emotional feeling.

It was earlier recorded: 'The prison-like appearance was intentional; there was no softening influence of curves or decorations of any kind. The result was deliberately to cut off the inmates from even a glimpse of the outside world.'

In my time an experiment with a bit of freedom had arrived. Male inmates who could be trusted to behave themselves and return were allowed out into Spalding Town one afternoon a week. To ensure no sinful straying and by way of extra punishment, women were curtained in purdah, in a uniform dress, designed to crush any throbbing excitement – in case any still managed to exist! What a sight it was (some would think it distasteful) to see the paupers drifting out in their funereal suits; shuffling along the Pinchbeck Road, like a plague of black beetles, aimlessly to wander about the town, with nothing to do but to stare at life, in a world so apart from their own.

A little way towards the town, a rich man used to stand by his gate. In full view, this good Samaritan, well-fed and smartly-dressed, handed to each pauper a gleaming threepenny piece. And they in turn, in a show of self-abasement, made their obsequious 'thank you,' one by one; not forgetting, of course, suitably to doff their caps. Once during the summer school holiday Nurse Purdam allowed three of us older boys to go and beg. 'Thank you, Mr Banks,' I said, feeling more than a tinge of envy – that this wealthy man, on show at his gate, seemed to be so favourably endowed. So ended a valuable lesson: that some folk had the wherewithal, not only to live well, but to give a mite or two away. And I wondered how long it would be before I achieved a similar state.

My growing perception of the uneven distribution of wealth probably connected me to the only sermon I remembered; confidently delivered by the vicar from the pulpit in the Spalding Parish Church (the High one of which I had become a press-gang member). His words struck a cord. In short, much as it appeared otherwise to me: property does not belong to individuals. They are only 'stewards',

172

with responsibility to look after the property under their control, and pass it on to future generations, likewise to be blessed with this privileged entrustment. The question that arose in my inquisitive mind, agitated by bouts of sinful envy, was simply this: who appoints these favoured stewards? Why didn't I get offered a stewardship? Why was I overlooked? Where was I on the day those lucrative assignments were given out? I suspected there was favouritism.

In earlier times child abuse in the workhouse was widespread. In 1837 there was a public outcry when it was learned that a five-year-old of lower intelligence, and suffering from a physical disability, which made him incontinent and dirty, was constantly flogged for it with a birch or splatter, by the workhouse master. Two other children aged three and four were similarly beaten. Eventually a complaint was made and various officials were dismissed. But one way or another it would continue (but not in my day, for which I would have cause to be grateful).

The adult inmates were kept busy doing the most degrading of tasks. Bone crushing was one, until it was abolished in 1845. If the slightest bit of meat or gristle still adhered to the bone, this was gnawed off by the hungry workers. The cranking of multi-corn grinding was another regular occupation. It took approximately 8,800 turns of the wheel to grind four bushels of corn and that was a grinding lot of turns.

Picking oakum, by both sexes and all age groups, including the very old and small children, continued right up to 1904. (Oakum is a loose fibre obtained by picking old rope to pieces, some tarred and knotted, and used especially for caulking.)

The workhouse schools were brutal places, too (before state schools were attended). Beatings and floggings were common, from masters, often illiterate, brutal people, picked for the lowest wages the Guardians could negotiate; in fact, they were not much better off than the inmates.

It often takes time for institutional cruelty to come to the surface and, be exposed – usually inmates would not be believed. Much has been recorded, a lot went by unnoticed or ignored – rocking the boat proved difficult.

By comparison with the previous century, what cruelty, if any, existed in the 1930s? There was the regular 'imbecile' scorning: '... sticks and stones ...' There was also the sourness of Miss Bristow (the wounding, salt and vinegar one), who made that ice-cold quip: 'It will be a cardboard house, the same as yours,' thus dashing my childhood dream of ever escaping to a family home.

And spare a thought for poor little bastard Barry, who had abruptly been moved from his unmarried mother and the confining security of the workhouse nursery. Now aged five, sitting bewildered at the infants' table, now considered a mature child inmate, with mother visits only one hour a week, the same as the rest of us. How I came to feel sorry for him. Now regularly wetting the bed, he received the standard workhouse treatment. Nurse would take the offending soiled sheet and place it over his head, a signal for some of the children to pinch his skin through the sheet with their fingers and thumbs. Never would I ever forget the outline of his quiet sobbing, looking like a twitching ghostly statue – with no mother or family to turn to. And no wonder I was alarmed. I, too, had been a regular bed-wetter. Luckily for me, brother Stan came to my rescue. If my bed was soaked, he would help me hurriedly make it, with the sheets still wet, so as to bluff everyone, including the nurse. And being quite determined, Stan would get me out of bed several times in the night and sit me on the standard workhouse po – some of those times I never consciously remembered, so I must have peed to safety in my sleep. Thankfully, I was soon cured – Stan's treatment mentally disciplined me. (*My problem wasn't an emotional one, it was simply due to lack of any previous training, and the fear that the bogeyman*

174

was sitting near the po, under the bed, eager to bite my wee-wee off!)

Monday, Wednesday and Friday evenings were the bath nights for the boys; the alternative weekday nights were reserved for the girls. Sunday evening was less intense, we stood up at a basin and cleansed ourselves with a flannel as usual. The older children supervised the young. Bearing in mind the scolding we might receive from Nurse Purdam if the bathing was running late, there was always a thread of anxiety running through this onerous task: more especially if the bathroom was left the least bit untidy, or the giant baths were not hard-cleaned with the brand of 'Monkey' soap (a white tablet of abrasive cleaner, used for rubbing away the scummy bodily dirt, which left a bold filthy line around the bath). 'Monkey' soap indeed! Why didn't they call it 'Monkey Grinding' soap? It had to be used with all the elbow grease we could muster up and down, round and round!

Organising bath time could be a stressful occasion. One boy, not much younger than myself, made a habit of playing up. He delayed getting undressed and would give out some cheek. Eventually I slapped him, but he still remained difficult. So I slapped him again – such a trial had he become. It doubly annoyed me that he seemed to thoroughly enjoy his provocation and punishment. He never cried; he just grinned and grinned. This provoked me to further desperation; to avoid a bad-tempered telling-off by our Mother-nurse for not getting a move on, as I was then considered in charge. But why did that lad provoke me, time and time again? God only knows! I never found out – not having the time or depth of understanding to even consider the boy's peculiar stance, which caused in me too much frenzied reaction.

Wednesday lunchtime (dinner time, for the likes of us) was fraught with yet another difficulty: the 'good for you',

175

roly-poly pudding. The jam filling was nasty tasting, so bad faces were pulled all round the table. I used to gulp it down with sickly feelings, I can tell you. But you can imagine how disturbed I felt when brother Stan, sitting next to me, emptied most of his own pudding on my plate. Ugh! – what a rotten thing to do. How I hated him for that! I couldn't protest out loud. Nurse would have come down like a ton of bricks had she found out. The things you're forced to do for brotherly love.

On Thursday, we had nutritious lumps of scrag-ends of mutton, no doubt supplied by a local butcher to fulfil his keen workhouse tender. The meat part was edible but, unfortunately, it was attached to gristle and various greyish pipes. The rule was a simple one: to suck and chew the gristle and meat from the pipes and leave them gleaming clean. Usually, there was trouble. Some children had to be persuaded to pick the pipes clean. One girl in particular, Rosie, was considered by Miss Bristow to be downright *saucy*, blatantly leaving on her plate some of the meat and gristle still attached to the pipes. Miss Bristow cut and scraped it off, fed the girl's mouth and held her nose, until, after much wriggling she swallowed it down. Afterwards, feeling sickened by this act, she often went into the toilet, placed fingers down her throat and heaved the lot up.

Sunday meals were special, as you would expect. Instead of porridge we had a boiled egg; two, if cook had been generous. What a treat that was: eggs laced with plenty of salt, munched down with bread and marge, remaining forever my favourite Sunday breakfast. For tea, to supplement the usual piles of bread and marge spread, which first had to be finished up, there followed a treat: a slice of fruit cake, in which every child hoped there'd be a piece of cherry – preferably a whole one. If lucky, there'd be shrieks of delight, especially from the grateful infants. We were never bodily starved, we had to work through any emotional starvation by ourselves – counsellors had not been invented. But it must be said, in the spirit of fairness: Spalding Poor Law Institution (forever my 'Workhouse') was always efficiently run – like that damn mechanical clock, which banged away the time in the hall from the very moment we were smothered away from the outside world. Not once did I hear a hungry child cry, 'Can I have some more, please?', that request made, by the ungrateful Oliver Twist, which so angered the Victorian workhouse beadle, in our day known as the porter: to be exact Porter Stone.

Apart from some jarring experiences and the other happenings more trivial, still alive in a memory of so long ago, there must have been something stirring of that then unmentionable thing: the growing sexuality of boys and girls, cooped together under one roof – confined like animals, but not strictly tethered. I must solemnly report – never a jot! At least not that I observed. We weren't repressed, just wide-eyed innocent; as indeed were a lot of grown-ups and better for that, some might say.

One evening after settling between the spotless white sheets of my bed, one of the older girls suddenly shrieked through the dormitory door. 'Gerry,' she said, 'nurse wants you to wash your hands!' (Whatever for, I cannot now remember, we washed and scrubbed so often.) I jumped out of bed, always ready to obey and, if possible, keep trouble away. Down I went through the now dark living quarters. The electric lights were switched off promptly at nine o'clock: this saved money and it ensured that there was no alternative to bed. (Upwards, from twelve years old, a few trusted children would be allowed to sit out the dying embers of the fire; just talking in the dark about this and that.) Along the final passageway, I could plainly see a careless child had left the bathroom lights on. Beams were glowing around the ill-fitted door I was about to open. My word, what a surprise I got. There she was, our very own Nurse Purdam,

177

sitting starkers in the bath. She violently swivelled her head round, and glared at me uncommonly coldly. 'You dirty boy,' she said. 'Get out!' I fled from the scene but not before getting a glimpse of her naked back although, I have to confess, that experience never even stirred my blood.

The workhouse life had come along so thick and fast that my old life soon receded into a faded memory, except I began to recall some bits and pieces, which I tried to join together to form a picture, so often incomplete. But between the teeth of biting reality, my growing imagination and awareness managed many spirited birthings, but far too many proved stillborn.

Well, it was something like that – children have such vivid imaginations. Most acutely felt was the yearning that went on secretly within my mind – that emotional screw boring away until it strikes bewilderment, which in turn gnaws and gnaws trying to find the way.

But hold on! Wait a minute! Aren't many children subject to suffering: inflicted by personal abuse, physical or mental (often a mixture of both), some in the guise of untroubled family living? Luckily for me, throughout my early childhood and now my institutionalised living, by comparison, I only suffered pinpricks. No brutish parents or guardians ever savaged my way. And for that deliverance I would have been grateful, had it crossed my mind at that time.

29

Sometime in the spring of 1932, Stan and I went as usual to the dining hall for the regulation family visiting time, which neatly slotted in after Sunday school, as I have previously explained. To my complete surprise, also sitting at the table with my elder brother and my mother were a smartly-dressed couple (which instantly indicated to me that they were comfortably better off than most, in those dreary days of our world depression).

Allowing as much disdain on her face as she could instantly muster, the smartly-dressed lady of the couple looked at us and through us, as though we were devilish apparitions blocking the way on the road of her life. Turning to my mother she said in a voice, not too loud, but which we could clearly hear: 'Oh!' (in the sound of deepest shock) – 'you still see them!'

I would always remember that incident so well, the shock of being called 'them!' And again a gnawing pain came across my chest, triggered by an instant grasp, the grasp of understanding: we were despised and not wanted.

Excluded from the conversation I sat politely and wondered: suppose these 'wealthy' folk took my mother away and left Stan and me alone in this lonely place; no wonder I pained and felt a bothersome panic – why don't strangers stop their meddling?

The couple turned out to be Aunt Flo and Uncle Edgar, who had travelled all the way from Yorkshire. Much upset was my mother's sister Flo at seeing Mam in such a degraded situation. She never said one word to Stan and me. Edgar gave me a quick glance or two, but seemed more anxious to keep his bowler hat firmly on, whether to cover a balding head, to maintain his dignity as he sat bolt upright, or to be ready to make a quick exit from our Big House, I could not tell. Porter Stone eventually released him when he popped his uniformed head around the door and called: 'Time please!' after the Regulation 60-minute 'family-time' had once more come to an end. Edgar and Flo then vanished from our lives forever, but, to be fair, they were Mam's only visitors from her other five siblings. Despite their haughty attitude (certainly to Stan and me) I very soon forgot them; too many other things were becoming my concern.

Though rejected by Aunt Flo, thank God for at least some consideration: that I wasn't of a different colour; that it was easy for me to pass myself off as one of *them*. But just imagine the field day some affixing bigots would have had, had all bastards been permanently tarred and feathered, or pigmented in a distinguishing colour, or even worse, had the Devil's horns protruding out of their heads. Such a merciful relief that I escaped all that.

> If God made the bees,
> And the bees made honey;
> Did God make me?
> Does that sound funny?

From the time I understood the condemning meaning of the 'bastard' word (and that was quite young – remember that village lad saying: 'You're one of them!'), now, every time I heard it in its swearing use, it truly made me cringe. The many prefixes added to the word increased its power of scorn: 'dirty', 'rotten', 'stinking', not forgetting the effing blasts and many others just as distinctive. They all sounded so personal and condemning, especially if you're actually 'one of them!'

180

I had somewhat timidly tried to ignore all the single and double expletives freely flying about. Even although they were not aimed directly at me, nevertheless they impinged uncomfortably upon my mind. Among strangers, any disparaging talk about bastards I used to listen to and say nothing; thankful that I did not look like 'one of them' or the 'bastard' they were cussing. Yet I must admit that I was deeply affected all the same.

Now past the age of 10, sudden relief came to my rescue. My previous uneasiness of mind was appeased by some logical reasoning – and the penny dropping with a clang!

Such a gloomy state had I allowed myself to sink into that I had failed to work out why my friend, whose parents were conventionally married, was often called a 'silly bastard'. Under such circumstances, how could that be? And then I began to notice; he wasn't the only natural-born child of wedded parents to suffer this way, as well as children conceived by nature only for which such scorn would be duly expected. My eyes already widened, now widened further. Eureka! for this sudden discovery that some 'bastards', although not true ones, were also suffering from that virulent word. What a wonderful enlightenment: that the 'bastard' expletive had such a wide coarse usage, and could be loosely aimed at anyone – not just poor me! This discovery would trigger my mind to reason: if you can't beat them, you don't have to let them beat you. And that was that!

So, bastard – you crafty bastard! You have separate meanings, especially for double bastards, like William the Conqueror, that murdering bastard, cruel, as well as illegal; born on the wrong side of a royal bed (with certainty, he was a king-sized bastard, if ever there was one).

I had found some peace at last, from the realisation that I could use the 'bastard' expression without wounding myself. How slow had I been to learn, long trapped within a bubble

181

of guilt, that words can be used in different ways, with more than one edge to their meaning.

After such relief, and all the newly-found confidence I had gained, my cussing language exploded: You bastard this! You bastard that! Rude words flowed out from me in every known swearing combination. Just think about that! From me of all people. I couldn't stop the wordy bouts of instant relieving, as I steamed out those oafish sounds. What a 'bastard' I had become! And how I was enjoying it...

While lambasting in full spate, now sounding like a swearing trooper and steadily growing full of confidence, I suddenly heard a quiet voice, coming from a bystander. Attracted by my cussing a well-dressed man had stopped and was eyeing me up and down. Then looking directly at me he spoke telling words of advice, the gist of it being: 'Don't swear like that, it might offend some people's feelings.' After that admonition, off he went. I was impressed by the stranger's manner and his obvious sincerity. So I calmed down somewhat, thought about his anxious advice and used the twinned-bastard expressions much less often: only when desperately needed to relieve my baffled feelings; not really intended to scorn anyone. But no longer did I cringe when I heard *that word* bandied about. In fact, I started to smile to myself, in the blissful knowledge that it wasn't being aimed directly at me: they're just letting off their surplus steam at some other poor victim; someone who has offended them, now getting a smack of the blasting verbals – thus proving that some words can be both wounding and soothing at one and the same time.

30

After my early childhood experience of attending the friendly Methodist chapel in the village of my birth (where everybody knew everybody else's bit of scandal, and often much worse), the sudden transfer to the (High) Spalding Parish Church came as quite a shock. Especially to a child unmoved by kneeling. That one could be so desperately lonely in a House of Worship seemed unbelievable and any comfort from the word seemed missing. Sitting there, fumbling with my reasoning and trying to follow the chanting and responding that went on in this place, proved at first to be a daunting experience. Luckily, Stan, as usual, came to my aid and sorted out the right pages on which to find the words in use, repeated *ad infinitum*, until I knew them off by heart.

Apart from the boys in the choir and children attending with their parents, we workhouse children sat with the rest of the town children, at the very back of the church. In charge of us was the verger, assisted by a beadle, whose face never lit up – so deeply did he seem troubled by the fear of rising sinfulness in our young minds. If we transgressed in fidgeting ways, or visibly showed our thoughts were wandering from the pages held in front of us, he eyed us sharply, back into a show of solemnity and duteous piety, exercised along with standing, kneeling and reverently placing our palms together while responding to sacramental words, which I soon learnt off by heart and trotted out in parrot fashion.

Though meaningful to many, that disciplined submission has been described by someone more skilled in writing, as:

'...the formulaic liturgies that confront worshippers with the same drab vernacular week after week...'

Looking back, as often one does to try and understand; it seemed to me that I was but a bit player in a crowd scene, enacting an ancient ritual in a working museum and blind to any relevance the words might have to me.

During the three years I attended this loving, forgiving, condemning church, not once did any member of the congregation ever smile my pauper way. So far as I remember, neither did they glare at me in a distasteful fashion. But is there anything more soul destroying than being completely ignored? Even our Mother Matron, who regularly attended this House to Worship, shot out like a bullet from a gun with head erect and eyes in front, giving her pauper family not the slightest flicker of recognition. (It was as though we had been shipped in and were of a different culture; of strange habits and disturbing features, to stand us apart from churchy devotees. By such did I feel a barrier.) In the pecking order of this religion, although paupers were allowed in God's House, it would also be expected that they would experience some personal relief at being freely delivered from their sins – if not their gnawing feelings.

And I further considered: These praying folk were the controlling elite of Spalding Town. Drop a bomb, kill the lot and local civilisation would grind to a halt. Who would we paupers look up to then? Just think about that! Oh child! How you do imagine things...!

Most folk are interdependent – we pauper children were quite different; so obviously dependent, hopelessly so at that. The vicar's sermons flowed over my head (except that one about the stewardship), allowing me some precious time to sit and dream, until the next supplication began and my knees bent in unison, like the involuntary actions of an automaton. But why did they waste their time preaching to me about sin? Why should I pray for forgiveness? At my

184

young age, living confined like a monk, I had no opportunity to sin. And why burden an ignorant child to pray for the sins of the world? Living in such restriction, of both body and mind, how inadequate I felt, forlornly going through the motions of my regulated existence. Entrapped, I had no option but to act in unison and pretend that I was joining in, as I waited patiently for the ending of the impressively ritualised performance.

On one occasion the curate confronted us workhouse lot and told us in no uncertain fashion in his fine posh voice (or was it mock-posh? I couldn't tell the difference, although it was a sound I found easy to mimic): 'The children from the institution will receive an annual book prize of less value than that of the children who attend of their own free will.'

The books were always full of simple goodness and light; of a wonderful world which had passed me by. Rather would I have had a regular delivery of one of the exciting boys' blood and thunder papers: the *Rover* or *Hotspur* to name but two, and read about people like Desperate Dan and other make-believe characters to tickle my nerves and excite my feelings, but best of all to give my mind an occasional escape.

If envy is really a deadly sin, then I must confess I did once sin. The Curate owned one of those newfangled wrist-watches, which would eventually replace the fob pocket watch and chain, previously an essential possession. Every time he took the sermon, before he commenced, he carefully unfastened his watch and placed it by the side of his sermon papers (Good! I used to think. He'll not overrun his time.) Now let me detail my sin. I wanted one, desperately so! However long it took, whatever sacrifices I had to make, I would own one of these handy timepieces. Placed fully in view, on my wrist, it would not only let people know how conscious I was of passing time, but also that I could afford this latest 'showy' innovation.

Towards the end of the service, after looking forward to a punctual end, I became gripped with apprehension (as weeks went by the feeling grew stronger). As the choir and various dignities moved in procession through the chancel towards the nave, my concern began to fret. Supposing, I speculated, one of those large memorial slabs tips up, opening into a large cavity, not only swallowing the choir – but also the churchwardens and the vicar! I used to suffer an uneasy feeling, until they reached the left-hand turn and passed the font towards the base of the tower, where they serenely disappeared. Simultaneously did I worry that the hymn might run out before they'd reached the vestry and the organist (poor fellow) would have to improvise more tiddly-bits than usual, to keep us in a pious mood, before we faced that outside world again, full of confounding realism – each according to their own – but mine seeming worse than most.

Impatient, but trying to be as polite as possible, I worked my way towards the north porch exit. Instead of leaving by way of Church Street, I sometimes slipped immediately to the left past the west door and the tower, along a path leading through a wicket gate to a side road named The Vista and then left along Church gate for a short distance to the entrance of Ayscoughee Hall Gardens, but never ventured inside.

This reminded me of happier times when Mam used to take me to visit this public place. How exciting it had been to walk around the long ornamental pool, to read the names on the fine war memorial (checking how many Greens were lost in that Great War, and asking Mam if she knew any of them). In those days peacocks strutted in the gardens, on the tidy lawns dotted with Grecian statues, sadly some with arms and heads missing, not due to vandalism, just normal wear and tear. We always snacked on those occasions in one of the rose arbours, then along the wall on the River Welland side. We ate pork sausage rolls purchased from

C.W. Scupham & Son (adjacent to the Corn Exchange) and always a cream cake from a local baker. And that wasn't all. In those days there were swings, a roundabout and a see-saw solely for the use of children, in a playground off Love Lane. What an excitement all this was: a trip on a powerful steam train, a wander through the town, then tasty food followed by play which was provided free. One thing made me a little nervous: all those notices, 'Keep Off the Grass', which I always obeyed from the time I could read, convinced me there was an invisible keeper purposely spying on me (how extremely well-behaved we were in those respectful days – 'frit' to death by the threat of the birch-cane landing on our tender bottoms).

Now arose a problem. I would have to run pell-mell back to the workhouse barracks. Any lateness would be closely questioned, and one of the children might snitch on me, even inadvertently, causing trouble – trouble, trouble – as if I hadn't enough!

By way of variation I ran several ways home. Always back towards the Stone Bridge, built in 1838, and then, depending on the time and mood, sometimes through the market, then either along Hall Place or Red Lion Street into New Road then Pinchbeck Street to home. Alternatively, I used Double Street to Broad Street, cutting out Bridge Street, the feeder road to the other ways.

Even in the workhouse there were the dreams I heard about (and some I personally experienced). One elderly female inmate (permanently imprisoned), told me with sheer delight how she dreamt and dreamt of entering Heaven. Describing all the bright gold and silver accommodation among the dreamy clouds; the gentle tinkling bells, and the angels flying about with lovable pleasure on their faces. I got the clear impression she was more than ready to die. To be removed to her Elysium – the abode of the blessed after death, where timelessness was endless, day and night had

187

merged and a state of ideal happiness would finally be achieved in her new House in the sky. Following all she described to me, and with my own workhouse experience, I saw no future problems following death if Heaven was the Home that took me in. In the meantime, I had my punishment on Earth to contend with, in a different kind of Home.

Yet another sudden shock was coming my way. In December 1932, brother Stan attained the age of 14. As hastily as possible, in order to save on workhouse costs, he was sent away and placed in service on a farm, at nearby Gedney Hill. One day in early 1933, Nurse Purdam abruptly said to me: 'Say goodbye to your brother, he's going away to live on a farm.' I had mixed feelings (not uncommon in those times). Good, I thought, he's escaped to freedom. But deep within I knew I'd miss him – what a solid rock he'd been! So off he went, this 14-year-old, partially disabled with a 'wasting disease', unable to lift his right arm beyond a swing towards the horizontal without pushing it upwards with his left one. It was some time before I heard from him. To all intents and purposes he might have been banished to far away Australia, or Canada, following the route of many *white slaves*: those thousands of abandoned and cruelly treated children – made faceless by a do-good intention.

In church one Sunday, held in a surge of lonesomeness, fed up, and further stimulated by a dare mood of self-pity – I *flipped*! From my lowly rear position (in sidewards view of an ancient hollowed-out coffin, which gave me the creeps), I was able to observe, as usual, what appeared to be well-dressed citizens of settled respectability, occupying the middle and front pews. They always fervently took part in the singing and praying and seemed expert at bobbing up and down. This state of affairs I found somewhat confusing. Why did these good people need to pray? They seemed to have everything; in stark contrast to my having nothing but the suit of clothing on my back (and this was owned by the Poor Law Guardians). I was much too young to put together this particular piece of life's jigsaw. Then, I could only believe my ears and eyes – how I tried to understand...

Here I am (I reasoned), as low as I will ever be: no money; no home; with parents incapable of offering me any form of security. So I began PRAYING, PRAYING, PRAYING LIKE MAD! And why not? I really needed to pray. My entreating was simple, yet it continued to be unanswered. Were my desperate thoughts too worldly? Was that the problem? Just consider: *Please God all we need is a cottage, a roof over our head – no need for tap water, a pump will do, or even a well, so long as we can be a family again.*

But social relief was not offered by the church, nor was it to be expected; only the balm of spiritual comfort was available, and that could not resolve the desperate need that life had thrust my hapless way.

Between my bouts of self-pity, there arose spurts of grief for the old life I was sorely missing. No wonder at times some anger bubbled up to sorely fester; as might surely be expected in the mind of a frustrated prisoner: alive and kicking, listening, thinking, and building up to worst of all – darkened silent brooding.

> Autumn passed away,
> Now was dreary Winter.
> If Spring went astray,
> Would Summer fail to bloom?
> Leaving only deadened dreams.

During one particular Sunday, sitting in the church, fed up to the back teeth I violently wrote rude words in the margins of the *Book of Common Prayer*, with a stub of pencil I had found lying on the floor, small enough to be concealed from prying eyes by being covered by my guiding fingers:

Shit! Bugger! Damn! Sod the vicar! Bugger the curate!

Thus did I write, desecrating several pages. Gosh! I thought afterwards, my soul will rot in hell, or I will be struck down by lightning for this blasphemy. But later, outside the church in the fresh air and bright shining sunshine, I became convinced that God was probably smiling on me, after allowing me some relief from my childish petulance.

But had I known beforehand of the following reported accident, it would surely have trembled me out of my act of violation, in, of all places, a consecrated House of Worship.

Tales of Divine punishment have often been recorded. On January 18th, 1665, the then Minister of Spalding, Robert Ram, officiated at a very distressing mass funeral which occurred after a roof fall had killed twenty-three townspeople who had gathered in one of the Old Priory buildings to watch a troop of dancers. After the names of the unfortunate dead, listed in the register, Robert Ram made an additional note: '...that the accident was God's will and judgement.'

[To further prove the point, just consider what happened to York Minster, in 1984, when a supposedly Heavenly bolt from the blue struck and caused a disastrous fire, which destroyed the Minster's south transept. Disturbed faithful members of the church were convinced it was due punishment, following an ultra-modern sermon by the then newly appointed Bishop-Theologian Jenkins; and his open-minded questioning of the 'certainty-wallahs', which was too much to stomach by some of his ancient, mind-set flock.]

A kind of visitation did come upon me, one which gave me a sense of escape. One night, without forewarning, my dreams changed. I couldn't wait go to bed, such was the excitement which repeated night after night. Vividly do I recall being able to fly by simply flapping my arms for wings (as strong as an angel's, and instantly sprouted for my needs). Deep in my sleep I took off from the workhouse yard, over its high wall, past the porter's lodge and far beyond the town of Spalding. I flew over mountains. I flew over seas, until at last I settled in a field next to a jungle. It soon became obvious to me that this strange country was Africa. And I was free, free to travel a million miles! But every time I landed I heard the beat of drums and warriors would appear in their brilliant head-dresses, brandishing their spears and running warlike towards me. What a fright that was. Flapping my arms frantically, I usually took off long before the spears began to hiss about me. If on the odd occasion I failed to lift off and froze in terror, but before I was mortally wounded, I woke up in a state of jumps and found myself back in bed. But night after night I couldn't wait for this breath-taking adventure and experience such a wonderful freedom, to a life far away from my walled-in prison.

(Those dreams must have been influenced by the cinema, showing the Great White Trader, *Trader Horn*, a weekly serial showing this adventurer blasting away the animals, selling the skins and ivory, and on the lookout for a goldmine or diamonds. The natives (meaning the local inhabitants) kept calling him *bwana*, which I found out meant, 'master' or 'sir' – titles I also had come to know, only too well.)

Isn't it often the case, when you think you've reached rock bottom an opportunity comes along. Now around the age of 11 (perhaps more capable of deeper feelings) to my surprise there came an offer. The curate on one of the few occasions he spoke directly to us, announced that I, along with others, had been selected for instruction into the rites of Holy Communion; so we could then participate in the Eucharist from the very front rows of the church. To attend on an empty stomach, while our thoughts and moods were

191

undisturbed by the usual worldly feelings, at the early hour of eight o'clock.

In my mind, not surprisingly, there arose a theological problem. An older boy, full of knowledge on such matters, turned to me and said: 'I understand that only those who have been christened can be confirmed, that's why we have been selected.'

A worrisome feeling grew huge in my mind. Here was I, about to move up the Establishment ladder only to be thwarted because my mother, for whatever reason, now of some importance, had failed to have me dangled and dribbled over at the font. Not easily overcome, I made a conscious decision to allow it to be assumed that I had been signed with Holy Water and keep my dark secret bottled up. But the bother that caused me. Supposing I was found out and accused of misleading, or worst of all, lying by silent implication. Luckily, no one asked me that dreaded question, so I behaved in the same way I did when folk were discussing bastards: realising that I could never beat them, let them assume I was a normal human being – just like them.

Another advantage came with the instruction. We attended The Chantry, in Church Street, once a week, where they also served us a refreshing cup of tea. And sometimes I sneaked a look at the curate's daily paper, *The Times*, which was full of events going on in the outside world: going on I tell you, outside and over my head. What a deprivation that was: no daily news to keep us informed; not even a children's comic!

Among the many things the good curate taught us was the essential signing of the cross (in the most economical way possible, he advised). I assiduously practised this art until I became proficient; working at it mainly in the street, as I walked back to the barracks in the dark – such was my intense desire to at last be one of them.

The great day came and no less than the Bishop of Lincoln

arrived among us. They seated him on a throne-like chair in front of the nave, not far from the pulpit. Wearing a mitre (which to those ignorant of such higher things, is a tall cap, deeply cleft on top), and by his side was his symbolic crook; more correctly known as a crozier, a most useful tool for gathering together those who have strayed from the fold. This august human being, who wore the regalia of his high station, looked like a cross-dressed mixture of Santa Claus and an ancient druid. The capes and folds of clothing covering him were richly adorned as you would expect on this awesome occasion, in which I was now in full participation and, at last, seated in front of the church. Such was my high emotional state that I failed to notice whether or not this good Shepherd was also displaying the amice apparel, amice, orphrey, chasuble, maniple, daimatic, tunicle, stole, alb, sanctuary slippers, or any other queerish garments in keeping with this great occasion (in truth, I had not the foggiest idea that such things existed). Eagerly did I await for the rite to begin and my nervous first step on the extended Establishment ladder. But would I now become one of them? And if I did – how might I show it?

Such was the spookiness of this great occasion, that the dear old bishop appeared to have winged in among us from another world (which impression was probably intended). Our confirming Shepherd looked to be a kindly man; most certainly well fed. He had a ruddy complexion which contrasted with his bodily attire (whether this was caused by good solid food or liquid refreshment of the stronger kind, I would never find out). But why shouldn't he look like Friar Tuck? Some clergy can look so dejected if they are pale and skinny.

When my turn came I walked towards him and knelt down (can you imagine that? – a bastard pauper receiving from a grand bishop!). In due accord he did his *laying on of hands* upon my brilliantined head. The words he uttered

I soon forgot. But to give full credit to his labouring, he *did us* patiently one by one.

[*Not as duly chronicled, in 1712, when a certain Bishop Wake confirmed 2,000 candidates at Spalding (on that splendid day the church was brimming full). But 2,000! However did the bishop manage? There was probably a simple answer: some Bishops merely gave a general blessing which would allow large flocks to be confirmed.*

The Revd Samuel Westley certainly disputed Bishop Wake's reputed performance, alleging that most likely, one way or another, some people were counted more than once. Westley sounded somewhat sniffy about this astonishing claim.]

(An alien visitor descending upon our earth learning about Revd Samuel Westley's displeasure and Bishop Jenkins's problems (among others existing and forthcoming), might be forgiven if they got a clear impression that there was some discord and difficulty in yielding between our various religious followers.)

31

Life in the workhouse continued its set dreary pace. Most of the events described by my new family in the first days of arrival eventually came to pass. In turn, I passed the same information on to newcomers, to try to cheer them up a bit; so often lost and despairing did they look. I enjoyed attending the local Westlode Street State School. That was a precious freedom for five days of the week. The teachers imparted the knowledge and I enjoyed digesting it. Discipline was strict but that never bothered me. If the odd chastisement kept pin-dropping silence in the class, it meant that the majority could get on with the lesson, while the few disruptive ones had to toe the line. I had no quarrel with that. I listened with open eyes and mind – my teacher was the main contact with the outside world. (Teachers, you have more influence than commonly acknowledged – especially to *outside* groping children.) There wasn't a lesson I truly disliked. Like a sponge I absorbed to bursting point the elementary education which was spread over me like enriching manure, during the too few years I attended this school: even the skill obtained by disciplined repetition of that boring times table; which became a useful calculator permanently fixed in my mind.

On Christmas night, presents were delivered in a pillowslip at the head of our beds. Much thought went into this; we had previously been asked what we hoped Santa Claus would bring. As you can imagine, cries of excitement went up, starting in the early morning. Later in the day we joined the grown-ups in the main dining hall. There we had the

195

'blow-out' Christmas dinner, with thruppenny silver coins mixed in the pudding (needing the advice to chew carefully). What a find that was for those who were lucky. And later in the evening (after a 'knife and fork' meat tea) a concert party entertained us. A local butcher, who was a dab hand on the piano, bobbed up and down as he played all the favourite songs – rattling them off out of his head. We all sang loudly and joyfully and were soon lulled into a delirious state of Christmas-tide forgetfulness.

How could I ever forget those morale boosting, simple songs. They were uplifting like the power of hymns:

> I'm H.A.P.P.Y. I'm H.A.P.P.Y.
> I know I am, I'm sure I am,
> I'm H.A.P.P.Y. – etc. ...

> Show me the way to go home,
> I'm tired and I want to go to bed...

> It's a long way to Tipperary...

> Pack up your troubles in your old kit-bag...

But what bleak prospects those poor devils had (and I was doubtlessly one of them), singing to bursting point, on Christmas Day in the workhouse – making the most of living it up before the light of day drearily shone over us again.

Usually a conjuror also performed: Professor No-Ko (or some such outlandish name). With great panache he'd waved his wand and kept repeating his own magical words: 'oko-boko, little drops of cocoa' – would you believe! (instead of the usual: hey-presto). Later we went back to our respective quarters – goodbye Mam, again. (How I missed the friendly blaze of the fire we had at home; the roasting of a few chestnuts, an orange and a few sweets, a modest present (one recycled game on Christmas Day, 1930. I didn't complain; I knew we were desperately poor). And how I loved singing around the piano, with sister Win rattling out the tunes. That was the real Christmas I pined for – now but a faded memory away; feeling miles and years gone by.

The regular one-hour Sunday family visits almost became a duty performance. (There was frustration, aggravated by restriction; sometimes that eased a little, but time dragged on. If the past was now buried, the present was in a hole.) Over the years my mother had changed from dutiful cooperation with the staff to downright disobedience, ending up almost totally withdrawn and introspective, in a somewhat disorientated way. There seemed less and less time when a chink of her former normal self remained. She now also appeared to do nothing but stand and stare out of the women's dormitory on the first floor across the way, in full view of the children's playground. I could see her and she could also see me, but we never waved once. Any contact, even waving contact, was far too emotional and distressing for both of us. *They* were still the target of her frustration and anger, having *robbed us ends and sides of hundreds and thousands* and so cruelly dispossessing us of our *rightful* home. And in this place the Matron was still poisoning her with that white powder she so craftily placed under the meat at mealtimes. Now on permanent strike: refusing to work, which as anyone with a grain of understanding was unthinkable rebellion for a workhouse inmate. Without question, lurking in the background would be the rising tide of officialdom's despair – what's to be done with that obstinate woman?

In the children's quarters the food was basic but good (despite the grisly, tubey mutton, and the nasty tasting roly-poly pudding). I never felt any pangs of hunger, unlike many thousands of poverty-stricken children living outside in family homes. My clothes were of good quality: waterproof footwear and two suits – the second one for Sunday. And my day-dreams and my night-dreams had become an important part of my escape. There was also the church outing to Skegness, our annual seaside holiday lasting all of one day long. And not only that, some other mixed events came along, sometimes disturbing, sometimes soothing, and at other times they could be testing. It was during this period that my attitude changed somewhat. Recovering from fretting and pining, I was now looking and thinking; instead of just being a beaten acceptant, what were my possibilities? What can be done and must be done? And even more important, to work out fact from fancy. Quite a tall order for someone workhouse-placed, in short supply of stimulation.

> *Worry, worry – seek and find!*
> Troubles, troubles – every kind!
> What is more, I'm telling you,
> *They didn't do this, they won't do that!*
> *Should I do this, can I do that?*
> To help me seek and find...

During those three long years (long, because there seemed no ending of any year and the time imprisoned in them), I never received a birthday or Christmas card, nor any newsy letters (except one from Stan which I will come to later). Even the sounds of a violin playing in the distance did not reach me; such was my feeling of isolation.

One routine day, starting like most of the others, there arrived at the Workhouse a postcard for me. (It was still the handy means of sending a short message.) I handled it somewhat suspiciously, this was an entirely new experience. Who would want to send a postcard to me? On one side there was a picture of Skegness clock tower, closely surrounded by benches and people sitting upon them. (This was before they removed them to widen the traffic island for the fast-multiplying motor car.) On the message side the words were few and the sentence to the point: *See you at the clocktower at 3 o'clock and we'll have a good time. Win.*

(This was in 1933, two years after becoming a workhouse inmate, and it emotionally stirred me up quite a bit, in my now eleventh year.)

Those words bubbled in my mind: *See you ... have a good time. Win.* Although he had not forewarned me, Oscar had obtained permission for sister Win to meet me during the church annual outing – and ... *have a good time.* So intoxicated did I become with this sudden postcard news, that it affected my self-control for a time. I read and reread it. Carried around in my pocket and during the school day I placed it in my desk – message side up! '*...we'll have a good time.*' My sister was going to meet me, permission had been obtained. So inattentive did I become in class (quite contrary to my normal behaviour) that the teacher gave me a glancing look, but she never discovered the postcard which was disturbing me so much.

After weeks of growing excitement, the great day arrived at last. The powerful steam locomotive pulled us away towards the sand and sea and duly arrived (after shunting about a bit at Firsby Station, to get on the Skegness branch line). With our usual crocodile discipline we walked to various places: to the sea for a paddle, to Butlin's for the fairground rides, limited by the cash allocation Nurse Purdam had been given. For the mid-day snack we went to the Pavilion in the Tower Gardens where we drank a beaker of milk and ate a sticky bun. But trailing around with a large family was not only inconvenient, it was not my ideal way of fun. The little one's hands had to be held tightly, and the carrier bags with the wet towels began to feel like a lead weight. Roll on 3 o'clock!

After receiving detailed instruction where to join my

199

family again, Win and I sped off from the clocktower. What a freedom that was, just the two of us. She treated me to ice-cream and more Butlin rides; especially on the dodgems, where a notice read: 100 SMILES A MINUTE! Indeed, Billy Butlin's 'True intent was all for your delight!' We chugged in a boat along the waterway, from south to north along the promenade and back the other way. And then we finished on the boating lake and I rowed the boat with quite some skill. But all too soon my freedom ended. Back I went to the railway station, to join the family 'crocodile' again. My whiff of freedom had ended. Frustration set in again, that I was still one of 'them'. How I resented my confinement and my lack of personal freedom, especially on a seaside outing.

That lump arose in my throat, thankfully invisible – no pain in the chest this time. I had become adept at deflecting most stings of trauma. So back again, back to the workhouse to batten down my emotional hatches and get on with the only life possible – for the time being; my life being! – still being! – cocooned in a drab existence, wrapped emotionally in a shroud of uncertainty. What next? God only knows, I couldn't even begin to guess.

I saw my sister Win once again during my incarceration. One summer Sunday she travelled the winding 40 miles or so to visit us during the family hour (and that was a kind thing to do as it probably affected her feelings). She was dressed in a fashionable flowery summer dress and stood out like a sunbeam, against the institutionalised, regulation blue of my mother's uniform. We quietly talked about this and that which seemed to be the thing to do, when words of relevance cannot be easily found.

At a nearby table sat the women's ward, a loud-mouthed bully, Jinny, something or other; a long-termer, full of confidence or so it seemed. 'She's always causing trouble,' said Mam, and quietly related one or two incidents. Win's

200

ears pricked up like a hunting dog's when she heard something which she thought amiss: it was a loud disparaging remark about unmarried mothers which was highly provocative, and certainly painfully personal. Boiling with fury Win suddenly arose and directed her short temper upon the unfortunate inmate, Jinny. Leaping out of her seat she shouted to this workhouse crone: 'Come here, I've got a bone to pick with you! Off flew Jinny, through the exit door, fast to the limit her legs could carry her. Now think of the trouble after we had exhausted the visitor's family hour and Mam went back again to face the barrack bully (quick tempers can relieve, but much too often at a cost to others).

I felt discomforted by this loud scene, having sense enough to understand that this sort of behaviour, in the circumstances, was nothing short of uselessness. Perhaps it's just as well my sister never found enough spare time to visit us again. What a shock it must have been when she saw the drab workhouse scene and her family in such a helpless condition. That is possibly why she *flipped her lid!* She probably desperately fretted over us. And that was all she could do, on a domestic maid's wages of ten shillings (50p) a week; yet another household drudge, expected to be grateful for the only chance life had to offer.

It might prove to be the case that the more comfortable way to resign to a prison sentence is not to be bothered by outside people – even those who exhibit kindness. Certainly not by emotional letters or even the common postcard, and not personal visits which end up troublesome. Within, my mind developed a feeling that if ever I went to the grown-ups' convict prison, I'd rather not hear from anyone from outside the holding walls – not even those sincere visitors of a righteous disposition.

And now to that letter I spoke of, the only letter I received, the one from my brother Stan. A letter that was to send my emotions into a state of turmoil; the memory of which would

201

never be forgotten. Unexpectedly it came, and it would be more accurate to say, 'out of the grey' rather than 'out of the blue'. It was enclosed inside an envelope so no prying eyes could see it. I recognised the handwriting so I started to read, expecting something exciting: how it was good to be outside and free! Instead his words numbed my mind; they scared me! If I followed his request he'd surely get into trouble – of that I was convinced. But those words – would I ever forget his desperate message. Here is the gist of it: 'The work is hard. I cannot do the heavy lifting, I'm sleeping in a cold outbuilding. Have to get up at 4.30 a.m. to feed the horses, and work on until 7 p.m. Tell Matron and see what she can do.'

Tell Matron, indeed! Rocking the boat and getting him into trouble (reminding her that he was too slightly built for farm work; had a 'wasting' disease and could not lift his right arm above the horizontal without the aid of the left one – and he was only 14 years old.)

So institutionalised had I become; so goody-goody defensive, in order to avoid any repercussions, that I hesitated. I kept the letter in my pocket and told no one. My decision was indecision, but not by deliberate intent. If Stan had been waiting to be rescued, he must have felt disappointment. His youngest brother then at the age of ten didn't know what to do. Where did that letter go? In my pocket for quite some time; it burned me so badly it was *lost* in the end. That was the only letter I received from Stan, followed by a period of silence. Some months later he cycled over on one Sunday visiting day. He had grown a few inches, bodily filled out and looked healthy in his suntan. Not a word was ever mentioned about that letter of concern. Somehow he had managed to change his first master and now lived in at a Mr Bower's farm. Although his new boss was an exacting master (as you would expect in those hard times), Stan looked confident and now content with his lot

– at least for the time being. (Never one to overuse words; when much later I asked him about his earlier experience (the cause of that letter), he simply remarked: 'It was a rum do!' An understatement that spoke volumes.) There are times when you have to leave things alone, but often I would wonder: suppose? suppose? – had I shown that letter to the Matron, would it really have made any difference? But that's not my soothing excuse: was I by now getting a defeatist feeling that workhouse paupers had fewer enactive rights than imprisoned criminals? With no ongoing welfare for those sent out of sight, as though they never existed; like the 'white slave' children, previously mentioned – too soon forgotten and many brutally treated. But that's the way it was and usually silently accepted – rocking a rigid boat would then be unthinkable, at least, by those on the receiving end.

32

Just to prove that life is not all doom and gloom, a most exciting invitation came along. In my twelfth year I was selected, along with five other older boys, to join six lads from Boston Workhouse for a holiday at Frieston Shore, along 'The Wash' – that huge toothless, washed-over socket, on the eastern side of our land. On the first stage of our journey we arrived in Boston, conveyed there by the Lincolnshire Road Car Company, in the livery of Lincoln-green. Supervised by Porter Stone, we arrived at least two hours early, alighting at the market place, full of bustling, friendly people. I liked Boston, it smelled of fish and vinegary chips and suggested hidden history. With time to kill before we caught our next connection, the good porter decided to allow us to wander freely about the place.

Snatching this bit of precious freedom, we walked across the busy market place bristling with people as this was Saturday. I viewed them in the mass, this crowd of strangers, busily talking one to another; whirling round in eddies, foraging for the market bargains. To be lonely in a crowd can cause bouts of yearning. Where were those familiar, inbred village faces which I knew from top to bottom? Then (and this was fascinating) we continued along a narrow thoroughfare by the delightful name of Dolphin Lane, into an open space called 'Pump Square' – a splendid memorial to our Victorian forefathers. In the centre of this square (so it has been duly recorded), once were two subterranean rooms, or vaults, of neat workmanship, with arched roofs. These man-made cavities were used as a reservoir of water (and it is said, to house convicted prisoners). The ancient pump was no longer spouting water at the stroke of its handle when I passed through Boston. Instead, an ornamental replica stood forlornly at the east end of the square; a reminder of the past, and my dear old village birthplace.

Yes, Boston caught my interest. It seemed so big and congested, with its wide market place leading outwards onto narrow lanes and alleyways of surprising interest. Watched over by the lofty tower of St Botolph's Church, locally known as 'The Stump', thrusting skywards, giving the appearance of seeking the very Gate to Heaven. There is ample evidence of past prosperity, provided by the neighbouring rich farming land and the trade brought by the visiting sea-going vessels. Yet some disgruntled character, a long time ago, had written a rhyme, which was not only narrow in thought, it was slightingly full of ill-will. The writer remains anonymous; no wonder, just consider what was written:

> Boston, Boston, thou hast naught to boast on,
> But a Grand Sluice and a High Steeple,
> A proud conceited, ignorant people,
> And a Coast where Souls get lost on.

On the day of my visit the town seemed to be in good heart. So who could have been so despicable? (Writing rude words and not owning up.) The answer may lie in a single word – the use of 'souls' instead of 'lives', it sounds like a smack of religious condemnation, from a narrowly held view of the world. So was it one of those pesky Puritans who, in 1607, caused so much disruption in the town? Where they had to be locked-up in the Guildhall before being duly tried. What relief must have been felt by the remaining Christian town people, after those rigid nuisances had finally sailed away.

205

Good riddance to those Puritans!
Boston will not miss them,
When they're blown across the seas,
Taking their pious baggage with them;
Pushing their luck in a Brave New World,
In the colony of Boston, in New England,
There called 'God's Own Country' –
A land ripe for exploitation,
After subduing the red-skin heathens,
And stealing their Mother Earth.

In Pump Square, at the appointed time, we boarded the coach otherwise known as a 'puddle jumper', except there were no puddles about; the sun would shine the whole month through. Porter Stone handed us over into the care of a man from Boston. (As I've forgotten his name I'll refer to him as 'G', our temporary guardian, and as such he had a commendable influence on our young lives. Obviously a devout man, he led the mealtime grace and on Sunday marched us off to nearby Frieston Parish Church, which was expected and not considered unusual, for both children and the attending congregation. There's no doubt about it, set deep inside G was a layer of practical moral sense, adhered to without any fuss; simplistic and capable of imitation, especially by a wondering child. That set apart, life's experience had already taught me that religious folk do not have the exclusive rights to moral influence. On the contrary, I was fast discovering that the irreligious can also play an important part. And quite often, didn't I discover that there can come moral stimulation from the remorseful; now consciously facing up to their own stricken anguish: Why, oh why! did I cause such distress?

After a winding journey of some five flat Fenland miles, collecting and dropping off passengers we arrived at our destination: Plummer's Hotel at Frieston Shore. It was situated only a few yards from the embankment which was connected to the first floor of the hotel by a footbridge, to a spacious room of some length, where we children bedded down on mattresses. On the ground-floor, using wash-basins at the public house, we carried out our minimum ablutions, as skimpily as you would expect of children not closely supervised and faced with ice-cold running water. The long room where we slept and ate had probably been the hotel's restaurant or lounge. By the time we children stayed there, the whole place was run-down and showing a state of neglect – yet to us it became an earthly paradise; freedom to roam and do much as we pleased. But what a come-down for this fine hotel, that its last paying guests were 12 pauper lads from the Spalding and Boston, Poor Law Institutions. [*The Plummer's Hotel in 1805 was said to have room for 20 guests (nearby, but first to go out of existence, was the Marine Hotel with 23 bedrooms). The guests came mainly from Yorkshire and the Midlands. They came to enjoy the two-day horse race meetings held between Frieston and Butterwick, until the 1860s. Most likely on the then deeper foreshore bounded by the old 'Sea Bank', illustrated clearly on the maps. And some visited the area to engage in a spot of shooting on the sand marshes; not to sniff the fresh Wash air, nor to pick the saline fleshy leaves of samphire, or to rub themselves in the mud of the creeks, to soothe 'the screws', a painful rheumaticky condition.*]

The sea and hoped-for sandy beach were nowhere to be seen. The tide was out when we arrived, exposing a well-worn path towards the shore. 'The tide will come back again – twice a day, you'll see,' said G. He further explained that when the tide returned and started to fill the creeks (some as deep as rivers), we must return at once, otherwise we could get cut off and drown. None of us could swim. At low tide we walked about half a mile before we found the sand and sea, observing all the wild life, listening to their many sounds. Several times we went the two miles or so to watch the fishing smacks and sea-going ships chug in and out of 'The Haven', the sea outlet from Boston. We waved to the crews and they waved back. This sight stirred within me a thought of possible adventure. Even so I willingly went back to the security I now knew so well. We stripped the fleshy samphire with our teeth and developed quite a taste for it. Sometimes in the evening we sat on a bench on the embankment and G joined us. We discussed many things. In particular I remember adoption being mentioned (but surely not for a 12-year-old). Yes, I thought to myself, I would go along with that in order to gain my freedom, but as soon as I could I would seek out my Mam and live with her once more.

Every Sunday and Bank Holidays, visitors would turn up to walk about, or sit on the bench and sniff hard at the bracing sea breeze. One retired farmer came along, driven by a chauffeur in a posh motorcar. G soon chatted him up, explained who we were and the rest of it. Luckily for us he was passionately fond of samphire, except, unlike us, he liked to have it cooked. A bargain was clinched: if we would collect samphire for him, he would reward us. And so we did, obtaining thruppence each for bundles of the stuff. He was pleased and so were we. We'd have a special treat the next day: a packet of crisps, some goodies or a bottle of pop – our way of living it up.

1934 had a burning summer, at least at Frieston Shore. Wandering about in swimsuits all day long, we singed our skins badly under the sun. G was not only kindly but resourceful. He produced a massive bottle of olive oil from which he poured some over our tingling skins and bade us rub it in. The flesh cracked and the skin shred in strips which flapped about on our backs and the olive oil cooked it, well done! We fried in the day and painfully endured burning sensations in the night. But thankfully we fully recovered – after which our skins darkened, leaving us decidedly foreign-looking.

Another thing forcibly struck me. On Sunday afternoon the young Master of Boston Workhouse cycled over with his wife. To my complete surprise, instead of being hesitant and looking downwards, the Boston children gathered around them and spoke in wild excitement about their great adventure. I kept in the background, but I observed that all the children showed signs of being fond of this couple. After living under the efficient but frigid regime at Spalding, in truth, I felt more than a tinge of envy – that this couple not only seemed to act as substitute parents, they also showed affection.

Another surprising thing came about, making me quite nervous at first. Instead of seating us in the very back rows of the pews, G directed us to sit at the front of the church surrounded by the regular congregation, where we appeared to cause no alarm to the good people of Frieston. The vicar seemed pleased to see us and to cap it all, one lady member of the congregation gave me a beaming motherly smile; though so institutionalised had I become, and suspicious of 'outside' people, I never smiled back in response. I later regretted that. And something else happened, which was quite astounding; the Vicar invited the 12 of us to take tea on his lawn. The sun shone, the table was laden with sandwiches and tasty cakes, all prepared by the ladies of the congregation. It was so hot, before we were due to go back, the Vicar offered us a final drink of 'pop'. No wonder my memory of Frieston is one of friendship and kindness. The Master of the Boston institution again turned up, and personally asked me how I was – just fancy that! Another man from Boston visited us. I believe he was the main mover in arranging the Frieston visit (a Mr Swain, a local councillor?). He also chatted to us. I had quite a conversation with him: this kindly man of action. After nearly three years of routine and indifference his personal interest was almost unbelievable, but most welcome. During the month we were away no one from Spalding turned up – not even our beadling, Porter Stone. But what did that matter in the face of such wonderful freedom to roam and explore to our heart's content?

On returning to our Spalding Home, the six of us must have presented an alarming sight. With new skin growing, some burnt bits still hanging free, old skin tanned like leather and with more than a smudge of dirt engrained upon us, Nurse Purdam took immediate action and ordered us to take a bath, to cleanse our polluted state, in case it became infectious. Proof indeed that we were firmly back into her custodial care and the regulations.

33

After the freedom of that memorable holiday, we were once more mainly confined to the exercise yard and supervised visits to the communal lawn: usually for a picnic tea and occasional games of cricket (organised by the Matron's sons). Proving more adventuresome, Nurse Purdam allowed a few of the older children to go for a walk along a lane leading off the Pinchbeck Road, where we sometimes managed to fish for tiddlers. On one of these expeditions Ernie managed to insert the fish hook deep into a finger and had to go to hospital to have it released.

Otherwise, apart from attending the family visiting hour, we children played tag, ran races and kicked a ball if we had one. On one exciting occasion we flew a kite, on such a long string it fluttered towards Spalding. Eventually it broke free and disappeared from sight – how I envied it!

One of my duties was to collect a small jug of milk from the cookhouse for Nurse Purdam's tea, until I forgot one day and was sacked for forgetting to perform this chore, which did not displease me.

Word had somehow reached the cookhouse that I had been singing and clog-dancing after the fashion of various music hall variety entertainers, especially Gus Elen who was regularly performing in the early 1930s at the end of the *Pathe-Pictorial News*. It was now the turn of the cook to request a performance of 'Arf a Pint of Ale', sung in my best cockney accent:

> Now for breakfast I never think of 'aving tea,
> I likes me 'arf a pint of ale.

At dinner I likes a little bit of meat,
And 'arf a pint of ale.
At tea I likes a little bit of fish,
And 'arf a pint of ale.
And for supper I likes a crust of bread and cheese,
And a pint and a narf of ale.

At the very end I used to vary the last line and sing out in a cockney accent: And a *gallon* and a narf of ale!

And believe it or not, that little flourish got laughs. Who knows, I might become another Charlie Chaplin who also served some time as a workhouse inmate when he was a child.

'Before you go back, come and visit your mother,' one of the cookhouse inmates requested. She led me through that same side door used by my mother when she had so swiftly disappeared on the day we arrived in this place – the door to the women's section. Beyond this door was a highly polished, longish, spartan-like room where I observed all around were high-backed chairs. I had completely forgotten that my mother lived in this room a few seconds' walk away from my latest comic triumph. She was an active 55-year-old (with another 25 years still to live) now living in confinement – a kind of debtor's prison – paying her debt not in money, to society in a punishing way.

Sitting around with nothing apparently to do (so it appeared to me) were the women inmates of all ages – some more capable than others – all resplendent in their spotless, plain-same uniforms of light blue with thin white vertical lines, not stamped with arrows as was regular in that other prison place. (In the midst of such confinement and frustration, no wonder blackened rumours did abound of unlit candles being misused in a darkened dildo way.)

'Over there, your mother is over there,' said my forceful guide pointing to one of the high-backed chairs amidst the seated circle. 'Over there,' chorused the other inmates, now catching on to the excitement which was to disturb their quiet lives for a few minutes. Mam appeared shocked to see me, my visit was so unusual and completely unexpected; and strictly speaking it was against the rules. I turned towards her and we spoke a few empty words with the entire audience listening in. The words were easily forgotten. I then turned to go. 'Kiss your mother!', one female inmate loudly said. Again they all repeated this request, in a singing, almost shrieking way: 'Kiss your mother!' they all bid.

I had never to my knowledge kissed my mother in all my ten or so years of life (folk in the village where I came from were not outwardly demonstrative – there are many other ways of showing affection; I knew the signs, kissing was not one of them). Under such intense pressure I had no alternative but to move towards Mam. I kissed her on her right cheek. She remained immovable, like a marble statue, and the kiss felt cold and utterly impersonal, then planted on this human being whom I knew to be my mother; now living in deep isolation – shut up, heaped up and certainly lacking of human spirit. There was an abject air of defeat about her. I also noticed the ever-widening streaks of grey hair that were beginning to show in this grim location. That was another shock to me: she was getting old! Mam might die in this place and leave me on my own.

Afterwards I sensed that I had been guilty of gross bad manners. I had intruded without prior invitation into Mam's sanctuary of private suffering. I was not supposed to visit this *prison room*. Visiting time was on Sunday afternoon for one hour in the main dining hall. By now I was used to the official way of doing things: one hour every week on Sunday afternoon was the space allocated in this institution for *Mother* time. This additional intrusion into both our lives, so suddenly without preparation, was far too disturbing and left behind nothing but emotional drain. How can you

213

wind up the threads of your emotional life in seconds and free them down again, without you hardening your innermost feelings to form a protective shell? Quiet weeping would not ease the pain; noisy blubbering is next to useless – not that I ever bothered.

So don't forget in future: visiting time is on Sunday, between three and four o'clock. Other times are not only inconvenient, they are sorrowful and disturbing – and another thing, stop singing that damn silly song! And try not to keep reminding yourself of this burdensome, confining; that there is no escape from this place: that rescue is but a false dream.

34

During the first winter of 1931/2, I had not seen and had heard very little concerning my Horton father, now aged 78. He was still in the infirmary hospital wing at the rear of the main workhouse range of buildings, and most likely still suffering from the effects of his foot injury (miracle drugs were not yet available). Visiting was never considered, so far as I am aware, even if I had wanted to visit him the authorities would never have allowed this to happen (sinners could not meet their bastards). To be fair, I made no request, nor did I think of such a thing – my own problems were hitting me hard. He was old enough to cope with his own. In this Poor Law nursing home for the destitute sick, the usual way of escape for the discarded elderly was by way of a coffin, the cheapest kind, without adornments made of shining brass; planted in a hole beyond public gaze (in the paupers' plot in the cemetery). And most certainly not sporting a fine headstone with an appropriate inscription, in Horton's case: HE ESCAPED AT LONG LAST.

In front of the Infirmary, in full view from all its windows was a large lawn on which we children played games: rounders, football and cricket; although any 'six' landed in the nearby vegetable or flower patch.

The lawn provided a welcome break from the children's secure wing and we looked forward to going there and the limited freedom it provided. For a special treat Nurse Purdam used to arrange for us to have tea on the lawn on sunny days and this extended our freedom into the early evening. We children sat around in a circle, eating our bread and

215

marge pieces, one by one, never forgetting to say 'thank you' aloud for every single one. It was an agreeable experience in the glow of the sun; except that I disliked being seen by the elderly, infirm inmates as they passed by and usually stared: like a zoologist would on finding a rare specimen feeding in the forest.

Embarrassingly, one summer day a girl in my school class, living *private* somewhere off the Pinchbeck road, all of ten, walked along the field next door and waved a friendly hand to me. I ignored her. How dare she invade my privacy and shaming poverty state. Before she gave up she came several times and brazenly waved. Although I cannot deny that I was deeply touched, this outside intrusion was too much for me to accept. But maybe, who knows, this could have been my very first romance.

Another day (during the summer of 1932) while sitting in our tea circle, much to my surprise and unease, I saw Horton sitting on one of the garden benches earnestly talking to his pauper chums. They seemed to be all ears for he was a good storyteller. I knew that from the tales he had told in my childhood; countrymen can usually spin a good yarn or two and he was in full flow. This nearness to the man whom I knew to be my father began to bother me. I had grown up by a big spurt since last I had had contact with him, nearly a year since, so I was completely unprepared for this encounter. I explored my recent memory of events: he wasn't a criminal; on the contrary you could safely say he was far too honest. He'd never knowingly sold a rotten fruit or vegetable in his entire life; had never been cruel; was always sober, and that was something to be thankful for. Some families had to suffer cruelty and drunkenness. Not our family. Our main problem had been caused by the irritating habit of money passing us by. A lot of problems can be resolved by throwing money at them, but our present problems were perhaps too complicated even for that. I was, in any

216

case, feeling a kind of independence, reconciled for the time being that my life was firmly clasped in binding hands, in a house bigger than some castles: a kind of public boarding school for children, but not one where children of better-off parents go home for the holidays.

But as might be expected, I continued to ask myself the main question: How long do I stay in this place? Prisoners in gaol know their term and they get remission for good behaviour. I am trying to be calm, but a little explanation would help. No one talks, except the children with the same problem, and they know nothing – only wild occasional feelings of misplaced optimism and speculation, and that irritates and gets me nowhere. Perhaps I could run away and join a ship sailing to America; several members of the Horton family had done this in the past. I remembered the Horton farm pictures hanging on the *room* wall of our farm cottage. Suppose, just suppose, I ran away and reached their home in America. What would they say to this sudden appearance of family blood? After all, they (*they* again) do say that blood is thicker than water.

The American Horton family looked prosperous, so that way seemed hopeful. Who knows, they might come over and rescue us from our present awful plight? So I imagined the 10th Cavalry galloping through Spalding to wheel sharply into the workhouse and (without permission from Matron, or Porter Stone, on duty at the gate) springing the old man to freedom. They might even release me, even though their proud, cherished name had now been changed to Green. But I already knew that escapist pipe dreams only happened in the local cinema and there we screamed and howled with delight, coming back to reality with a bump, when the projectionists flicked the switch to turn on the lights and we walked outside, to confront our real and only life.

The American Family Saga – extracts and comment:

Sam Horton was the son of George, who farmed as a grazier near Boston, Lincolnshire, and died in 1831, comparatively wealthy. He left around £3,000, which he distributed around his family without any complications. Sam, at the age of 17 (in 1835), being venturesome, decided to emigrate with a companion from his home in Gosberton Cheal, where he then lived and jointly farmed with his brothers, George and John.

Sam landed at Castle Gordon, New York, after 21 days on a sailing vessel that encountered stormy seas, lost its rigging and was blown off course. Of those aboard 17 died of starvation. He was hospitalised six weeks in New York City before he regained strength and found work in logging camps near Troy in Herkimer County...

He married Alpha Lucina Perkins on 14th February, 1841. He was then 23 and had returned home for a brief visit to claim the legacy his father had left him. From '41 they ventured into farming in Medina County, Ohio. After six years, including two bad crop failures, this farm was sold in 1847 and the family moved back east to a farm in Niagara County, New York, where they lived for three years.

There, they bought 220 acres for $12.00 an acre. In its early, rough stumpy condition the Horton farm produced very little cash income from grains. This led to their keeping of five milch cows to fill their need for milk and butter at home. They had cows – they had milk – but now they had no outlet for it. Fortunately, his enterprising wife, Alpha, had learned the process for making the large, round stone cheese, then the only cheese found in food stores. As one way of realising a better cash return she made several cheeses (one a day) from the milk produced by their five cows. Sam then called on every grocery store for miles around to find out whether their cheeses would be saleable. They risked borrowing to build a small factory in 1866, on the strength of the discovered demand.

From such a humble beginning the business seemed unstoppable. Sam's son George Byron (hereinafter: GB) took over in 1872, and by progressive management in 1908 he was operating 12 cheese factories with an annual output of 2,500,000 pounds of cheese and owned seven dairy farms (1,240 acres of land) and 100 acres of choice hardwood timber. GB was once elected State Senator but was ruled out as legally disqualified, as he held a federal post office position, a tiny county office but enough to bar him from Senate service. He also held several important state appointive positions: Member of the State Board of Agriculture; Member of the State Tax Commission; delegate to the 1907 State Constitutional Commissioner. In his local community he was President and Master of this and that Society. A veritable shaker and mover. (After his death, in the form of a tribute, the local community had erected a memorial stone.)

With business booming in the early 1880s, GB had built a fine new country home. Somewhat trend-setting, he decided on a '...two storey, five master bedroom, brick with slate roof and a tower on one front corner, as was the current architectural fad. Still proudly standing, it was described in a local newspaper as 'the finest farm home in the state of Michigan, if not in all the United States'. Nowadays, it could be described as somewhat Disney-like. The snooty English might call it 'Parvenu's Place'. When I visited the house I was most impressed with all the different wood panelling and especially did I stare in the attic, so large that the birds within could fly around in a complete circle.

At the time of his death in 1922 (the year I was born), GB left a $300,000 estate; built up over the years from his own inheritance from his father, the immigrant Sam. How the inheritance was dissipated is explained in forthright terms by GB's son Sam, who eventually had to come to terms with his brother Norman's stock market losses (he being plain unlucky, or just reckless in the extreme: not only buying stock with cash, buying stock 'on margin' – a small percentage down and the balance to follow).

GB's will, far less watertight than it should have been, suffered from mixed interpretation by various members of the family who ganged up on brother Sam, the isolated family executor.

Sister Alice '...opened up with a shameful tirade, attacking father for ... even thinking of making such an absurd will... I certainly do not agree with his queer plans...' Then she decreed: WE HAVE DECIDED not to do what the will says at all – to keep the estate open until mother dies – to let Norman run the estate until mother dies – that you, Sam, must resign as executor and let Norman act as sole executor...'

And so, given enough time, the icy dawning of 'if only' seemed bound to come: 'For several years after my father died and his estate went to the dogs, I kept getting letters from the beneficiaries, who were in a quandary as to what happened that so completely ruined the work of two generations... A horse and carriage was driven through the will ... only one (No. 8) of his 8 intents was carried out. His other 7 intents I regret allowing the other beneficiaries to trash the will, with a near total capital loss to all heirs and to mother's income...' So wrote Sam's grandson, Sam.

And now the knife goes in: '...while he (brother Norman) aimed high at "riding father's coattail" as they say, to a Michigan State Senator's seat, with we heirs financing his campaign ... with his stock market losses and the fallen value of farm land due to the depression, Norman's estate shrunk by a lot more than his full 1922 inheritance of $100,000. And not only that, by conniving with the "dissenters" over the will, Alice being his main supporter; Norman managed to "broach" the whole estate to fund a senator's

220

life-style ... for 12 years Norman faked like a rich country squire...'

After the Wall Street crash in the 1930s, some bankrupts jumped out of skyscrapers – with fatal results. And some shot themselves, Norman was one of these. Causing a brownish stain on the floor of his study. (His suicide occurred in 1933. At that time I was 11 years old and a poverty-stricken, stigmatised inmate in the poorhouse; facing life as it came: silently and in bouts of wondering. It would seem that the degree of woe and the passage to beyond can vary enormously – from smarting to smitten.)

But to be fair, it was duly recorded that Norman was quite a productive senator: introducing 46 bills during his senatorial career, 22 of which were enacted into law. It was also reported in a lengthy newspaper tribute that '...he was a captain in the World War (1914–18) and in private life he was a delightful, loveable companion. In business he was upright, and in the management of his own and his father's estate he did his best to meet conditions.' And then it kindly concluded: 'We all have troubles; it seems that man is born to little else, but we do cling to life with tenacity, and with faith and hope, and look forward to better days. So when one destroys oneself we know that the power of resistance has been overcome by a superior force which no one can measure.'

Unquestionably, this would be a bad period for the proud Horton family; of both the American and the English remnants, now lacking use of the name. Had I then known of their problems I might have felt some sort of sympathy. But life is like a slippery snake: it changes direction and loses its skin from time to time. In 1933 the body was naked – not of a stony-heart, simply stony-broke! The rescue of Horton, my father, by the 10th Cavalry would not take place in Spalding; so that was yet another useless daydream, on which to waste away some struggling time.

Returning homewards after that bout of trans-Atlantic wishful dreaming, what of help from Horton's other children of his widely-sown seed? Although George (Horton) Mawer (his first bastard) was brought up by his own grandparents and never knew Horton as a close father, he didn't fail to apply a little subtle blackmail when requesting £100 to set up in business, making his plea by finishing up with the words: '...after all, you are my Father'.

Who agrees that 'blood is thicker than water'? Not the bastard in this case and can you blame him? Not only was he stigmatised but forced to live with his life well and truly blighted in the scorn of all onlookers, by his most unusual birth certificate, arranged by his branding 'grandfather' – downright revengeful, to say the least.

And what of his surviving legitimate son, Thomas, now small-farming in America? He would have enough problems of his own. Now married with a family of two to support, not only would he have been disgusted by his father's *tacky* behaviour but also affected by the world depression. In any case, Thomas had made his forthright views well and truly known to his father when he returned home in the 1920s. The son's estrangement was not only geographical, it was deep set in a straitened furrow, as you would expect of those times. Can you imagine the shock this strictly brought up lad would have received, shortly after his arrival in the USA, when he learnt that his father had *done it again!* This time with Lizzie Green, his former surrogate mother (the housekeeper) – no wonder his family blood was thinned to water and hard-frozen.

Surprisingly and vividly, on a summer's day, there he was, my father, sitting on a workhouse garden bench, and although I was too far away to hear Horton's tales, I must confess I was all agog. What was he yarning about? The bad corn yield in 1875; the drought of '87; or the good years from '91? His religious upbringing (he attended

222

Gosberton Parish Church in his younger days) must have given him faith in good years to follow bad: 'Tighten your belt and it will come out right in the end – the Good Book tells us so.' The trust that man had in a Supreme Power over us.

So far Horton had had nearly 80 years of living, to my precarious 12. He was certainly old enough to be my grandfather and also, without much stretch of the imagination, old enough to be my great-grandfather (remember, he was born in 1854 and I was born in 1922). No wonder my hard questioning had begun – especially about the cock-ups of some horny men.

> *A pox on ancient fathers,*
> *Who manage to come and go,*
> *And on all random, randy ones*
> *(The fumblers and the bold).*
>
> *So pray to God for guidance*
> *(He made us one and all);*
> *But might He be responsible,*
> *For allowing Adam to Fall?*

On that relaxing sunny day we were so near in the flesh, but so far apart in reality. Several months had passed by since last I had seen or spoken to Horton and my understanding (or misunderstanding) of my life had been mulled over and over in order to reach some logical explanation for its present outcome; which was certainly then out of my control. A gap of resentment had widened and swayed from side to side as I looked for some reasonable certainty until uncertainty took over again. I must confess that more than a little self-pity came my way as I steeped myself in repressed anger; perhaps the worst anger of all to be directed against another human (but how could I shout out my anxious thoughts in my present situation – they simply had to be hidden). Sorting out fundamental truths is sometimes difficult, especially with limited understanding and no helpful explanations. Is it better to bury them deeply inside? But that often causes festering and discharge at some future time which more often than not arrives. Perhaps it's better to pretend that some things have never happened, but in all honesty – can you do that?

For now, I had no other option but to stay put in the workhouse; to make the best use of any opportunity that came along and, for the time being, accept this slice of life given to me. The fearful truth had already struck home: Horton could not help me now, or in the future. He had already supplied me with his set of genes and that was it. He was my father and my father could not help me. But I reasoned further: this had surely happened to other children in their lives, they had lost or never known a father or mother, but they had somehow overcome this problem, sorted it out, often with great strength and accomplishment.

Such frantic thoughts brought me both comfort and hope – who knows what the future might bring? I'd soon be 14 and out of this place and earning. Getting rid of my dependency must be my very first aim – that was now as far as I could dream.

Another interesting encounter occurred on one of those sunny garden days which also made my mind jolt a little, but only a little, by now I had become somewhat shock-frozen. One of Horton's pauper friends from the bench approached me to ask a question: 'Is it true that Mr Horton still has a 50-acre farm in the Cheal?' he queried, 'He keeps talking about it.' Do I believe this, I thought? A 50-acre farm – whatever next? And then the answer came strongly through: he was living in past time, of years and years ago. I was living in the present time so I had to try to make both times meet. If I said no, he would lose face. That must never happen. I rather liked the idea. We owned a 50-acre farm in Gosberton Cheal, success at last! 'Yes,' I replied, 'Mr Horton does own a 50-acre farm in the Cheal.' Well aware that I was misleading, I said this without a qualm – how could I let the old man down? No one ever queried my answer so I must have been believed, and Horton's stock would have risen on the garden bench that day. At least, that is what I hoped. And even though I had told a wicked *ligger*, I didn't give a tuppenny damn! Nor did I wash my mouth out with cold water, as Horton used to instruct us to do, in order to cleanse our mouths of wicked *story telling*.

Now my reasoning was gathering apace. We were certainly not going back to the farm and the fragile security I had thankfully known for a few years. Some children in this place had never known a family life. I was lucky and could draw on lots and lots of happy memories to sustain me. They had never known another place. Nine years of good fortune were behind me to help me face the world. But that's looking into the past – the future was my pressing problem. Father Horton was in the same situation, but he was never going to go through the main gates to freedom; except the special kind of freedom that comes to us all at the end. This was to be his last home on earth. Yet he had worked so hard with such honesty and blind faith all his life, this end was unbefitting and brutal. The things kids think about when they try to square wobbling circles.

On that first occasion on the workhouse lawn, George Horton (my life-giving father) did not notice me and I was thankful, and relieved in my mind.

I was pleased my father had not found me!

My Heavenly Father had not found me either. His mysterious ways had ceased to bother me over-much, not even when I listened, ever hopeful, to the vicar. Something was missing! All I wanted was *out* from this place. Even a cottage with a leaky roof would do – anywhere! But not transported to

225

Heaven! I was too young for that. Just blazing mad at times! Is that unreasonable? But why blame God, He's not an estate agent. He's likely more concerned with the poor in spirit, not how to accommodate them in down-to-earth dwellings.

Several times did I see Horton before he discovered me, his lost and last son, squatting a few yards away like a North-American Indian at a warriors' pow-wow, but without a pipe of peace and pride of tribal place. Perhaps his friends had pointed me out. His own eyesight was failing and I had changed a little, so instant recognition was perhaps more difficult. In any case, when I saw him moving towards me I kept my head well down, and would have bolted into a rabbit hole, but on this well-kept lawn none was available. He moved steadily and purposefully around the ring of feeding children and at last he caught me out and peered hard for me on that sunny day: a tall old man with a black flowing beard, a vivid reminder of my past before my present predicament began.

Clearly determined to seek his prey, he finally fixed me in his sight and then asked: 'Where's your mother?'

'In the women's ward,' I replied.

Taking seconds to absorb my informative reply, he then asked: 'Where's Oscar?'

'Back in the Risegate,' I replied.

And then, in a continuing probing tone: 'Where's Stanley?'

And I replied, 'Working on a farm.'

'Oh, he's got a situation,' he concluded. I was most impressed by his use of the word *situation* – it sounded much more dignified than job. Then he moved off, seemingly satisfied with this first interrogation, leaving me uncomfortably charged with emotion. All the children of my large family were lapping up this conversation, no doubt by now beginning to wonder about this stranger's connection with my past, now somewhat mysterious life.

Several times Horton successfully sought me out and almost without variation he would start: 'Where is your mother?' And I would repeat my short reply, and he would follow with the rest. Never once did he ask me how I was, nor for that matter, did I of him. How strange – he was my father – I was his son. My short life's experience and recent contact with senile people made me acutely aware that Horton's memory and concentration were rapidly failing and this perhaps was a blessing – a relief from stark reality. How much relief I would never know. He was living within his old memory world – the eternal problem of living too long. What was I to do? What could I do? Nothing, simply nothing but sit and helplessly listen. My life was starting and his was finishing, it was as simple and as cold as that. Yet another subsistence, slave-bound smallholder had gone bust and ended up on the organic muck heap. Whatever his problems (even his failings) he never deserved this imprisonment.

Every time Horton approached me on the lawn (and much to my annoyance he always did when I was sitting in the workhouse *family circle*), the children listened in with ears that must have been flapping like an elephant's. My self-esteem (what little I had left), was in danger of crashing to the ground. Often I would feel so angry with this man who had carelessly planted my seed, yet had always carefully planted his produce seed on his farm. Like the scandal tabloid press, my pauper friends soon smelt a rat and were on to me like a flash. 'Gerry, who is that old man who keeps coming across and asking you questions?' they asked. 'Just an old man I knew in the village,' I replied. From the series of questions no one guessed the real relationship (except Nurse Purdam, who knew the truth but kept quiet about it). And that is how I wanted it. I'd had enough of emotional bending so I wanted to escape. It was time for a divorce. But such stark separations contain elements of anger,

227

frustration, sadness, loneliness, freedom and remorse; not necessarily in that order, or at the same time.

Goodbye! Goodbye!
We're both in deep distress.
We are so near.
Yet far away –
In a pickle of a mess.

And there's nothing we can do
(except in silence, say unsaid):
Goodbye Old Man!
Goodbye My Son!
– I wish I was Dead and Buried!

If he was absent when I was on the lawn, Horton would be peering out of the window, watching us play games and he would search out for me in particular. I felt his persistent eyes boring at and through me, and occasionally I gave him a quick glance and noticed his intensively peering face. (Perhaps our nurse had noticed my trauma after all and had requested the ward sister not to allow him out to continue his disturbing questioning.) My occasional glances in his direction began to turn into remorse. I felt a wave of pity for him. He looked so lonely and forlorn at that window, his last hope of contact with me – his very own flesh and blood, the youngest of his mixed brood, the carrier of some of his ancient genes.

I then thought of happier times; he had never been cruel; always kind in his way; and never forgot to bring me a pennyworth of peppermints from his weekly visit to Spalding market – although I would have preferred a packet of fizzy sherbert, but politely never said so. He was my father, the only one I was ever likely to get; except the Heavenly Father, and my relationship with him seemed fairly botched

228

up. With my intuitive perceptions dashing hopes of blessed happiness, I slowly sank into worldly realism, bending towards cynicism: a condition that encourages cocking a snook in contempt.

Except for taking time off for meals, Horton stood staring out of the window, and I continued mainly to ignore him. What else could I do? Even if I had wanted to make some small amend, my scope was strictly limited. My nosey friends were all around, it was going to be difficult, but eventually I devised a plan. After cricket I volunteered to collect the equipment, and took my time over this task, until the other children were out of sight around the corner of the building. Then looking up and directly making eye contact I stood still for a few precious seconds. We gazed intently at each other. My mind felt numb in the search for feeling. Nothing of happiness welled up inside me. No anger came, just a sense that a bridge was missing and I couldn't leap across the gap. He never waved nor did I. We just stared across an immeasurable chasm, our bottomless abyss of despair. Then furtively I turned away, back to my new-born life, leaving him behind: the secret father of my early childhood, the one who gave me human life – the true cause of my being. I never saw him again after that summer of 1934, now 12 years of age, I was fast growing up as you would expect. So better not to sit too tightly on judgement, of folk so closely and painfully felt.

> *Heed your Mother,*
> *And your Father –*
> *As earthly as you can.*

> *Consider their mixed Blessings;*
> *Weigh their transgressions:*
> *Humanly – if you can!*

35

For many of the elderly patients, Spalding Infirmary would be their journey's end. Although in its day it served a desperate need with every best intention, this gaunt Victorian building was a place to be avoided; with difficulty if you were ill, old, destitute and had no caring family to look after you. No wonder people would say when *surplus* children came along: *'They'll be a comfort to you in your old age.'* But no matter how well the Infirmary was run, it must have sent a shiver through the spine of those who knew it might be their last place of abode on this earth. They also knew it was part and parcel of the workhouse complex, dreaded by all despairing people – especially those who had lived too long and now felt 'in the way'.

Within its red-brick walls there existed all kinds of patients: rejected, senile, ill to dying. Without question, some of those odd in mind and considered beyond the point of being usefully acceptable within society, might easily have ended up in a place called Bedlam (the hospital of St Mary of Bethlehem), had they lived within its tentacled grasp during the heady days of its reign.

Thankfully, my own experience of the infirmary was not to be permanent. And to be fair, I had no reason to grumble. During the winter of 1933 I was also admitted to the very place where Horton now existed. Drawing on what other people told me, I had contracted pleuro-pneumonia: which was pneumonia complicated with pleurisy (marked by a pain in the side or chest: double-pneumonia, *so it was commonly said*).

I spent the first night in the men's ward, a depressing room in the usual drab green and brown workhouse colours. Most of the elderly patients seemed in a state of dying, or permanently lost to our world. A vociferous complaint was made about me on the following day: I had been coughing all night and disturbed their sleep. The patient opposite me demanded that I sat upright in bed to help the coughing subside. He was most probably right, but I was in no fit condition to carry out his request, which further ruffled the poor fellow into a state of vexation, for what to him was unreasonable behaviour on my part.

The very next morning, faced with this patient's vehement protestation about his loss of precious sleep, caused by my irritating coughing, the ward sister, after due consultation with the doctor, arranged for my removal to the women's wing. There I was bedded in a much brighter ward, next to a bedridden old lady who treated me with motherly sympathy. Also in this smallish ward was an elderly senile patient, who habitually hid all the cutlery under the sheets after each meal. Regularly once a week, the nurses turned over her bed amid much sound of clattering as the missing knives, forks and spoons clanked onto the floor. In the night this poor woman also got out of bed and screamed for Sukie (her favourite sister who had long since been dead). She never cooperated when requested to swallow pills or any liquid form of medicine. A wrestling bout would then take place between her and at least two nurses. One would restrain her on the bed and the other would hold her nose, until she opened her mouth to breathe, and then the medication was expertly popped down her gullet. After a time I found this battle quite entertaining. In those times this action appeared to be both necessary and acceptable; rocking this regulated boat could not be allowed.

Good fortune came my way over the period of a month or so under their beneficial treatment. For meals I had special

231

tit-bits; jelly, blancmange, eggs and slices of fruit cake, as well as meat and veg. Can you imagine the delight, after the plain fare I'd been getting? I could hardly believe my eyes when meal times arrived with this delicious food on a plate, on which the name 'Green' was boldly written in ink. During my time as a patient my mother and brother, Oscar, made regular visits: for one hour, as usual, on Sunday afternoon, in keeping with the rigid workhouse rules.

One of the cleaners kindly brought me the weekly children's section of the *Daily Mail*, and I read all the words several times over. There were no books to read, no library going the rounds. Was this because reading might excite the patients, and delay their recovery? If 'getting your head in a book will not get you a living' – such mental activity would not help to cure.

Once, in the middle of one dark night, when patients were supposed to be fast asleep, I developed a burning thirst as if I was lost in the Sahara desert. Not wishing to shout and cause a disturbance I eventually hit upon a plan. Every night the nurses placed a stone hotwater bottle in my bed. I gingerly fished it from the bottom, now below my feet, unscrewed the stopper and took a long refreshing swig. The water was no longer hot. It was still lukewarm and very refreshing – the things you do to try to maintain independence in your life.

To relieve my constipation, from which they decided I was also suffering, a nurse inserted a tube-like instrument up the outlet orifice of my bum. She squeezed a ball attached to a tube. A surge of hot 'soapy' water entered my bowels and proceeded to softening the hardened faeces into a flowing motion, which they then caught in a bedpan. Jokingly, this remarkable instrument was called 'the village pump'. That was truly a surprising new experience for a wide-eyed, innocent lad. And another problem arose. After a time it became obvious that my head was lousy. The lice were breeding so fast my skull became overcrowded and some fell on the pillow, which a nurse eventually noticed. With my head held over a basin the little blighters were washed out in droves, especially those huge red-blooded ones, which I enjoyed catching under my fingernails and then plopping them dead on the nail of my thumb (a method which I had picked up by watching the lousy people in my native village, engrossed in their primitive habits).

One other thing I should mention. It probably speeded up my recovery somewhat. After some few days I heard someone nearby discreetly whisper: 'If he doesn't stop coughing soon, the doctor will have to insert a needle into his lungs to release the fluid.' Improvement or not, the very next time the doctor 'walked the ward' and asked how I was, I told him I felt much better and managed to suppress that irritating cough. Before I was discharged from the care of those tryingly tested nurses, they supplied me with a vest lined with cotton wool, which I had to wear next to my skin. It eventually dropped to pieces and I was pleased to be rid of it (it heated my body so), but not before the summer came. Nurse Purdam saw to that. Having been confined to bed for so long, my leg muscles had so weakened that for a time I wobbled about like a drunk. That was my hospital experience; in the days when often nature was the only cure, or you needed that extra bit of luck; described by some as divine intervention, sincerely believing that miracles do really happen.

One thing would live on: my gratitude for their care and attention in battling with an illness (often fatal) with only basic treatment to command and very little of that.

36

One normal school day (one free of any pressing agitation) my after-dinner return to classes was abruptly delayed at the school gate by a strange woman. Although unknown to me, she was obviously aware of my identity. Without any preamble she abruptly posed a question that contained its own answer: 'You are Gerald,' she affirmed. 'Yes,' popped out my immediate reply. For such was the urgent tone of her voice, an instant answer seemed vital. Then quickly followed my suspicions. Usually only official folk called me Gerald; those close called me Ged or Gerry. Gerald stood out too far against the familiar Toms, Dicks, Georges and Harrys. At that time I didn't know its ancient derivation: that it was made up of elements of *spear and rule* – suggestive of a conqueror which I desperately needed to be.

But even if I had known that, I would still have disliked it: it stood me out so much, especially in class. GERALD! – the moniker I wanted to lose. It used to make me cringe so. To stand out was the last thing I wanted in my faulty, bastardy state.

The strange woman continued: 'Would you like to stay with my family? I have asked Matron for permission and she has agreed.' After I had gulped a surprised 'yes', she pointed directly across the road, to a modest end-terrace dwelling. 'I live there,' she said. And I agreed to visit from Friday evening after school to Sunday evening after tea. But just think about it – this sudden turn of events. Matron had actually given her permission for me to leave the workhouse for a whole weekend. (And that wasn't all, these

234

visits were to continue, although at the time I didn't know that.)

What a joy this breath of freedom proved to be. For two days every weekend I now had Matron's permission to escape. One emotional problem always beset me. Every Sunday evening, as I snail-paced back to my workhouse home, passing the tramps queuing along the Pinchbeck Road; the homeless flotsam and jetsam, hoping to be admitted to the workhouse casualty ward in charge of the Labour Master, to be bathed, deloused, given a mug of tea and an institutional sandwich of bread and cheese, there always arose a lump in my throat, not out of sympathy for the tramps, for my own hapless condition. This to-ing and fro-ing of my life would raise a high degree of mental turmoil when the Big House once more came into my view; awaiting my timid entrance back into its soulless routine.

Naturally, I wondered who this stranger was. So far as I was aware there were no known Green relations living in Spalding. Apart from cousin Irene Rawding (daughter of my mother's sister, Kate) who lived in Lincoln and used to visit us on the farm and always sent a newsy letter at Christmas, none of my mother's five siblings kept in regular touch.

The stranger's name was Mawer (Elizabeth), married to Thomas (Tom) Mawer. Jumping to a hasty conclusion I first thought she was related to Mary Mawer, the unfortunate maiden Horton had impregnated and did not marry – thus breaking the code of decent behaviour. No wonder I easily concluded (exposed as I was only to pure living) that my father Horton was a loose, sinful bounder. And all his moral spouting was worth less than nought! No wonder my outlook oscillated from frosty to bleak, with dreariness in between.

Elizabeth explained to me that her husband, Thomas Mawer, was the son of Horton's sister, Alice (my Aunt Alice, whom I never met because she was born in 1852, died in 1906, 16 years before I entered this world). Tragically, she was widowed in 1893 (as previously related) when her husband Joseph Mawer committed suicide at the age of 40, after his entire potato crop was destroyed by frost after being loaded overnight on a railway wagon. Can such a plight be imagined? In the days when suicide was a sin and very little help (if any) was available to bring up five orphaned children. Brother George (as expected), then having a few bob in the bank, helped his sister to survive until the children grew up, thus proving beyond all doubt that my father, George, was often the family's benefactor. (Born 29 years after this tragic event, I was never advised that Joseph Mawer was my uncle. By then he was all but buried in the fog of history; to me, anyway.)

When you sink below your bottom depth, where you've been busily scraping along, how on earth can you cope with that?

You claw back your life to the rugged bottom once again, to reoccupy the lost ground; where at least you can survive – whatever is left if you cannot do that – at the very least!

Thomas Mawer, my newly-found Spalding cousin, was some 35 years older than me – old enough to be my father. Tom was a softly-spoken man and he always seemed somewhat subdued. And no wonder! At the age of 20, having secured a clerical position with the London and North Eastern Railway (which was quite an achievement for a working-class lad, and a permanent job for life) – yet another unexpected tragedy happened.

In brief, Tom fell victim to a crude piece of farm machinery. To fill in time before starting his new career, he hired himself out to work on a threshing rig: the old way of working with a steam engine, driving a threshing drum, and an elevator (jack-straw) to move the surplus straw into a stack. He took the working position by the space over the flailing 'fingers' of the drum, whose purpose was to violently shake out the corn.

236

Whether Tom lost his balance, or caution, after several hours of hard unrelenting work, is not known. It only takes the briefest of moments to meet with disaster, especially if the machinery in use is crude and unguarded. However it happened, those threshing *fingers* grabbed Tom's arm and tore it off. So at the age of 20, with future prospects settled, he now ended up on the scrap heap, where he lingered until the age of 63. For the rest of his life of 40 years he was constantly tortured by 'phantom-pains': those curious ghost-like sensations that appear from a missing limb. In those far-off days there was no relief. When the nerves *worked up* it affected his mind. To those who were close he was reported as saying: 'I'm crucified every day of my life.'

Eventually, after the usual legal haggling, he was awarded £200 by way of compensation – for loss of a secure career from the age of 20. (At £2 a week; around two years of his future potential pay. Or, to put it another way, invested at $2\frac{1}{2}$ per cent, it would have produced an income of £5 per annum: the then going interest rate on a Post Office Savings account. In addition to this capital-sum settlement, Tom Mawer received the princely sum of seven shillings and six pence from 'the Parish' (now 37.5 pence). This pittance was approximately a quarter of the then low basic agricultural wage.)

The Parish official brought Tom's *relief* every Thursday. Just to make sure that they were not frittering good money away on a needless cause, the poor-relief officials insisted that Tom report to work, digging gutters for the local drainage board; where he was expected to be agile and use a shovel alongside able-bodied men (thus demonstrating that they were duty bound to sort out the malingerers from the genuine needy – which in this case they instantly did).

Mary Elizabeth Mawer, for that was the stranger's full name, went to work at various menial jobs; there simply was no other option. She slaved away in the local laundry

237

or on the land to supplement the mean parish allowance made to husband, Tom. Yet, despite all her problems, she offered me a touch of freedom during those precious weekends. She never went to church and I cannot remember her banging any particular religious drum. That she was kind there was no doubt. She was also fiercely independent, which in those days people had to be. That there were folk outside the workhouse walls in such dire circumstances should not have been a shock to me, but it was. In contrast, my life was feather-bedded. No wonder there appeared to be a deep feeling of bitterness pervading this home: so near to the surface, a continuous grieving.

One Saturday evening when I was walking in the market place, in the area called 'the Stones', I was suddenly accosted by two youths still under 20 years of age (the 'teenager' word was not then invented). It was customary for young men to imitate their elders; put on a serious demeanour; wear a fob watch, and after reaching the age of 18, begin to smoke a briar pipe, and some even started serious courting, which often went on steadily for years.

'Hello Ged,' these two lads said, appearing to speak in unison. They were out on the town for the evening, 'chasing' girls, addressing them with ice-breaking words, such as: Does your mother know you're out? Have I seen you before? Or even more daringly innocent: Can anybody come? 'Here,' one said, and then the other, 'Here you are.' And to my other surprise they began emptying their pockets of all their copper coinage. In all, the fortune amounted to ninepence (the then going hourly rate for farm labourers slogging away in the field). I was overcome by this generosity. I'd never owned such a princely sum of money in all my life. They were also curious to find out how I was – knowing full well the house where I now lived and the home where I as born.

It wasn't the sudden gift of this money that affected me

so much; it was the recognition they gifted me with. They remembered me as a person: a boy named 'Ged' from their village and that deeply moved me. To them, I was a person known beyond the workhouse walls, who had once lived away from his present life. These youths (Ken and Harry Gedney) had confirmed my identity and background: 'Ged' from Gosberton Risegate! Someone with a past, still existing in the present, and hopeful for the future. Overwhelmed, I thanked them (and would do so again much later on in life). So can you imagine the heady freedom I gulped at the weekend when I visited cousins Tom and Mary? What a change from being locked up all day long, except to go to the *pictures* on Saturday, and church on Sunday, both under close supervision. Now, for a precious time, I roamed all over the place like a heady explorer – such was my need to discover that another world still existed.

Once I walked out along the West Marsh road to observe the spring tide as it rolled in along the river Welland, forming a moving wall of tidal water. Apart from the regulars who got drunk on methylated spirit, passed out in the street and had to be wheeled into the police station, there was plenty of public-house drinking. At the turn of the nineteenth century there were some 60 pubs in Spalding (one always handy on the corner). By the time I speak of the number was under 40. In the early days when competition was at its most intensive, the proprietor of Ye Olde White Horse, a 600-year-old hostelry, wrote the following blurb which he displayed outside with pride:

My 'White Horse' shall bite the 'Bear'.
And make the 'Angel' ply;
Shall turn the 'Ship' her bottom up,
And drink the 'Three Casks' dry.

It was reported that this bit of enterprise increased trade

239

for a considerable time. The town's principal hotel, the White Hart, was still flourishing when I perambulated around the town. Its colonnaded entrance seemed to indicate that it did not welcome visits from the rabble *hoi polloi*. When I passed by I always waited a while to watch the customers come and go. And I marvelled (not without some envy) that such a fine world existed and I wondered how long it would be before I ascended the entrance steps of such a posh place.

Nearby was the Corn Exchange which I had visited shortly after my deliverance into the workhouse. It was the only time I was allowed out with my mother, along with a crowd of adult and children inmates. We attended a dress rehearsal of the local Spalding Amateur Operatic Society. That was an eye-opener I can tell you. Apart from the pleasure of what I thought was a splendid performance, I also marvelled that some folk had the time and opportunity to act and sing, as well as attending their normal work. On that evening all the women (those privileged to be offered such a treat) wore civilian clothes, the men their usual black funereal suits. Separating ourselves as much from the other inmates (out by only a matter of feet), my mother and I had walked arm in arm to the theatre, during that short-lived get together, which ended when the final curtain came down and we walked back again, through the gates to our respective quarters in the place which had now become my home.

There was so much of interest to take in as I strode about the town. Particularly did I notice a few furtive beggars from time to time. They were the unemployed, often badly wounded soldiers – the heroes of World War One. One poor wretch in particular, both legs severed, wheeled himself along on a home-made cart. Much dodging of the police took place, as this type of begging was strictly against the law.

During those days of weekend freedom my pocket money

240

usually increased; sometimes nearly beyond belief. Charlie, my second cousin, who was still single and lived at home, used to give me thruppence every week. He was in regular work at the local sugar beet factory. Oscar would give me tuppence, so added together that was quite a small fortune.

One Saturday, Cousin Mary Elizabeth took me with her to her local confectionery shop along New Road, which in those days was still a bustling part of the town. (Even that quaint passage-way, The Hole in the Wall, contained several thriving businesses.) Double-yellow road markings were nowhere to be seen. Entering the shop, a tall man approached to serve her. After duly making her required purchases, she finished up making the following remark, which completely took me right off guard: 'This is Gerald, he would like to work in your shop.'

From what seemed to be a great height (he had served in a guards' regiment during the World War), he answered with the following words, which to me made a full and final point: 'He'd have to wear skirts to work in this shop.'

After which he gave me a swift, sorting glance, as though he'd seen a stale bun on his shelves. Walking homewards Cousin Mary explained: 'That was George [Horton] Mawer who owns that business.' Nothing more. I supposed that she took it for granted that I knew he was the bastard child of that maiden, Mary Mawer, whom my father George Horton had cruelly failed to marry (long before he fertilised my maiden-mother). That was the only encounter with the man who was my half-brother, whose family blood had decidedly thinned. Eventually he sold the confectioner's shop and set up a new business in a private hotel at 16, Welland Place, along the London Road, until on retirement he sold this property to the Welland & Deeping Drainage Board. Something else of interest I was told much later on in life by Alice, the daughter of Cousin Mary: George [Horton] Mawer looked after his 'Aunt' Mary until she died.

241

I soon put two and two together: 'Aunt' in those days was sometimes the 'mother', in this case the ruined Mary Mawer: this was one way that desperate, unmarried mothers, respectably covered up their straying past. Many times after that did I pass my half-brother's shop, but never bothered to glance inside. I now knew enough about life to get his uncomplicated message: Goodbye! Hello does not exist.

Without the slightest question of doubt, George [Horton] Mawer didn't owe his half-brother, Gerald [Horton] Green, as much as a second glance. *Considering his background* I was inwardly pleased that he had done so well and used our mutual Father's gift of £100 to such success. Indeed, this seemed to me like a good omen. As well as that rich American Horton branch of the family, here was another *family* success. So allow me some comfort from this hopeful thought: perhaps in time my turn of success might come. Didn't one kind workhouse Board of Guardians visitor say to all the assembled children: 'One day one of you could become Prime Minister? What a giddy, astonishing thought that was.

Always ready to seek enlightenment, in those days there was little else to do on Sundays, I walked along Westlode Street and stood outside the much more modest Salvation Army Citadel, determined to storm its walls. (I had previously thought of attending the fine, red-bricked Methodist edifice in Broad Street. Approaching the entrance my nerves suddenly failed me – stopped me in my tracks by a troubling thought: that this imposing House of Worship was by far too grand for the likes of me. In any case, these Methodists had never attempted to claim me as one of their fallen flock, as the Catholics always did of their own.)

This time I succeeded and boldly went inside, clutching a warm penny in my pocket which I would give in the collection. Now here was something quite startlingly different. Uniforms abounded – the congregation here were Christian soldiers, fighting the good fight; intent on saving souls: of drunks and dregs, as well as their own. And I even felt a surge of excitement when their band began to play. With such playing and singing, it seemed to me that in this place of worship everyone could enjoy their stay. The Sally-Ann was often reviled and scoffed at, so I felt some affinity with them; for wasn't I also burdened?

No one spoke to me in this humble citadel: perhaps, for the simple reason that I followed my new High Church practice, of sitting in the very back row. And, being of a shy nature, I slipped out immediately after the service ended, with a feeling inside that I had strayed into another holy domain, where I had still felt lost, deep inside – thank goodness for my human spirit!

37

1934 turned out to be an eventful year. Not so much because the great depression was receding; not even because of the ever looming war; a change of personal direction was the cause. Dare I call it direction, or would another rudderless, sailing boat set off?

After three years of incarceration in the workhouse prison, the hopeless slide to near insanity, caused by the helplessness and bleakness of it all, something seemed to click in Mam's mind. Her cries for help had been useless. Her wild beseeching: 'I want my clothes! I want to go back to my *rightful* home!' and, 'They are poisoning me!' had got her absolutely nowhere, except irritation from the staff. Other bovine-like inmates, coldly subdued in this dreary place, seemed more contented to serve with resignation their bleakly-restricted lives.

Help simply had to come from another direction; for surely the only help still open to her was self-help. Somehow, deep in her mind in '34, a spark began to splutter. How and exactly when I shall never know. Perhaps her chronic depressed state had finally bumped to its lowest depth and now, at long last, a climb upwards had begun. Whatever happened, in the early autumn of that year, she took off and fled full-pelt out of the prison gate (or through the gardens and fields at the rear of the buildings), leaving Porter Stone in a state of agitation, more than likely angry at this flagrant breach of security under his dutiful watch.

Women inmates were never allowed out, except under strict supervision. Where on earth would this demented woman find to go? It is well known what some women can get up to if you let them loose on the streets. 'Mark my words,' some people would say as they shook their thinking heads, 'nothing good will come of this.'

The first I heard of this mad adventure was at teatime on the day of her disappearance. Matron appearing somewhat agitated came across and questioned me closely: 'Do you know where your mother has gone to?' I replied in the negative. In truth, if I had known I would never have told, for at that very moment my mind either froze or ignored the news I had just heard. Then after the initial shock my innermost feelings (the limited feelings you still retain in a workhouse) instantly began to quiver a bit. Secretly I became excited by it, but nonplussed all the same. Where on earth would she go in that dreadful workhouse frock with those monotonous thin streaky-white vertical lines? And no hat! – my goodness that would never do. (Clearly did I remember that black hat trimmed with red roses that she wore on family outings before she was incarcerated.)

She surely could not go far dressed like that. But I had forgotten: the general public would have no idea what a workhouse dress looked like. So, most likely, no particular notice would have been shown; except a good old British, polite sidewards glance. For the time being the authorities would have to let her enjoy her sudden freedom; until the hue and cry really got under way and the dogs and deputies were unleashed to burst upon her and drag her back into public safe keeping.

Soon, everyone was baffled. Obviously, she had found a safe bolt-hole. By creating this turmoil, she had also turned the worthy workhouse system on its dreary head. Protesting was one thing but this kind of rocking the boat could disturb the inmates' delicate equilibrium.

After tea on the second day of her freedom Oscar came to see me. He was deeply mystified. Where could she be? Forthright Nurse Bristow, then on duty, had a ready answer to this irritating problem. Without hesitation and brusque as usual, she said to both of us: 'It would be a good thing if your mother is found dead, then you can get on with your own lives.' I was too nonplussed, and probably too institutionalised, to show any outward feeling or venture a reply. Even so, I had never thought this way before. What a sensible woman; what a good idea; what a neat official solution: Mam's quick pauper funeral, then complete freedom to live our own unfettered lives. No loose inconvenient ends; our embarrassing problem buried out of sight, even if not easily out of mind.

Although I was also mystified I never lost any sleep at night, or lost my normal appetite, and I attended to my lessons as usual. But this sudden news had caused unexpected excitement in my life – a tingle in the pit of my stomach. Whatever next! Mam, they'll think you're mad!

How would she cope with this sniff of freedom after three years of tight rules and regulations? Imagine: to walk free like other people; the very air seems fresher; the trees, the leaves and birds much more alive; to see and rub shoulders with other folk, free to go uninterrupted about one's own private business – no longer restrained in both body and mind! Outside the workhouse walls a busy world still existed and she was getting a lick of it; not a taste, sometimes you have to lick before you taste and then take a hungry bite.

We had always visited Ayscoughee Gardens, as kids when we visited Spalding. Mam was especially fond of the pleasant surroundings and I remember even as a tiny child sitting in the alcove by the ornamental pool which, to me, stretched a long way right up to the war memorial. These were very happy memories. I also grew very fond of these public gardens, and still retained those contented times stored within my memory – the times, now seeming long ago, when we could walk about as we pleased!

AYSCOUGHEE GARDENS!

This proved to be the answer we were all puzzling over. She had gone back to a place of happy memories, not to the morgue, as was so cruelly suggested by Nurse Bristow. With her small stock of pennies she had bought a meagre snack and drank from the water fountain, after walking openly through Spalding town. At night she hid away (perhaps behind the war memorial?) until the gates closed. Then she settled down on one of the seats in the rose bowers (then along the wall next to Church Gate). And there she hid and shivered, bleakly all alone until the next morning when the park keeper opened the gate to the public. She had not prepared a plan, at least, no long-term plan, this was pure desperation, an impulse to break to freedom; perhaps in the hope that at long last something helpful might turn up. But only God might know her thoughts and learn of her utter misery, as she awaited the sun to rise on yet another deaden day.

Nurse Bristow's subtle hint of possible suicide was always a real possibility, but folk in Spalding well know that if you want a quick suicide (apart from shooting yourself), the best way would be to jump into the fast-flowing River Welland. What a missed opportunity for her to fulfil that nurse's cold-hearted prediction. On the way to Ayscoughee Public Gardens, along Church Gate, all she had to do was keep to the right-hand side of the road by the open bank and throw herself in. Peace would have been hers within a few minutes. Another casualty of life to be recorded by the coroner. Yet another pauper's coffin, holding a wretched death, to be buried outside the boundary of a consecrated cemetery; assuming the officials had retrieved her body.

Yes, indeed, trauma can be thrust upon us from the next split-second to the end of life. No respecter of birth, station or condition in life, it seldom fails to pay a visit – at least once, but often several times, though unwanted. It can call with a sudden raw, unexplained savagery, or with a creeping stealth, without invitation or encouragement, leaving its

247

afflicted prisoner damaged, bewildered and striving like a drugged, hapless sot, trying to maintain a foothold balance in a maze of depressing debris; then aimlessly to stagger along a dark frozen tunnel of utter despair and isolation. Turning inwards; reaching outwards; upwards and downwards – through many imprisoned ways. To inwardly scream out through time and still more time; until some hopeful passion beams into life, to lighten the heavily inflicted mind. *But, most helpful of all, other folk show signs of appearing normal again.*

Instead of throwing herself into the river, she turned left off Church Gate into Ayscoughee Gardens and went in to sit in peace and quiet along with normal society. But surely, with such a hue and cry, this strangely-dressed creature would be bound to cause suspicion; especially after two days. No doubt her escape would have been reported to the local police who would be on the lookout for this loony wretch and return her to the state she had been in: ordained protective custody.

Eventually she was spotted, as you might expect in such a small town. With such meagre resources at her command, her time of freedom was bound to be limited. Fulfilling his duty, Porter Stone set out to recapture her, along with members of the workhouse staff. She saw them approaching and decided at least to give them a run for their money. They closed in upon her but she eluded them for a few minutes by jumping into the ornamental pool and wading away from them. It was a one-sided contest and she was recaptured, but I'll bet not before a lot of screaming and struggling, and a soaking from head to foot.

'Porter Stone got hold of my head and held it under the water,' she later told me. And I believed her without further questioning. (Whether this was deliberately intended, or was purely accidental, is sometimes open to question when a *victim* makes a complaint.)

248

It might be wondered what the exasperated Porter thought as he and his staff subdued this maddening female: This will serve to teach her a lesson – she'll think twice before escaping again. Think twice, indeed! Such rebellious thinking. But sometimes a failed venture comes in handy if the experience is used for guidance in the future, when an intense desire starts to froth and bubble again. (After all, didn't Dick Whittington 'turn again' before he finally succeeded?)

The next Sunday visiting hour took place in the Infirmary where Mam was now occupying a bed. She had suffered from exposure during the two nights she had remained in the Ayscoughee Gardens, not helped in the least by that cold-water ducking. Though she was still recovering from her self-imposed ordeal, one thing stood out a mile: she seemed to be more of her old determined self. This stolen whiff of freedom had been a poignant reminder, that out there life still went on. She had opened the window just a chink and sniffed a draught of beckoning. So instead of being brought low and craven, this woman still oozed rebellion. And that in an institution can set alarm bells ringing; where bending or breaking the rules is just not allowed to disturb the tranquil pace of unvaried living.

During her short stay in the infirmary wing, two doctors turned up to question her, apparently with some concern. They asked her about her life in the workhouse, and she took this golden opportunity to *tell them straight*. Among other things, she wanted her *outside* clothes, the ones she was admitted in, so that she could return to her rightful home. *They* had robbed us ends and sides up – of hundreds and thousands! And in this place, not to put too fine a point on it, Matron was poisoning her food – 'She turns white every time she sees me scraping off the poison, which she secretly places under the meat.'

At last someone was listening. And there seemed no doubt

249

about it, she was pleased to get these festering grievances off her chest. The doctors listened intently, only occasionally intervening to pose another question. Seemingly satisfied they left to go their respective ways. From such apparent concern, something might happen, and as far as my mother was concerned – as soon as humanly possible. There being no alternative, Lizzie Green moved back to the drab workhouse ward and continued her protest by ignoring all the rules as she woodenly stood, appearing fossilised in time, gazing out of a dormitory window, imprisoned within a psychopathic state and bound in transfixion.

38

My mother was physically fit, 54 years old, in 1934. She was still being uncooperative; still standing by that first-floor window, still stressing her passionate desire to be released to freedom. Her short periods of normality fluttered between her outraged feelings of frustration. The outlook wasn't improving. Perhaps the treatment needed to be changed by a new prescription, which in those days was not available.

Come to think of it, I had for some time become reconciled to seeing both my parents gazing out of workhouse windows. An angry, battling mother, and an 80-year-old senile father, were regularly viewed by me with some dispassion. Now 12 years of age I would increasingly consider my own pressing needs: my hopeful transition to freedom.

Sometimes, on yet another drab day, an excitement occurs that fairly takes your very breath away. Excitement! I bubbled over and trembled with it during one Sunday family visiting hour. Turning her head very close to me so that other folk nearby couldn't overhear, Mam made a most astounding pronouncement: 'Don't worry next week if I'm missing. I'm going to get out,' she said. I was, to say the least, astounded. The audacity of it! The memory of her recently failed bid for freedom was still fresh on my mind. But before I could voice my cautious institutionalised misgivings, she continued to advise me: 'I'm going to go to sister Kate's in Lincoln.' She had learnt from past experience. This new plan made good sense and I remember replying with some such words as: 'That's right, don't hang about in Spalding as you did last time, they'll only catch you.' And, thankfully, she nodded. On that Sunday I felt more grown-up than usual. I was being told things; had been trusted with a startling secret. Since her last failed attempt, she had worked out a better chance of escape. Her mind seemed to have taken a spirited turn. Yet some folk, without the slightest question of doubt, would there and then have pronounced her *mad*.

True to her word, during the next week she breached the outer boundary of the workhouse and moved towards freedom for the second time. After finding a side-ways exit, she turned right when she got to the main Pinchbeck Street, then over the railway crossing and left along Park Road and into the station by a less-frequented way. Sound planning: she doubly avoided passing in front of the workhouse (in full view of the porter's lodge), and being seen in Spalding, had she walked through the town in her outlandish uniform.

Matron came over at teatime and told me the expected news and repeated her previous searching request: 'Your mother is missing, do you know where she has gone to?' Without as much as a blush (putting on a most unctuous face, like the local parish parson praying in full fling for the fallen souls of every sinner), I was also careful to show a most concerned expression, and to subdue any show of guilt. Then, acutely aware of the advantage I temporarily held over her, I forgot the moral lesson of the great and good George Washington (who had never told a lie in his life) and lied, and almost failed to hide my exultation. 'I've no idea where she is,' I said. And so convincing was I in this false performance that she believed me and immediately retreated back to her office. As hours of freedom passed into days I no longer speculated. She's made it! She just had to be free! I was still inside, but what did that matter, my own chance to *escape* would eventually come.

My Horton father would remain in this place (in his case forever). What did it matter if I stayed another two years, until I could be officially freed? Mam had disappeared, she was outside, and somewhere free! And that perception relieved me; I would have to soldier on.

Unquestionably, the alarming discovery that Lizzie Green was missing must have brought on bowels of fluttering inside her fellow inmates. And turmoil among the workhouse staff. Matron was cross. Porter Stone was cross. That crazy creature had done another bunk. This time she had gone too far (or, at least, far enough, which is what I fervently hoped). Every previous minute ticking by without recapture was yet another minute of relief for me. Get away, Mam, I willed her, get away from Spalding! The odds towards the end of the first day were hopefully lengthening. Her giddy flight to freedom now seemed highly possible.

I have already given a description of the first two evictions of my life, now was to come the third: the unexpected eviction from the workhouse. *Mad* Lizzie Green had made it, she had reached Lincoln. This latest eviction came so suddenly that I again felt like a ghostly actor on the stage, almost invisible and with no talking part; hanging about amidst the scenery, only too aware of other players performing.

Without a whiff of warning I was collected from school, this time not by the relieving officer in an Austin Seven motorcar, by the plodding Porter Stone on foot. So low in the hierarchy did he fit; leaving a distinct impression that the main difference between him and the paupers was the smart uniform in which he performed his duties. Although, to be fair, he was also in receipt of a meagre wage for which he would be most grateful.

Now some distance beyond the prime of life, he was still courting. Sometimes, during my weekends of freedom, I used to see him 'walking out' his long-past-blooming lady friend. The porter's position was open only to a live-in single man. In those desperate days he was lucky to be in work. Marriage was out of the question. But he might just as well have become a monk, and be justified for his fleshly

253

repressions. Sexual commerce was unthinkable; tampering, downright sinful!

During the 15-minute or so walk he did explain the bones of the expected action that was about to take place. My mother had returned. She wanted me 'out' and it seemed that she was going to get her own way. After three years' incarceration, what a sudden frantic victory! For me this was yet another disturbance, yet another stark change of direction, without any other possible choice. Imbued with growing excitement, I stood and listened (as though watching a film). This was yet another shaky part of my life, playing out to the full, without any hope of enthusiastic applause.

But to be suddenly taken away from a school which I liked and in which I was flourishing; to be moved from institutionalised security to a giddy, mad, unexpected freedom, how would I react? More to the point, how did I react? Politely, quietly and with great observation. My understanding trailed a little behind; that had to catch up sometime later. My outward composure covered a welling excitement – Mam had succeeded! I was going to be free! Visiting hours, locked-up hours would disappear. I would be able to walk about the world without that constrained feeling. Controlled to *do this, do that, at this time, not that*, and forever being gazed upon for any outward signs of childish rebellion, which normal kids, with normal parents on the outside of this place, so often get away with. Any problems connected with freedom were far removed from my mind. Something always turns up, it always had, and it always would. But was this to be yet another some-day, come-day, go-day, God send Sunday, time? Such a thought never entered my head. Patiently I waited for life's next momentum, whatever grind seemed fated to come.

My mother's sister Kate was a skilled seamstress, an expert maker of coats and dresses, and that was now on show. She had fitted Mam out with a smart set of civvies

and they seemed most fashionable, too. She looked so smart
and different that I couldn't believe my eyes. This outfit
had transformed her from a raging, babbling workhouse
zombie into glowing self-assertion. The clothes and sniff of
freedom had put Mam firmly in charge of her life once
again, and the three imprisoned years puffed away like steam
from a fired-up kettle.

'You are sure that you have somewhere to go?' asked
Matron of Mam, particularly looking sidelong at me; doubtless
being genuinely concerned over my future chancy welfare
(as you might expect of a widowed mother having the sole
responsibility of raising her own two sons, of near ages to
my own). 'Yes, we have,' said Mam. 'My sister Kate in
Lincoln has offered us a home.' And she said this with such
determination and vigour that I felt like a person renewed.
(Matron had the responsibility of having to prove an important
point: that alternative accommodation was available before
release could be granted.) Brother Oscar nodded his head to
back up Mam's statement that we had a home to go to and
would not be vagrants wandering the streets. There being
no further cause for her concern, Matron sanctioned our
release. We were free, free to walk away without as much
as a backward glance; backward glances, like repeated honey-
moons, can sometimes be most disappointing. (In the years
to come I would have plenty of time to ponder the unknown
risks we took on that crazy, eventful day.)

Mam briskly started to walk out towards the workhouse
exit, leaving Oscar and me to follow. It was as though a
Queen of England was leaving her palace. With her head
held erect, clothed in her fashionable attire, neither looking
to the left nor right, she headed straight out of the workhouse
main gates; at long last to escape the clutches of that turnkey-
warder, Porter Stone, whose authority against her had abruptly
crumbled – most likely to the poor man's utter relief. From
her appearance and confident attitude, it seemed that, like a

queen, she would not have been surprised if people had already gathered in a crowd to line both sides of Pinchbeck Street, ready to clap and wave her on her regal way. It was like stepping on light air, we were free, nothing else seemed to matter – in the glowing sunshine, who cares a fig about the future when the past has been defeated?

We passed by Kings Road (late Stepping Stone Lane) where a well-spoken man had once accosted my friend Ernie and me. He offered us thruppence each if we would pull a heavy roller and a chalk marker at a nearby tennis club. Yes, no more, no less, that is what actually happened and we were pleased to be of use. Unfortunately, we overlooked the ticking passage of time. Arriving back late to the workhouse we were refused tea: serve us right – teach us a lesson! Matron came across and interrogated us at length. Being responsible for our welfare she would have to write up a report. Seemingly satisfied, she went away. I drank water from the tap, jingled the pennies in my pocket and blessed my unexpected good fortune. My lost bread and marge tea was not a great deprivation and only bed and sleep separated me from tomorrow's breakfast and the goodies I would buy at the school's tuck shop.

A little later I noticed Billingtons, the toyshop situated on the corner with New Road, and I recalled the day when I responded to a bold notice displayed in their shop window:

JOIN OUR CHRISTMAS CLUB
Goods set aside

During October of 1932, all of ten years old, I selected the lowest-priced toy (a racing car for sixpence) and deposited one penny, in return for a club card on which a smiling assistant carefully noted my investment. All the workhouse kids were agog! That Gerry would eventually own that toy, so boldly displayed in the window. After some weeks going almost completely without goodies, my club-card penny entries

256

added up to the required sum of sixpence. I then became the proud possessor of that racing car. My *family* gazed at me in awe, temporarily forgetting their uneventful routine. That evening I opened the box, wound up the car, and my word, didn't it whizz across the linoleum on the living room floor. With shrieks of glee the infants caught it and turned it around – to scorch back and forth. Several times they missed catching it and it hit the wall or the table leg. The mudguards became dented. And then, as always happened, the spring driving the motor started to slip each time it was wound up. Instead of full speed, the car started to judder, until it finally stopped. After that we rolled it towards each other; until it looked a sorry sight. At the end of the evening I gave it away to a starry-eyed infant (in any case, it was more suitable for a five-year-old). But I had shown some independence; planned a transaction; taken an opportunity that had existed and thereby given some amusement to a few of my fellow creatures; short-lived though that was.

On the opposite corner to Billingtons stood the Peacock Hotel, where many visitors to the town parked their cycles in rows, unchained and unsupervised, because none was expected to be stolen. The cycle then reigned supreme. It was there my mother abruptly stopped, as though hit by a weighty cannon ball. The plan (whatever the plan was) was suddenly changed. We would not go to Lincoln that day (if at all) instead, we would stay in Spalding and seek an interview with our family lawyer (whoever that gentleman was – God only knew!). With immediate effect we were going to evict the present occupiers from our dear old lawful home. To get rid of those occupying usurpers, as she had just done with Porter Stone. If not by today's teatime, then tomorrow! We would take immediate possession, forthwith! Without a bed; without a chair; a table; spoon, knife, fork, and even far worse, without capital to set us up in farming once again. Yes, we would straightaway go back to Gosberton

Risegate; back to our farm and directly reverse the injustice *they* had perpetrated against us. And regain some of the *hundreds and thousands* we had so unjustly been robbed of. Mam was once more gripped in a violent, emotional lab-dab-sweat. Without any doubt Dr Jekyll had ascended; changing normality into a form of obsessive madness and during such fraught times Mr Hyde went missing – probably 'frit' to death!

Oscar and Mam had quite a street altercation, I can tell you, before she was dissuaded from pursuing instant litigation (and some good lawyer had a lucky escape from a tightly wound-up, forceful client). All this time folk going about their normal business, politely appearing to ignore us, discreetly giving us brief glances. I didn't mind that. What I did mind was seeing my workhouse family on their way home from school, passing us by with surprised and curious stares. They said, 'Hello!' Utterly embarrassed, I turned my back and ignored them. What a story they would have to tell Nurse Purdam and she to repeat to the Matron: 'Mark my words, they'll soon be back inside!'

A little calmness managed to filter through, from God knows where, to descend upon us. Mam's tactic changed again. We would now throw ourselves, without warning, on our relations the Mawer family (where I had spent those weekends of freedom) and put ourselves at their mercy by requesting a night's lodgings, thus putting off any more vital decisions until tomorrow, depending on whether summer or winter was the mood of the day. It was during this wild continuing uncertainty that I fervently willed my 12-year-old brain and body to grow up as fast as possible, so that I could leave this insecure world far behind and take all future decisions affecting my own life, to decide myself where I would live – preferably somewhere permanent, like most other people. And above all, not to rely on strangers. Surely that's not asking too much?

But that's the thought of today. We're going to Lincoln tomorrow, some little distance away. Surely that alone will make a new beginning. How long will it be before I could conclude that this was the dawning of a brighter beginning? The next day (yes, the sun did shine) we travelled to Lincoln, with only the clothes we stood up in, no worldly goods to carry, except our own emotional baggage and that, thankfully, was invisible. Stopping for passengers and freight, at stations every few miles apart; reading the many advertisements which in those days were boldly sited in the fields alongside the track; there's no doubt about it, you can't but feel excitement as you puff along coupled to the power of swelling steam from a snorting railway engine.

(Many years later I was told how my mother had managed to reach Lincoln, by train in her workhouse uniform. For a hat she tied four corner knots in a large white handkerchief and fitted that on her head – how stylish, how daring! Just another harmless eccentric going about her private ways. When she requested a ticket of the railway booking clerk, she found that she was a few pennies short of the full fare. This kind man issued her with a ticket anyway, perhaps sensing the poverty state she was obviously in. Would he ever know about the drama he was playing a part in, when he handed over that little green ticket to freedom?)

Some years later brother Oscar passed on some information which bothered me far less then than it would have done if I had known it during my workhouse days. Although the Poor Law Institution was the last official safety net for the destitute and homeless, there was yet another net casting around for society misfits: those considered 'funny' in their ways. This net was broad and deep, designed to capture certain categories of human being who had *lost the qualities that are normal, desirable or proper to its kind.*

The 'net' referred to came about with the passing of the Mental Deficiency Act of 1913. This leap forward was hailed by a magazine called the *Eugenics Review* as, 'the one piece of English social law extant, in which the heredity has been treated as a practical factor in determining its provisions.'

This *tidy-up* Act (broad sweeping and cleansing) permitted various categories of 'degenerates' to be shut up in asylums on the strength of two doctors' certificates and a magistrate's order. As one might expect, there was both approval and outcry. Many Anglican clergy, including bishops and arch-bishops, nodded their approval. The scientist, Ernest William Barnes, who became a distinguished Bishop of Birmingham (1924–53), apparently approved and forthrightly declared that Christianity is trying to make: '... *a spiritually eugenic society... When religious people realise that, in ... preventing the survival of the social unfit, they are working in accordance with the plan by which God has brought humanity so far on its road, their objection to repressive action will vanish.'*

One of the many against the Act was G.K. Chesterton who, with equal resolution, added his own ten-penny worth: '... *the aim of this measure is to prevent any person who these propagandists do not happen to think intelligent from having any wife or children. Every tramp who is sulky, every labourer who is shy, every trustie who is eccentric, can quite easily be brought under such conditions as were designed for homicidal maniacs.'*

And that, without much doubt, would include raving mad, degenerate females who rocked the workhouse lifeboat by blatantly disobeying the rules.

Before this latest family upheaval, one Sunday, after the family visiting hour, Matron warned Oscar of an impending action. After her first escape, moves were being made to certify our mother insane (now we know why those two doctors gave her such close questioning attention). Her final escape would have been to Lincoln lunatic asylum, where they have full use of restraining methods for subduing those who are inconveniently difficult. To name but two: the

260

padded cell and the straitjacket (more kindly called a waistcoat) with its long tapering sleeves and buckles to fasten the victim's arms at the back.

It would seem that my mother was destined to go to Lincoln, after all. And accepting that this action might have come about (officialdom's answer to a very trying problem), how deeply affected would our family have been – not least, my ever-wondering self:

> Supposing that had happened,
> Supposing I had known:
> That my Mother was a loony,
> And confined in a bin!
>
> It's not so much the sin of it,
> The disgrace is bad enough!
> It's more the anxious feeling,
> Did God mark me the same?

39

There are some decisions that can cause consternation; especially the ones that are forced upon us. And, perhaps, here's a bit of peculiar reasoning; sometimes a hasty decision (even a panicky one) can turn out best of all. Perhaps not realised immediately in the long unwinding years to come, which for me had already well and truly begun.

When tomorrow came our choice was strait and narrow as a furrow. So we boarded the local train to travel to Lincoln, some 36 miles away. The alternative was starkly looming: to wander the streets and become vagrants, without a penny piece between us, once more risking our loss of freedom and being transported back to the Big House institution.

On that short, hopeful train journey many shades of living flashed by. I noticed all the advertisements, sited in those days alongside the track, providing a small rental income for the farmer and tempting the passing railway world to buy the latest fad and invention. It was an exciting time to be alive. All the world seemed to be on the move – even penniless me!

Over the track we rode, out came the sounds rising from the points, which seemed to beat a humming tune:

Clickety clack! Clackety click! Diddly dee – diddly dum!
What a life . . . Can be fun, even if – on the run!

It was beyond a kindness; much more a supreme sacrifice, that offer of Aunt Kate and Uncle Charlie to provide us with food and shelter. Their modest, terraced home at 16 Ashfield Street, Lincoln was situated in the lower part of the city (often smothered in smog from the coal-fired chimneys), where in the main the struggling workers lived. They would probably still be in a state of shock at having had sister Lizzie suddenly turn up; wildly disturbed in the appearance of an escaped convict. And not only that, lumbered with her youngest, still dependent, bastard son. A fast-growing child needing an adult's food and clothing; a complete drain on their own struggling lives. How their kindness would be tested...

Cousin Frank, the youngest son, was unemployed at that time (as were so many). He did odd jobs including selling an evening newspaper, much to his mother's shame. Later, he joined Ruston and Hornsby and stayed there for life, but that was long after I had moved on. When I lived with them the main source of income was provided by Cousin Irene, their only daughter, who had a secretarial post, with R&H. So with the means-testing of those times, any social assistance would have been out of the question. Unmistakably, hard times were upon them. All the more reason to appreciate their generosity in taking us in. They could have declined but having encumbered themselves, it seemed most likely that they were going to be stuck with us for a struggling time to come.

Perhaps it helped that Uncle Charlie was a member of the Plymouth Brethren and sincerely believed that whatever happened in life was down to God's true purpose – so sustained was he by his Christian faith, which he exemplified every waking day. 'Uncle Charlie's religion,' Aunt Kate often used to say (referring to the Brethren's bread-breaking ritual), 'is more like the papist's.' Aunt, by way of contrast, was a long-lapsed Primitive Methodist.

Escaping from the protective walls of institutional red brick, I had been jumped slap bang into a void. Or, to put it another way: I had become a missing person, existing on the fringe of life.

Now, I was about to experience a short trudging period in my young life. I had just moved through a confined monastic time; now it was to be trudge, trudge, trudge time – all over Lincoln. Instead of attending the big school by the Arboretum in the Monks Road, which I liked the look of; I was to accompany restless Mam on her trudges in and around the city, to savour her heady, new-found freedom. There was no suggestion or attempt to send me to school. I had become a lost child and had disappeared from the school system, not to mention breaking the law. Although this new life was fast becoming a prolonged holiday, it was not exactly the best treatment for a 12-year-old. Far too many valuable school lessons were being missed (surely to my future disadvantage). For the time being I was in limbo; waiting as usual for someone else to act and decide what I must do – it was back to come-day, go-day again, including Sunday.

At first Mam and I enjoyed our new-found freedom as we explored the City of Lincoln. She would lead; I followed like a dog on a lead. This was now my only education. Never before (and certainly never since) would I ever find time for such an extended introduction to a fine historical city. We trudged down Ashfield Street, turned right at the bottom, along by the River Witham; up and down the main street towards the Stonebow and back and then along Bradford Pool, sometimes to feed crumbs to the swans. Up Steep Hill we climbed to inspect the exterior of the fine cathedral (eventually sporting the Lincoln Imp peering out in stone). Many times we went inside and walked its length and breadth and on some days we sat and heard the choir and the organist practising. If outside was wet or foggy we lingered in the protection of that vast edifice. Afterwards going home by way of Eastgate or Minster Yard to join Pottergate down

Lindum Road and past the policeman dressed in white on traffic duty (some years before traffic lights were introduced). Up and down with some slight variation we repeated these walks many times – dum-de-dum – so many times! Always looking on, I gradually began to feel remote from the daily scene.

Eventually, as you can imagine, my workhouse shoes began to wear thin. Aunt Kate, being the practical person she was, gave me one shilling and thruppence (fifteen pence, old money) and bid me go to the shoe repairers. I sat on a stool by the shop counter until the assistant mended them. Thus did I come up against the practicalities of life – in the workhouse repairs were *free*, in the world outside it was *cash on demand.*

With such intensity did we take in all the historic sights. Mam even spared a few precious pennies to enable us to visit the castle and the old prison. We lingered long over the many interesting exhibits and sights to see; especially within the prison. Mam, in an intense, perhaps ghoulish way, inspected the prisoners' disused cells, the chapel where they attended service and were reproved for their many sins. After that she anxiously inspected, as indeed I did, the platform-drop which was used in its day to hang the condemned prisoners. She didn't approve of that!

One day we trudged a little further out, east of the city, to the end of Monks Road, then turned left to look at the modern prison (which in those days was surrounded by open country). Mam became quite agitated when we saw outside the prison walls a group of working prisoners in charge of two warders (dressed in a uniform and not unlike Porter Stone clones). We paused at the main gate and looked up at this fortress-like building. No doubt about it, the caging here was far superior to a workhouse. This building would be difficult to walk away from; there were no insecure bolt-holes. The wailing, warning siren was silent that day. There was one distinct advantage these prisoners had over her own recent incarceration: they knew how long they were in for, and possibly they could get parole for good behaviour. Her incessant sentence in the workhouse had been for life. No doubt feeling some sympathy for their self-inflicted plight, she then took a final gape and turned her back on the prison. We walked away – whether in relief or stricken by awe, I cannot truly remember.

During October and November in 1934, an event took place in the city of Lincoln which engaged and fascinated Mam. You'd be forgiven for thinking that she had no personal problems of her own – not forgetting mine. The murder trial of Mrs E.L. Major, of Kirkby-on-Bain took place at the Lincoln assizes. She was charged with murder on the 1st August of that year of her husband, Arthur Major. This turned out to be a deadly dual between the legal protagonists of the prosecution and defence. Full verbatim reporting was published daily in the main Lincoln evening paper, arousing much ghoulish speculation; heightened by the knowledge that hanging by the neck was still fully in fashion. And, furthermore, that the just reward could be awarded to a woman.

Mam fed on every word, it was almost as if it were her own neck above which the hangman's noose dangled. We now made sure we trudged up Steep Hill in time to catch a glimpse of the judge arriving and if we were around in the afternoon we watched him leaving. Mrs Major was found guilty and hanged, whether my mother approved or not! By that time I had moved on, to yet another temporary home – the fifth in a little over three years.

Uncle Charlie being of an inventive mind had developed his very own splendid version of the electric organ-blower; suitable for churches, chapels and some private owners. Initially, cornering the market so to speak, business flourished. He called his company: The Twentieth Century Organ Blower

Company. Much pride went into deciding that name. Well do I remember the smart embossed letterheads being rolled into the old Imperial manual typewriter, extolling the benefits and advantages of the electric blower against the hand-pump method of providing wind for the organ. Another one less boring duty for the verger, or sleepy choirboy, whose responsibility it was to keep mentally alert and fill the puffing bellows, in time for the responses and the hymns – especially the Alleluias. Diagrammed and fully illustrated brochures were also enclosed with the quotations sent on their way to prospective customers. To use modern parlance, this organ-blower invention was a 'breakthrough' and the demand seemed endless.

In the 1920s, orders poured in. Eldest son, Theodore, joined Uncle Charlie in the firm. They travelled far and wide (especially in Lincolnshire with all those out-dated hand pumps still existing in the numerous chapels and churches). To fulfil the contracts obtained, they allowed their customers to pay on instalments (without interest, as befitted Charlie's strict religion). Prosperity for a time deservedly came their way. Their mode of business travel was by that wonderful invention the motorbike and sidecar which gave them the mobility the expanding business required, at the lowest possible cost.

Whether it was the result of competition or the effect of the world depression, I can only speculate; perhaps it was a good bit of both. By the time I came to live with them, orders had dried up and the main occupation seemed to be typing out begging letters to numerous chapels and churches, requesting them to send the balance of their unpaid account. The letters were thought out very carefully and couched in a most polite, almost begging way – such was their desperation: 'We would be most grateful...' or 'Look forward to your urgent kind attention', as well as, 'May we respectfully point out...' followed by the odd etcetera. The more credit

267

they allowed the bigger got the hole they dug, until it seemed likely to swallow up their business, as well as any ambitious dreams.

All this restless trudging and searching, after about three weeks, started to pall. One day, by invitation, I walked by myself to Uncle Charlie's workshop (situated by the side of the Lincoln racecourse), complete with real carpenter's tools. At 12 I was nearly old enough to go out to work, so this was going to be a valuable experience. Who knows, I might have invented a machine to blow-dry clothes and made my own fortune. Instead, I made model aeroplanes: bi-planes to be exact, which places my childhood firmly in the pioneering days of flying. This activity gave me much pleasure. I also used to sweep out the workshop and practise on the old manual typewriter. Listening to Uncle C. as he composed and typed his begging requests, I there and then decided that I would be much tougher on debtors if ever I owned a business (and I most certainly was).

As a special treat on Saturday afternoon, the family managed to dredge up thruppence, so that I could go to the local 'fleapit' picture house, where I sat with many of the city's children. All of us craning our necks, looking upwards, only a few feet from the giant screen. (I'm not sure about the others, but I always ended up with a painful crick in my neck, slightly boss-eyed and with a blinding headache.) Nevertheless, 'the pictures' were an important part of my education at that time, especially the American ones, in which were portrayed some working people full of hope and confidence. I found this attitude difficult to believe and concluded it was only play-acting. I'd never observed much of it in our own subdued workers.

Now old enough to sense suppressed tensions – the ones not supposed to be noticed by children, I quietly observed my new family's life. That there was pride there, the sheer pride of outwardly showing independence, in the midst of

268

suffering hardship. More particularly did I notice that despite the desperate straits Uncle Charlie had fallen into, he always seemed to maintain a constant spirit of hopefulness: his unquestioning faith in God, that whatever came his unfortunate way was for a purpose. Not for him to whinge or question; better to kneel down and patiently seek a blessing – of good times to relieve his present desperation.

Now comes the tut-tut time, the bystanders' time, the experts' time and the shaking of the head time: that it would have been better for me to have remained within the security of the workhouse and to continue attending the local state school, where I was educationally thriving. In some circumstances that would have been right; but in our case had we stayed put, Mam would have been forcibly admitted into Lincoln Asylum – the final banishment, to push her over the edge of life. Would I have ever seen her again? Not even as a certified babbling drool? Most unlikely. So what is a few weeks missed from school compared with the destructive price then exacted by caring officialdom?

Although she had been helpful, Aunt Kate also had to be practical and became concerned about the cost of our keep. (There was no social support or automatic rehousing 'by right' in 1934). At 12 I had developed a grown-up's appetite and already my shoes had had to be repaired – largely caused by all that frantic trudging. Aunt Kate had a right to be concerned about how long were these poverty-stricken, uninvited relations, going to stay. Yet during all that anxious time she never made one unkind word to me, which, under the circumstances, proved to be very kind indeed.

Finally, a decision was made (as usual) over my head. It was arranged by post that I would be transported on the railway back to Gosberton Risegate, the village of my sinful birth; back to familiar surrounds but not back to the farm from which I had been so hastily evicted. Oscar then lodged with the Gedney family, and they had agreed to take me in.

Somehow a concession was wrung from the Poor Law Guardians to pay three shilling and sixpence (42 old pence) a week for my keep. Again, I was on the move to another home and more experience. And back to my early village school. This new prospect (despite the separation from Mam) filled me with nervous excitement.

On a dark November evening (I cannot remember the words of goodbye, even if there were any) I left with my bits and pieces in a carrier bag. Mam sobbed and cried: 'You don't like losing your own!' But it seemed obvious that I belonged to no one – not even myself! So off I went as there was no alternative – except the one I had escaped from.

Cousin Frank took me to the train and by the time I had reached the station I was fully composed and ready for life's next unfolding. Off with the old – on with the new, had long since become my travelling companion.

(Spiders spin their imprisoning webs; lions roar and eat their prey; the mouse is easily alarmed and even worms may turn one day. So when would I roar my madden rage and begin my life anew – and become independent? Not for some little time to come was the simple answer to that; for it was increasingly obvious that I still needed other people, by far more than they needed me.)

40

Immediately after leaving behind the bright lights of Lincoln, I noticed my reflection in the carriage window, against the blackness of that November evening. My life had moved into the low glow of paraffin lamps. Dull beams escaped from the windows of dwellings and the lamps along the station platforms as we puffed along the resounding track. A porter would silently appear and load the odd box and remove any packages addressed to local people. In some progressive villages a few electric bulbs pulsated out, some along the road supplied by a private generator; the forerunners of the lighting revolution then beginning to spread. So excited was I on the first train journey I had taken by myself that my spirits remained elated; instead of being depressed as might have been expected while travelling through such a gloomy scene.

I sat alone in the compartment of a non-corridor carriage. Suddenly I felt an urgent need to pee. Scared of being left behind had I got off the train to go to the station toilet, during its very brief halt, I partially opened the door of the carriage and peed, with great relief. I aimed down between the gap between the door and the platform with a surprising amount of accuracy. That was a useful lesson, I can tell you.

Oscar met me at Gosberton station (which was situated in the Risegate village). I gave my used ticket to the man on duty, walked along the platform and out of the station into the inky blackness of the night. Along Gosberton Road I looked across to the right and saw a light in the window of Station Cottage, a name which had been relinquished for the more up-market Riseholme (the 'Rise' from 'Risegate' and 'holme' to describe flat ground by a river, which is exactly what it was). After all, the old name had gathered about it by far too much past sorrow. This was a new name and a new beginning, under a substantial area of glass; despite Father Horton's too ready declamation: 'Bah, you can't eat flowers!'

Even so, a sudden sadness swept over me as I glanced at that lighted window. There would be no home welcome for me there. Mam's *rightful* home now legally belonged to another family. Instead of a vegetable garden at the front, there was now a wide expanse of lawn, and a willow tree had been planted by the Risegate Eau. Yes, my old home was still there, and certainly not forgotten, and never would be.

Home Sweet Home – was now where I happened to reside at present, where my basic needs were catered for, beyond which nothing else was expected; so I carried a loneliness within my being, which kept me tightly in its grip. But that was in the past. I had now reached another stage of worldly experience; not adoption, not even to be fostered. Although extremely well looked after, I would prefer to think of myself as a lodger and a temporary one at that. Such was my acquired outlook on life – my down to rock-bottom image.

If I belonged anywhere, it was deeply within myself. Supported by three shillings and six pence (42p) from the Poor Law Relief and whatever Oscar could spare from his meagre wages, I was only too deeply aware that I was still at pauper level. And not only that, I was now an item of curiosity in the village; having survived a term in the workhouse, which all poor folk dreaded – the ultimate in shame; on top of the shame of my irregular birth.

On Christmas Day in 1934 I felt especially low. Never at

Christmas had I been separated from Mam. In the workhouse we spent most of the day together, feeding, singing and being entertained. And I knew my Horton father was having his turkey dinner across the way. It wasn't that kindness was missing. I enacted Christmas as best I could, but an acute depression would not release me. Those damn precious memories! Why did they afflict me so?

My new *parents*, Mr and Mrs Gedney, were able folk, well used to bringing up children, having had six of their own. The last one, Jack, my age within a few months, was now to be my *constant* companion. I slept in a large double bed with brother Oscar. In the same roomy bedroom also slept four members of the family, in another double and two single beds. To be fair, it was a large bedroom and I never heard any complaints. Such doubling-up arrangements (which might one day be described as over-crowding) were perfectly normal in those days. At first I kept my few belongings in a carrier bag in an alcove by the side of the bed. Later on, as I began to possess a few more clothes, Oscar bought me a trunk from a shop in Spalding. This proved to be most useful as I began to need more room for additional possessions. Indeed, it was the beginning of owning things beyond my basic needs and a distinct enhancement of my life.

Having brought up her six own children Mrs Gedney extended her motherly attention towards me in a down-to-earth way; sloppy emotion was never shown. Didn't I now have food and a bed to lie on, clothes washed clean and woollen socks darned to perfection? When later I earned some money, she saw to it that I opened a Post Office Savings Account. 'It will grow at $2^{1}/_{2}$ per cent,' she said, I was most impressed; if I could save enough money there'd be no need to bother about work, at least not the kind I detested. Though I must confess, the one thing I really wanted was to grow up free of my stranded childhood.

This family was typical of most village folk in those times; only too aware that they had to turn out to work, however menial – not to do so would have been a family disgrace. It soon became obvious, as well as a lesson to me, that 'work or starve' was the fundamental driving force of every waking day (except Sunday when I prayed for hope and deliverance).

Without any further delay, I commenced attending the Gosberton Clough and Risegate elementary school on the very next morning of my arrival at my lodgings after leaving Lincoln (not to do so would have been unthinkable). The formidable headmaster, Donald Hector Gordon Ross (full of moral certainty and prone to losing his ranting temper), ruled intensively over his pupil-flock. He asked me a few details of my previous Westlode School experience, then issued me with a set of textbooks and bade me sit in his overcrowded classroom; where he struggled to teach around 50 mixed-ability pupils. No wonder the poor man would become overheated and suddenly lash out with his tongue.

After settling in and gaining a bit of confidence I started to read one of three books on a shelf in the living room of my lodgings. The last one I picked up was titled *The Life of a Philanderer*. Seeing me do this, after the first page or so, my latest mother asked me what I was reading and I read out the title. After which, only showing faint signs of nervousness, she said no more. This may take some believing but such was the innocent state of my 12-year-old mind that I at first believed a 'Philanderer' was a person who lived in 'Philand' (wherever that place might be); similar to a Laplander who lives in Lapland, if you follow the logic of my reasoning. Much to my amazement, a philander according to this account, was a man who kissed and cuddled a succession of girls in dark corners and hidden places. And the moral was plain to see: men who play fast and loose

274

with their own and others' affections would never be able to settle down and form a permanent relationship. No wonder Mrs Gedney was worried about the influence this book might have on me, assuming, of course that she had dared to read it – but to her credit, she never stopped me.

Yes, I was back in my native village again; in the place of distant memories, of hardship and dispossessions. Still a recipient of Poor Law Relief, delivered by an official once a week, who probably checked from time to time that I was still alive. Three shillings and sixpence (42 old pence) he delivered. That may sound meagre and it was, but enough to buy some basic groceries: with butter at 14p, Cheddar cheese at 8p; margarine as low as 5p (all for a pound), and vegetables free from the kitchen garden. Even so, one thing appears certain; my new mother didn't lodge me to make a profit – not even a penny-piece!

Another change affected me; instead of being one of the workhouse senior boys looking after and belonging to a large family, all similarly in a pauperised state but rubbing along with one another. Now I was to live one-to-one, a companion to a child brought up within the narrow security of his home and village. Suppressing all my own desires, I now followed my new brother about like a puppy dog, trying my best not to rock any boats as there seemed no alternative. I had had more freedom in the workhouse. Pictures on a Saturday afternoon, weekends of freedom with the Mawer family, who let me wander as I pleased. And now, what of any excitement in a 'back-of-beyond' village in which I felt so deadened. We sometimes visited the railway passenger station on Saturday evening to see who had arrived on the last train. At other times we went to check who was the last customer in Mary Pointon's village store (usually Mrs North, who arrived some five minutes before closing time at nine). There were other bubbles of excitement, which usually quickly burst; none exactly stimulating – plodding about in a country village was about as stimulating as a cold cup of stale tea.

And no wonder I rapidly became a stoic. I soon discovered that my 'cheek by jowl' companion had a fearful habit of losing his temper when he became upset, which was fairly often, for the slightest reason. And in my lonely, dependent state, I decided that no one had noticed my discomfort (to put it as mildly as I can). So a two-year term of pacification began. Had I lived in a secure home I would never have tolerated such fiery fits of petty anger. But someone did notice. Years later (some 60 to be more exact) a then fellow pupil would tell me: 'Yes, I remember you well. You lived with the Gedney family – and Jack was beastly to you.'

It's reasonable to suppose that if this fellow pupil knew of my 'temporary predicament', the whole village must have known. And I thought I lived my life in secret! I'd live long enough to learn that children are often beastly one to another – even brothers and sisters. And it's not unusual for them to remain closely in touch for the rest of their lives, after the growing pains have subsided; carrying forward no lasting ill feeling, as indeed I never did: better to move on than get bogged down up to your eyes in weeping lamentation.

On Sunday in the customary village way, children received their regular churching, at either the Methodist Church or the C of E (St Gilbert and St Hugh). My new family was C of E, so I continued that way – one way or the other it didn't seem to matter – didn't all roads lead to Rome? In charge of the tightly structured church service, was the stiffened Revd Hugh Finch Blackledge, MA. Dressed in his dark clerical suiting, sporting a pristine white dog collar, he presided over his small flock with all the confidence of exactly knowing what the sacred laws ordained.

Like so many thousands of vicars before him, he had been churned out by one of the grey-stone universities. His

276

dutiful existence was not only to marry couples in the only way then acceptable, as well as bury the dead; – his main duty was to keep the fear of Hell and Damnation implanted into the very souls of the timid, common people. The finest control that ever existed: the threat of everlasting torture for those found in the Evil net, come the Judgement Day. Yet, for the time being, so it would seem, their earthly punishment was more than enough.

During the two years I attended Gosberton Clough church the Rev'd Blackledge never spoke directly to me; never even called me by name (although he always did to others) and he never once eye-contacted me. But have some sympathy for him. Poor man, can you imagine his damaged feelings when I turned up; a living product of sin! But not only that – appearing to thrive as well. And looking so damned normal!

This devoted holy vicar never enquired of my spiritual health, so he never found out that I had been confirmed by his august boss, none other than the Bishop of Lincoln. So I sat and watched, lacking courage to walk to the altar and partake in the communion sacrament; politely resigned in my usual peering state, in other words, knowing my place of an outsider inquisitively looking in.

Ancient Mistress Dickens, who sang in a creaky voice and prodded children with her umbrella if they dare fidget during the service, also showed a degree of anxiety. Always sitting in a front pew next to the aisle, she shot out to be first-served with wine (not for her to risk any germs, not even sacred ones). If anyone beat her to it, she refused to go out and returned to her seat. Her action, although quiet and discreet, used to cause a ripple of speculation. For there seemed no doubt about it, she'd be elbowing ahead of the queue when the Pearly Gates swung open, then prodding a path with that umbrella.

In the fast-changing world we live in, some beliefs and

sins will be questioned. So take heart, when you reach my ancient age (despite much handwringing), 'bastards' will be so common they will no longer be treated as alien people. And many vicars and bishops will have rocked the boat, at times to near sinking; forcing some of the faithful congregation to be lost in utter dismay, as the gospel of direction is slipped about evasively, like the bending of weeds in the wind.

During the daily grind at the Clough and Risegate State School, instead of being intensively taught in a similar ability class of no more than 30, I now sat amidst some 50 children of mixed talent and various ages (up to 14 from the age of 11). Before, I had had no difficulty in keeping abreast of my work. Now I found that sums proved to be a difficulty; a lesson to be dreaded. With such a large and varied ability class Mr Ross's time was severely limited. Usually we were left to work on our own and to my chagrin I found that I was getting crosses instead of the usual ticks – which progressively clipped my self-esteem.

After a time, as he marked the red-ink xs, he followed with a loud groan. In no time at all I lost all my confidence and, so far as arithmetic was concerned, decided that I was stupid. Once I sneaked several answers from the teacher's book and worked out the sums backwards. Eventually there was one sum he hesitated to mark. Looking at me with his canny Scottish expression he demanded to know how I had got the answer. Being honest I simply told him: 'From your book.' Naturally he wasn't well pleased and uttered a moral condemnation – making me wish I could drop out of sight! Thereafter I lost any remaining confidence and learned to ignore all those red-ink crosses. To make his point more strongly, Ross would also sing a then popular song, revised to suit my desperation. And he sang it out loud for all the class to hear and witness my humiliation; as he criss-crossed in that damned red ink:

'I lost my way in a thick, thick sum [fog]
In a thick, thick sum [fog] in London.'

Yet whenever he instructed at the blackboard I always caught on. In truth the problem was a simple one. The textbook he gave me was a year or so beyond my previous instruction. He never relented, so I ploughed on, now accepting that I had become a DUNCE. And that 'rithmetic had now become my daily torment. (So much for the newfangled notion to come, that kids progress better if left to discover for themselves – such rot!)

Poor over-worked man, no wonder he lost his temper. He once carried a pupil across the playground and dumped him over a fence into an adjoining field. Another pupil (so I was told) he had once dropped outside through a classroom window, when in one of his rages. At times he would throw things, a cricket ball or any other handy missile. On one occasion he suddenly and violently beat me about the head, causing an old cut to bleed; all because my writing wasn't perfectly copperplate as was strictly expected. Another time a pupil's lip was cut and bruised, requiring minor first-aid. Regularly he would place the school's only football on his desk in front of the class, pull his penknife out and threaten to 'cut it to ribbons!' if our behaviour didn't improve. He administered the cane sparingly. In a most sincere face, just before wielding the blow, he would piously remark: 'This hurts me more than it hurts you.' But I never believed him as he openly struggled to salve his finer feelings.

Many years later a fellow pupil will confess to me that, 'all the time in his class, I lived in fear of him.' *So I wasn't the only 'victim'.*

Nevertheless, to make a fair point in his favour, he seemed deeply concerned about our future welfare, bothered that

279

most of us would end up 'dead-end' labouring on the land. He was especially good at moral precepts and many other bits of down-to-earth wisdom. One in particular caught my attention: *There's no need for you to burn your fingers in the fire, just because Johnny Smith does.*

That was simple enough, like that gem of wisdom from the Buddha (written 500 BC): '...*when you know in yourself that something is bad then give it up, and accept the good and follow it.*'

So there it is, straight and simple, to the point and from the horse's mouth: persuasion through moral sense, an important part of character building, especially for the likes of me, though often feeling abandoned, always hopefully listening and patiently awaiting any sign to widen my understanding.

41

So here I was in temporary storage, looking and pondering, waiting like a coiled spring to jump myself on; for the better, of course, I'd had enough of the worst. At the age of 12, with time on my side, surely my better moments were yet to come.

Later in November (1934), Oscar took me on one side and informed me of news I wasn't expecting: 'Horton is dead,' he said. He looked more embarrassed than sad. And I cannot remember showing any other reaction than one of outward indifference: as befitting a child who was used to submerging his innermost feelings. At long last: Horton is *Dead and Buried*! Fulfilling that plea he often made in the dark days before our first eviction, when he sensed that all was lost and ruination starkly faced him.

Good, I thought, he's escaped at last from all the misery heaped upon him in the last few years of his wretched life. Yes, I truly felt a sense of relief that my Father (the man who had sown my life-giving seed; who had also provided my first nine years of happy stability) had at far too long last, found his everlasting peace. Having suffered his Hell on Earth, he had now disappeared into thin air, or at least that's what it seemed to me. But my mind did further question: would he really come alive again, in solid form or apparition?

As sometimes happens after an occasion of sorrow, a few nights later I began to have a vivid dream. Was this to be my substitute grieving? It was so vivid that it forever etched itself into my memory. It was even more vivid than that workhouse dream, when I flapped my arms for wings and took off to a foreign jungle, escaping over the imprisoning workhouse walls. Where on earth do dreams come from? Whatever the answer, on some occasions they appear in remarkable forms: happiness, fear, love, hatred, and sometimes ending in nightmarish screams and a violent awakening.

In the first dream I found myself walking along a stony path under a blistering sun: After some trudging (much tougher than that trudging in Lincoln) there appeared before me a high wall of red bricks, boldly pointed in between with a layer of shiny-white cement. This wall extended on both sides as far as I could see, and looking skywards I noticed, somewhat fearfully, that it reached so high heavenwards that it was lost in a heap of cumulus cloud. There were paths both ways but they seemed endless – far beyond the extent of my vision. Resting awhile on the path to the left, I felt sure that I could hear noises on the other side – distant sounds of talking and children screaming with delight. It was then I imagined, that's where Horton is! He was there on the other side perhaps working contentedly in a restful garden, chatting away to the other inmates, while puffing away at his old clay pipe filled with ponging twist-tobacco. The dream ended like the completion of a film. So curious did I become that I vowed to myself that I would pursue this intense vision to the very end. Instead of hesitating the next time the dream occurred I decided to explore both paths, one at a time. It did return the very next night so I walked along the path to the right, but after a short journey I came across an impassable ravine, so I doubled my steps back to the first-tried path on the left which seemed more frequently trodden on. I trudged on and on in the fearsome heat, long past my first attempt. As I was beginning to lose heart, the wall curved for no apparent reason. And then with such abruptness, I could hardly believe my eyes, it actually ended and there appeared no barrier to the other side. Fearfully I approached the opening, fully expecting to see my father and perhaps even to finally wave goodbye (but not frantically so, the way I did the last time I saw him in the infirmary). For a minute or so I halted and listened hard. No longer did I hear voices and children screaming with delight; those previous sounds of life must have been imagined. I walked further forward now anxious to view the secluded side. By contrast with the stifling wilderness there instantly flowed a cool freshness about the place. Amid the silence nothing stirred – it felt supernormal. The sky that I now viewed was ice-blue in colour; as though it had been especially refrigerated to keep at bay any gloomy clouds of sadness. Into the far distance there rolled out grassland of Irish emerald-green; pristine and mowed close, sharply dividing Earth from Heaven. Not unlike the flat Fenland which I knew so well. The stilly chillness held me in awe, until the dream switched off again, never to be repeated.

So this is where my earthly father had vanished. His tranquillity had come at last. Of this I now felt deeply. So where he was, if he was, how he was, would no longer bother me – my troublous emotions had been relieved. In his memory, how should his memorial read?

> *Nowhere do I now reside,*
> *In my Eternal Peace*
> *Body and Soul I do not need;*
> *My death is Nothingness!*

Contrary to the usual expectations, the Poor Law Guardians had not only splashed out on a fine 'pine coffin' with 'brass furniture' – they had also given him a decent burial in Gosberton cemetery, a mile or so away from his beloved Cheal, the place of his birth. That would have pleased the old boy: ending up with a respectable funeral, blessed in a

283

House of Worship. His escape from the pauper misery of the workhouse-infirmary was now, thankfully, achieved (small wonder my feeling for him was one of deep relief).

His grave mound would not display a fine memorial stone, which crumbles away with the passage of time, its etched words of comfort temporarily alleviating the intense grief. Whatever the sentiments, it's a sad reminder of death; especially when the last fresh flowers have withered away.

A long column-inch announcement appeared in the *Spalding Free Press* of the 30th November, 1934. It was thoughtfully composed (by cousin Elizabeth Mawer, the one who had befriended me). With minor embellishments added and the absence of any scandal by omission, it truly followed the time-honoured advice – *never speak ill of the dead!*

Whatever was said or left unsaid, only the meanest minded would begrudge a tribute to a fine old farming man. Hadn't he battled long and hard, in good times and bad? Until he was swallowed up by that world-wide slump and the mountainous mortgage around his neck (as well as being disadvantaged by slavishly sticking to ancient farming methods, of which he was so proud). And there was one more thing which contributed to his misery: the unfortunate blessing of living too long. Small wonder that he had so many times wished himself: *Dead and Buried!* And sincerely meant it!

42

Although I had by now fully accepted the loss of my early childhood home, memories would often flood back, especially when I passed by the place, which was unavoidable.

Those were happy childhood days.
Spent on the cottage farm,
Long hours of sunshine (hoping for rain).
Tasty vegetables in the garden,
Mucked with toilet dung.
Fruit on the trees, rabbit in the pot.
Scaling the stackyard ricks,
Burrowing tunnels underneath,
Clambering steeply up tall ladders,
Climbing high in the trees.

In the year of my return, 1934, one item of interesting news in the *Free Press* caught my attention. It was duly reported that: 'Mrs Mark Bates, ... has drawn the horse Foxmasque, in connection with the Cambridgeshire ... Mrs Bates is entitled to £402.* Mr Bates said: "The money will come in useful, we can do with it."'

So far in my short lifetime, especially after my three years' incarceration, I could not but notice the creeping changes that had come about in my village. The sails had stopped flailing on top of the windmill. But far worse than

---

* Around four years' wages for a farm-labourer, it was indeed a tidy sum – to me, it sounded like a small fortune.

that the cupola had been removed, leaving a stunted, beheaded tower; forever to grate my line of vision.

Wild birds were still plentiful and nesting every season. Many a boy had a large collection of eggs, holed at either end and 'blown out' to leave the shell. Only take one egg from a nest, was the advice given. Unfortunately, other boys usually did the same – there was fierce competition to complete the most in a set. No wonder the wild life was disappearing along with the trees and hedgerows, both non-productive, and in the way of the newfangled, power-driven farm machinery.

The war memorial still attracted my attention. We used to recite the names from top to bottom (never expecting that some of our own generation would be added to the list: Robert Richardson and Leslie North, to name two of my childhood friends).

We often passed by the local smithy's workshop, next to The Old Crane public house, also doomed to close. There we children watched Jimmy Edgoose bashing white-hot iron into various shapes. In his role as farrier he shod the local farmers' horses. Sometimes we were allowed to pump air into the coke forge and we watched with some admiration as Jimmy shaped the metal with a drop hammer and finished it off with brawny blows, rounding the horseshoes on his anvil. But soon our village blacksmith would disappear to be replaced by enterprising mechanics: the up and coming new 'profession' of *Agricultural Engineer*.

The local vet, Mr Hackett, cautiously drove his large saloon at around five miles an hour. Village children on bicycles chased after him and some managed to overtake, while furiously ringing their bells in a state of wild excitement. Mr Hackett would smile and seem somewhat bemused, that his motorcar should cause such a resounding fuss.

At Woodthorpes, the wheelwright, we sometimes watched the workers prepare a metal vehicular tire: long spelt the *olde* way, distinguishing itself from the new pneumatic 'tyre', and not mis-spelt 'tire' by the Americans, who kept the original form. With clamps two workers would lift the red hot tire from the furnace onto the timber spoked wheel, which sizzled and smoked a bit when it was knocked into position with heavy hammers. All through this expert operation the boss would be casting his eagle eye to see that the tire was correctly positioned. Then it was cooled with buckets of water, which shrunk the band of metal round the rim of the wheel to the relief and satisfaction of his proud workmen.

The Risegate general store, run by Mary Pointon, survived on hope and faith; that at the end of the growing season there'd be enough surplus cash from the sale of produce to settle the many bills 'on tick'. Poor Mary! Trying to remain solvent: too much trust, far too much credit – ticking over like a time bomb before it burst and closed the village shop, which it did.

During the year of '35 I was to receive a lesson on the hard facts associated with living, which would last me for the rest of my life. Brother Oscar, who now laboured hard for a miserable pittance for Mr Burrell (a local chicken dealer) in his adjoining market garden, bid me spend the evening after school picking peas. Reluctantly I went, and dawdled across the field. Oscar picked up my hesitant attitude and shouted across: 'Come on, Ged, snatch hold!' He then threw a large hessian sack across to me, and pointed to the position where I'd begin my picking. I could have shot him dead for disturbing my life in this way. But after picking three sacks full, much to my surprise, Oscar paid me there and then. Would you believe, the munificent sum of one shilling and sixpence (18 of those large copper pennies; in those days, 240 to the £).

18 pence, a pittance you might say, but just consider the then cost of living: 5 pence, a child's railway return to Spalding; 6 pence, to attend the 'flicks' at the Odeon; 3

pence for a child's haircut, and still 4 pence left over for goodies.

And that was the lesson I learnt: that there appeared no lawful alternative to work. So would it slowly dawn on me that with my limited gifts it would be a waste of time daydreaming. The other way was the paupers' workhouse and I'd already had enough of that. Those heavy pennies I had worked hard for seemed the obvious way to escape from pauperdom. Apart from burglary at the risk of prison, no other freebie existed and I had too long been praying like mad for some relief – not so much in the mind; something tangible, however small – something I could feel and see.

We played football on Charlton's grassfield, after helping out with some daily chores to pay the fee. I also played in the school team, in the village colours of black and green. Unable to afford the luxury of buying football boots, I played in my civvy shoes and short socks, in the role of goalkeeper. Some girl spectators called me 'legs' – it was quite embarrassing. So many goals were let in, head-teacher Ross once enquired if we had been playing cricket – followed by one of his low groans.

In the summer evenings we often raced around the silt sloping walls of one of Mr Charlton's pits. It formed a splendid racetrack; exciting, almost like the fairground Wall of Death. Some aspects of village life were not that bad, after all.

But where have all those pits gone?
Long filled with tons of rubbish?
We used to ferret among the bits,
Hoping to salvage something useful.
Many old bottles were buried there,
Now sought by keen collectors;
If only they knew where to dig!

288

In my thirteenth year, perhaps ready to feed my growing independence of mind (and something to do to occupy the dull Sunday evenings) I varied my religious experience by once again attending evening service at the local Risegate Methodist Church; totally oblivious of the possibility that the good Rev'd Blackledge might choke on his rage at my scandalous display of indifferentism. More especially as I was still performing his C of E rituals every Sunday morning; but surely, if narrow experiences tend to produce narrow minds, I desperately needed to widen my own.

Often, the lay preachers of the Methodist Church performed like theatrical entertainers, outright and full of passion – not above thumping the pulpit to highlight some awful sin. The most passionate of preachers (so it seemed to me) were those who had been sinners themselves and had suddenly seen the light. Hell and Damnation were spread about like butter on bread in this otherwise friendly church. And you could almost smell the smoke from the singeing and see the Devil perched and grinning over the wound-up preacher's head. No question about it, the moral teaching in this church was loud and clear, and decidedly straight. So I listened and thought and wondered, my searching mind impressed; for I could not help but notice that in those days the preachers held to a strict, simple belief in the divine truths contained in the Bible. Not for them a fashioned morality: that some things only seem to be bad; that some bad might be excusable; and many doubts falling in between could become adaptable.

I learnt a few words of Heraclitus (570–497 BC), one among so many wise philosophers, who once scholarly stated (among other things) that: 'Everything is in flux all the time.'

Please tell me something new, wise man, especially with a hopeful flavour. I already knew the state of flux from past raw experience. No wonder the common people would often scratch their heads and wonder what on earth is the world coming to. But have some sympathy, it's frustrating being a philosopher. They regularly churn out thousands of words, hoping that precious few, containing the seeds of something meaningful, might sprout and grow to provide an insight badly needed by the many anxious seekers (including my frustrated self).

My thirteenth year arrived in 1935. I was still a lodger, owning a few personal possessions in a suitcase; still doubling in a large bed in a bedroom occupied by up to six males. During the day I was now much more mobile: I possessed a bike, which was an ideal form of transport along those flat Fenland roads.

Now considered a youth, instead of a child, a little freedom entered my life. Instead of attending Sunday school, I accompanied Oscar on various bike rides, ten or fifteen miles away along the many local roads. That was quite an adventure after the sameness of village life. On those trips I noticed many things, especially all the houses where complete families lived. And I began to speculate, as you might expect, on the reason for their good fortune or, more to the point, my confusing lack of it. One family at Surfleet had purchased a discarded railway coach (first-class, would you believe!) and now lived in it. In typical country, jokey fashion they named it: *THISILDO*. Yes, we laughed, but deep inside I was filled with envy. A dwelling like that would be blessed by me, and *ITILDO* would be its proud name – it will do, indeed!

Having no pet or private space to call my own, I tended towards being secretive. One day I set a sweet pea in an empty cocoa tin, watered it and talked to it whenever that was possible. I hid it behind the barns at the end of the kitchen garden. It flourished and poked its head out, until it grew some four inches tall. Then quite suddenly it faltered, keeled over and died. This saddened me tremendously, and I experienced a state of grieving for a plant that had provided me with companionship, without uttering a single word. This bereavement, unlike my Father Horton's death, did not vividly invade my night-time dreams: there was no red-brick, high wall; no ice-blue sky of peace and certainly not any reunion expectation. Although a plant is fully capable of living, I truly believed that its death was full and final and extended bothering would not be helpful.

For some time my mother remained in Lincoln, still a burden on the slender resources of her relations, who were desperately strapped for cash. As winter approached her trudging time ended, and she unsuccessfully started to look for work: scrubbing floors or anything menial that happen to come along. She certainly wasn't without will or courage, but the competition was very fierce. Not only did she remain unemployed, she appeared to be unemployable – too many applicants for too few jobs.

In those means-tested days, obtaining assistance was purposely difficult. There was no lawful right to a social income; most certainly not to a society outcast which my mother virtually was. To be judged, without question, to be one of the many feckless creatures outside the scope of any assistance, not even for her bastard children – especially for them! Relief still existed at a workhouse, the very place she had escaped from. My word, what a trial her new-found freedom had become.

Whether or not two strong-willed sisters in one household caused too much friction, I cannot say. But one day in the cold winter of 1935/36 she slung her hook and caught another train. This time she landed herself on her brother Will and sister-in-law, Kate, living at Alexander Road, Skegness, the seaside resort 'so bracing' just north of the Wash.

Again, she tried her best to obtain work, but to no avail. 'My face is my reference,' she would declare to anyone asking for such inconvenient details. But eventually her luck changed – twice in a matter of months, which proves that sometimes if you follow your nose (even in sheer desperation), eventually you might find a better lot to fall your way. Whatever my mother lacked, she never suffered from a shortage of gutsy courage – reckless though that sometimes appeared to be – getting into new problems while trying to escape from the old ones. Oh, how her courage was tested to the full (some would say wasted) in attacking her perception of injustice, time and time again! But sometimes hard striving can bring about a solution – after many hopeless beginnings. Pity it sometimes takes so long – life can ill afford too many bouts of extended self-infliction.

43

Living next door to Kate and Will were the Fravigars; ice cream manufacturers and retailers, with stalls on the bracing sea front. Working the clock round in the summer months they desperately needed a woman to 'do' for them. So my mother landed the job of live-in housekeeper. I next saw her in the summer of 1935, in my fourteenth year. But only for an hour or two when I visited the resort on the annual church outing, and again on August Bank Holiday of that year when Oscar and I cycled all the way from the Risegate, along those flat snaking roads in the sweltering heat.

It was during those snatched visits that I noticed a change in her demeanour: she had regained her self-confidence, had money in her purse and a recovered outlook of independence. Yet this same woman, except for that desperate escape from the imprisoning workhouse, would now be languishing in Lincoln Asylum; permanently locked up, probably restrained within a strait-jacket, and considered crazy as a fluttering bat; out of sight, out of mind, neatly stowed away by order, under the umbrella of what was then euphemistically known as 'protective custody'.

Unexpectedly, after the Skegness holiday season had ended, she visited the Risegate for two or three days (the exact time has escaped from my memory). I remember the visit well. Having visited Spalding one day she met me from school with an enormous pork pie and offered me a huge slice there and then, which seemed to give her immense pleasure. I ate it, never mind that I was minutes away from a huge evening meal. How strange that for whatever reason such a small incident sticks in the mind. There's no doubt about it, this sudden *confrontation* with my mother, sadly, bothered me to uncertainty once more. So I was pleased when she went back and left my mind to regain the outward composure which I now practised in order to cope. But, to be fair, that slice of pork pie was Mam's show of affection, trapped as she still was in her gnawing frustrations. Folk in our village did not usually display an outward show of their feelings – that would have been considered sloppy – and my mother was no exception to that unwritten rule.

Later that year (in November) I was invited to stay a couple of days with the Skegness relations. Yet another fraught occasion – switched on and switched off like a beacon: I did not enjoy the emotional strain.

My mother's second stroke of luck came after her seasonal work as the Fravigars' housekeeper came to an end (she was now aged 58). In October 1935 she obtained another position of housekeeper to a bedridden elderly lady, a Mrs Jackson, at 20 Queens Road, Skegness. It was a terraced house, having two large bedrooms and a roomy attic. Living conditions here were far from primitive. There were three modern innovations: a mains water supply to an outhouse tap; a gas supply to a fire and downstairs lighting, fully functional so long as the hungry meter was fed with shillings. And outside there was (that wonder of the age) a flush toilet. No bathroom, just the usual bowl in the sink. Sister Win was still in service, now working at the local Vine Hotel. Brother Stanley remained a farm drudge at Gedney Hill and Oscar and I still lodged in the Risegate village. That Christmas (with the encouragement of the kind Mrs Jackson) all the family was invited to stay. At last, after some five years, we were all together again. It was exciting but short lived. I full well knew that our circumstances remained dire and I could see nothing but a future at poverty level. Insecurity surrounded me and that stirred me into a hatred of poverty, that inseparable twin of deprivation – the walls of my prison, from which I began wondering how to escape.

Meanwhile, after that pleasurable break, I was still in lodgings supported by poor relief, still attending school and fast becoming aware of the disadvantages of being forever stuck at the elementary level. Out of sheer necessity, I drudged in the fields to earn money to buy new clothes. That is why it was so important for poor village children to work most of the school summer holiday. For six weeks I slaved away in Mr Cope's fields in Gosberton Clough, picking potatoes. It was a five-day week, eight hours a day with half-an-hour for 'snap' at eleven o'clock, when we thankfully rested and fed. I soon found that picking potatoes is not only boring, it is back-breaking work. Attacking this repetitive job with long bouts of day-dreaming was the best way to get it done – my mind lived in a different world, leaving my body to perform like an engine.

> *Potato picking in wicker baskets,*
> *Usually weighty with cloggy soil;*
> *How those taters made me pain,*
> *More, thousands, millions more!*
> *Until I'm exhausted and sore.*
> *How much more of this suffering toil;*
> *At four shillings for an eight hour day.*
> *There's not much fat on labourer's pay.*
> *Up the row, down the row,*
> *Round and round the spinners go.*
> *It's enough to make you scream*
> *And hate the world you're living in!*

I finished school in July 1936, all of 14 years old, and predestined to be 'farm fodder'. One of the multitude of poorly paid slaves, entrapped in a life of servitude, under the controlling eye of a 'master'; reluctantly joining those who knew and accepted their lowly place – without any thought or the faintest hope of escape.

Mr Ross, our headmaster, well used to this annual parade, said his goodbye to each school leaver and asked of each one what occupation they would follow. 'On the land,' said most of the boys in front of me. So I said the same, but added a desperately hopeful wish: 'On the land, until I can get something better.' How and when I would get something better was beyond me. The poor man gave out one of his low moans, at our expected replies, knowing as he did the deadend we were drifting into; not far short of slavery.

> *Oh, how I toil, a son of the soil,*
> *In fine and filthy weather.*
> *I know my place – in misery,*
> *To plod on so worthily*
> *– like a blinkered horse!*

Along with Jack I started at Mr Arthur Cope's farm at Gosberton Clough – no school holiday for us. His land spread over some 100 rich acres rented and around 20 acres owned. I developed a dislike for Mr Cope for the following two reasons: he was my 'master' for eight hours each full working day and four on Saturday; he was so efficient at detailing the daily tasks that no sooner had we finished the last punishing one, he immediately instructed us to start another. It was work, work, work! Picking and riddling potatoes, setting plants, hoeing and all sorts of collecting, bagging and slashing – especially the sugar beet.

> *Lifting sugar beet to lay in rows,*
> *From daybreak on a frosty morning,*
> *Makes the hot-aches come and go.*
> *Then chop, throw, chop, throw,*

Umpteen roots into tidy heaps.
Along those rows-miles too long!
How I hate the frost and beet,
And this flat unfeeling land!

Mr Cope, who seldom worked hard for long periods, used to be fond of saying: 'A good master works his men hard. Otherwise they become lazy and unemployable.' But that was the way it was: 'master' and 'servant' and they would also indicate their servants' inferior status when they repeated a well-used statement: 'After all is said and done, farm labourers are ten-a-penny. A working horse cost £50!' I also remembered Father Horton's saying: 'Study capital, not labour!' Is that what he meant? Money in the bank – labourers ten-a-penny!

I grew inwardly rebellious at the thought of being entrapped within such monotonous hopelessness. In order to appease my state of mind, I secretly carried about my person a small map of England with a line pencilled in from Lincolnshire to Liverpool. One day (who knows?) I might run away and board a ship to America, become rich and successful like Sam Horton my distant relation, who sailed there from the Cheal to seek his own fortune in the early nineteenth century.

During one railway excursion to Skegness in 1936, after I had left school and started work, I again visited my mother, now settled at 20 Queens Road, still employed to look after Mrs Jackson. Both she and Mrs Jackson asked me if I would like to live in Skegness; in short, to join my mother. Both women listened intently for my reply as I shuffled my feet, still wearing the shoes of past insecurity. Such was this sudden surprise that I blurted out a 'maybe' instead of an excited 'yes!' Nevertheless, this conversation was to unsettle me, and make me wonder: was this a possibility? I thought about it often and remained much unsettled. So one Sunday I decided to skip Sunday lunch and cycle over to Gedney

Hill, some 16 miles away, to see brother Stan and discuss the matter with him. He was at that time remotely out of touch, so although we were pleased to see each other nothing was settled and I returned to my lodgings (but had I cycled to Skegness and Mam, my previous dithering would have been resolved).

> *I skipped away from my lodgings today,*
> *To see brother Stan, still bound in service,*
> *And slaving away for his present master:*
> *Farmed out to provide dirt-cheap labour*
> *(To cut the expense of the workhouse).*
> *These desperate conditions make me seethe,*
> *Homesickness bites me hard and deep,*
> *How long this dreadful world depression?*

In the labour-intensive days I speak of Mr Cope employed: one horseman; one tractor driver; three general labourers and two youths. Additionally, during the busy season he would employ a gang of several women, and during the harvest gathering, at least one old-age pensioner would offer his part-time services. All these employees were essential to cope with the labour-intensive work on his 120-acre farm; all arable except for one grass field. We were still living in the days (of 1936) when human muscle-power and horse-power still reigned supreme. (Some 60 years later, in the 1990s, a local farmer advised me: 'You can take it from me that with such an expensive outlay for labour, in these days Mr Cope would have been bankrupted within six months.')

Unknown to me, amidst my growing agitation about the possibility of a change, something was secretly stirring. My Mother was requesting of Oscar and Mrs Gedney that I should now be sent to her new home, the latest one at Skegness, the one now occupied by my mother, solely on account of her occupation as housekeeper to a bedridden elderly lady. The security of tenure surely a bit shaky from the day Mrs Jackson eventually *passed away*. Indomitable Mam never thought of that, that this might be another shaky possession, leading to yet another eviction. Things tend to happen in threes: one bother colliding with another until the impactions become the final bother and crash into the buffer end.

It startled me somewhat one day when Mrs Gedney asked me point-blank: 'Do you want to go and live with your Mother?' To which I replied without a second's hesitation with the word 'yes' flung from my lips. And so it was arranged that I should go a few days before Christmas of 1936.

I couldn't wait for my freedom. I gave in my notice to Mr Cope, who probably thought I was mad in the days when work prospects were hard to find. From Gosberton I caught the green Lincolnshire Road Car Company bus to travel into the unknown once again, to live in a family home after five long years of impermanence. Now I was old enough to earn money, to create for myself some security. I was growing up if not grown-up. From now on I would seek whatever opportunity that chanced along – open minded – full of hope. Such youthful enthusiasm! – a determination to find a promising path and boldly move along it.

The last words I heard from Mrs Gedney were: 'It's like losing one of my own!' That deeply felt motherly touch, reminding me of my own mother's words when I left Lincoln over two years ago: 'You don't like losing your own!'

I remember leaving my native village, with my worldly goods packed in a suitcase, a shilling or two in my pocket, in a state of sheer excitement. This was no sad parting; it was a joyful relief to escape. To leave the struggling farming community, to no longer be a Son of the Soil, in a life of dreary bondage (at least, that's the way I saw it, having had my nose so close to the punishing ground).

As soon as possible after Christmas (which all the family again attended) I went into Skegness town to seek a *situation* (that 'job' word my father had used when he had stumbled across me on the workhouse lawn). Who knows, I might find a career that could lead to riches? Whatever the employment was it would be better than being idle. In any case, there was no dole money for a boy of 14 living with a mother in receipt of a regular wage (but then, there wasn't a fat lot of anything, not even for an unemployed adult with a family, subjected to the tight constraining rules of the then harsh means testing).

My luck was in. Boldly displayed in the window of Dutton's the newsagents in the main street, Lumley Road, was a notice in large script:

SMART BOY WANTED
Apply Within

And so I did, hoping that I was smart enough to be considered. Without much ado I was offered the job, which I eagerly accepted. What a boost that was to my self-esteem, that I should be judged to be 'smart' – in the best sense, of the word. I started work the very next day. Of great importance the job was permanent; subject to suitable references which I obtained in due course from Mr Ross, the headmaster and Mr Cope, my first employer. To my surprise both references were glowing and that was another boost in my life.

The 'job' although easy, compared with slaving on the land, had one annoying drawback. This caused me to be somewhat anxiously challenged. For six mornings every week I had to leave my bed at 5 a.m. Then depart from the house in the cold darkness and trudge through the snow about a mile into the town. There, from behind the shop in George Street, I collected a two-wheeled trolley and headed for the rail station in time for the arrival of the early morning train. Also in attendance was a much older and bigger lad from Averys, the main competitor to Duttons, just a few doors away also on the Lumley Road. It was customary to compete in loading the trolleys before racing back to the shop to be the first with the news. Hating such senseless competition (or so it seemed to me) I persuaded the other lad to win turn about. To my surprise not only did he agree, but did so with relief – vulgar, sweaty competition was simply not my style.

Waiting anxiously at the shop was the 'smart' manager, ready with a printing stamp to add the latest cricket score, in the space under 'stop press news', especially of games played far away. After that task was completed I left the shop with a sack of newspapers to be delivered, ending up along the hotels of the North Parade. After a few days a furious postman accosted me to complain that I was not pushing the papers fully through the letter box, thus making his letter delivery doubly difficult. I immediately mended my ways, much, I felt sure, to his relief – the things you have to learn in life!

After completing the paper round I rushed off home for breakfast, then returned to the printing works at the back of the shop where I busied myself oiling the printing machines, and reading proofs to Mr George (before he disappeared to the Avenue Club for his first whisky of the day). I was so proud to have a responsible job, the thought that I was being exploited never crossed my mind. As well as infusing discipline, this work also gave me needed experience, which I badly lacked. And didn't other working folk too readily offer this plum of advice: if you don't work you jolly well deserve to starve! Under such intense pressure, I had no option but to toe the line.

My wages were all of ten shillings a week (50p). But I was proud to be in work and earning, though my nights

301

were spent in such a state, checking the time on the alarm clock in case it failed to go off at the appointed time. Never once did I fail to turn up – such determined pride! In reality, to be employed was far better than the then alternative. Proudly I took my first ten-shilling note home, to give to my mother for my keep. She tried to refuse it but I insisted and we compromised: the note was handed over and I took two-shillings for pocket money, being one-fifth. (My mother's act was genuinely intended to be kindly, but kind people are not always the most practical.) A positive eye-opener in this job was the varied news I read. All the headlines from the *Mirror* to *The Times* and if possible more besides. And to top this up, at home we took delivery of a national newspaper, of which I became an avid reader. All in all my vision of the world was slowly expanding.

During March (in 1937), in a shop opposite I saw another opportunity notice:

> Errand Boy wanted
> Apply within.

Mr Robinson, the manager, took me on. At 12 shillings a week (60p) this was a decided improvement in my status. But, more importantly, the starting time in the morning was 8.30 a.m. in winter and 8.00 a.m. in summer – giving me two extra hours in bed. And I was allowed to take the delivery bike home; a heavy duty one, with a large container at the front to hold a basket; green in colour, with the name Lipton Ltd painted on a metal sign attached below the crossbar. On my half days and Sunday, many a local trip did I take. Once I went to Ingoldmells to look at the site of the new Butlin's Holiday Camp and I also cycled south towards The Wash and explored along the heaps of sand dunes, where wild birds were still plentiful; reminding me of my workhouse holiday at Frieston Shore, a few miles away.

After a probationary period I moved from 'errand' boy to 'smart' boy once again. The company offered me a three-year apprenticeship which I eagerly accepted, making me a 'bound apprentice in famous Lincolnshire'. Obviously my potential had been spotted...

So there you have it – wasn't I adventuresome! Still not 16 and I already had tried three occupations: from being a lowly farm-labourer, to a printer's apprentice (even if I was only a dogsbody who doubled up as a paperboy); and lastly into higher prospects as an errand-boy with a multiple-grocer, which had led to an offer of a legally binding indentured apprenticeship, with all the future opportunities that might bring.

And the weekly reward, just think of that: from a modest ten shillings a week (50p), to 30 shillings (£1.50) by incremental increases over the bound three-year period. At long last I was making progress; on to more security in my life. Not too much but enough to finally relieve my fear: that poverty and I might not keep walking hand in hand.

By the time I was 17 I had acquired a bicycle, a light-weight tourer. On this I explored for miles and miles. Especially did I enjoy visiting the rolling Lincolnshire Wolds. This added a spirit of adventure to my life and gave me a wonderful sense of freedom. Never once did I get bored. Over every hill and around each corner opened up new vistas of which my eye and mind could not get enough.

That life was tough I already knew; that life was a constant battle, many people kept telling me so. So why should anxiety harass me when my basic needs could so easily be fulfilled? Hadn't my Father Horton declaimed, time and time again! – rubbing it well and truly in, to the outer limits of boredom, that:

'You've got food in your stomach,
Clothes on your back

303

A good bed to lie on,
– what more do you want?'

And didn't I also clearly remember what 'they' (the uptight ones, of worthy intention) had so often well-meaningly asserted, that: In the end 'they' (the poor bastards!) often manage to turn out well. What more did I want than that!

But that's enough about me. The excess of ME was only intended to assist in describing life at the struggling level; during part of the nineteenth century and the early part of the twentieth. Since those days life has moved on (for better or worse, I'll leave others to say). Can you bear with me a little more? There are still a few jigsaw pieces to be fitted in so my innocent childhood's view of life can be better explained. Especially, how at the time it seemed so bogged down (in the mind as well as the body) in all sorts and manner of guilt – assertively then branded as sin! For wasn't I the very embodiment and living proof of corruptive ways – but isn't any landing a good one, if you can walk away from it!

EPILOGUE

Distant and cold though it appeared to be, the new Poor Law of 1834 at least provided a certain degree of security, which for most inmates was by far superior than their dispossessed alternative. And that certainly included me, following my last family eviction.

Overwhelmed though I was, especially during those first raw days of induction; then smitten by loneliness, dejection, and later rejection, even a workhouse must be given credit where it is due. Like a reliable timepiece it ticked out its total security around the clock. And that's what it was intended to provide me with: no more! – no less! (housing, clothing and food).

Like some privileged public schoolboys who lament their own miserable incarceration, as time went by (lots and lots of time!) there would slowly arise in me a feeling of some affordable affection for my old *alma mater* workhouse home. Yet, despite this bit of defrosting I would try my utmost not to see my own children enter a similar safe refuge.

And well you might ask, what were the feelings of George Horton's various offspring, however they sprang into life – in or out of wedded bliss? Not a lot as you would imagine, as they gnashed their teeth after one scandal followed another. (Perhaps I was fortunate to be the last of his line, by which time it seemed less thought of as a crime than sheer astonishment at the prowess, at age 68, of such a randy old man, far past the then dying age, and suitably nicknamed 'Staghorn'.)

When their own pressing needs began to grow (especially

thinking of the stretched-out men) would they themselves manage to easily overcome, if not always to fully understand, that the maddening 'thudging grip' protrusion can spray its way without a conscience? A shocking realisation if they had been exulted in their goodness, which would not only be unfair on their own purest intentions: it would be downright distressing for them! There really is no easy alternative but to 'rise above' all temptation, into a bright cloud-free sky; not to descend into a tempting wicked crevice: that's the purest way of striving; the way to overcome the excitement of temptation and avoid all the repercussions. But if all your good intentions flounder (as they are often likely to) then immerse your body in an ice-cold bath – another piece of good advice readily going the rounds.

What of George Horton's female victims, the two single (unmarried) mothers of his various bastardised children? What a cool customer he was: impregnating and then failing to marry them. No wonder in my early innocent days (and they lasted quite long) I would be astounded that such carnal calamities could take place, which appeared to be so dishonourable. This question badly burnt my feelings, so I urgently needed an answer.

Some 60 years would pass before I obtained a vital clue from George Horton Mawer's birth certificate; the child of Horton's first 'mistake'. Issued by the Sub-district of Gosberton in 1891: on the 10th August, some two weeks after the birth (it should be recorded by social historians as a quite remarkable document).

In column (6), the father's name was an all-knowing dash. There being no registered father, the child automatically took the surname of the mother, Mawer. There being no 'Father' entry and her declared occupation of 'Domestic Servant' it would be only too obvious that she was a fallen woman, deserted in her hour of need.

But why those surnames: George Horton? Perhaps marriage

CERTIFIED COPY OF AN ENTRY OF BIRTH

GIVEN AT THE GENERAL REGISTER OFFICE, LONDON.

Application Number....... 3684

REGISTRATION DISTRICT _Spalding_

1891. BIRTH in the Sub-district of _Gosberton_ in the _County of Lincoln_

Columns:—	1	2	3	4	5	6	7	8	9	10*
No.	When and where born	Name, if any	Sex	Name, and surname of father	Name, surname, and maiden surname of mother	Occupation of father	Signature, description and residence of informant	When registered	Signature of registrar	Name entered after registration
92	Twenty-seventh July 1891 Surfleet R.S.D	George Horton	Boy	—	Mary Mawer Domestic servant	—	J. Mawer Grandfather Surfleet	Tenth August 1891	W. Russell Registrar	—

CERTIFIED to be a true copy of an entry in the certified copy of a Register of Births in the District above mentioned.
Given at the GENERAL REGISTER OFFICE, LONDON, under the Seal of the said Office, the 22nd day of December 1982.

BCA 003796

Form A 302 (S.360233) Dd. 534651 30M 1/78 35M. 040-06

Christened in Oct 7 baptised on the 9th February 1892 by me W. Russell Registrar in the presence of J. Mawer Surfleet was still a possibility and the Horton surname was registered as a forename, so if a ceremony later took place, the lad could drop the Mawer tag and revert to his father's name – becoming less doubtful, if not fully respectable. (This practice had recurred in the past, although, if the marriage was much delayed, the handy hyphen might be used.) Even official birth certificates, so it seems, in desperation, can be refined – or juggled as you wish.

Yes indeed, and so the plot thickens. In column 7, the informant's name is boldly given as, T. Mawer, grandfather, occupier, Surfleet. This entry thereby confirming that the mother, Mary Mawer, was his daughter, absolutely without question.

Now the plot thickens further. On the 13th February, 1892, the original entry of the 10th August, 1891, was revised. The 'grandfather' description of the informant was deleted through by a stroke and added in the margin, under an asterisk, was this defining statement: 'Clerical error in Col. 7, corrected on the 13th February 1892, by me W. Russell, Registrar in the presence of T. Mawer, Occupier.'

So there it stands: had a genuine error of the relationship of this new-born child been made? Most certainly not – this was vengeance! It now becomes obvious that the cuckolded husband had discovered this blight on his life, before the birth came about (and surely the Registrar must have heard the rumoured-truth flying around his district, before he officially recorded the first entry, never mind the marginal additional 'error', pointing out forever that a carnal mishap had occurred).

How very angry Thomas Mawer turned out to be. His first entry, 'Mary Mawer' with the description 'Domestic servant' made the new-born child a bastard. To consolidate that bit of branding, the details of the 'Father' were missing and in column 5 only a single (maiden) name is listed, as the 'presumed' married surname of the mother is absent.

Although not specifically asked for, the mother's occupation (or other status, i.e. spinster) is also registered: no indeed, you cannot dishonestly cover up, the birth certificate is a two-edged tool.

But for goodness' sake, how many times in the wider world do we have to produce our birth certificate? This somewhat hapless child was brought up by his grandparents which was one way of resolving an awkward problem – and I thought that I had suffered from confusion, during my formative time of questing.

However, that carnal calamity could have affected my feelings far worse; that is, if I had known the stark truth: that my 'Staghorn' Horton, serial-rutting father, had committed adultery instead of the more acceptable fornication with a freely single woman. For coveting was strictly forbidden in the Bible by 'thou shalt not' divine command. In other times, now long gone, there could have been a stoning, especially of the woman.

There's no doubt about it, their sin was almost on a par with sodomy, then lambasted by the church. In any case, they were old enough to know better: George Horton was aged 37, and Mary Mawer was then 34 (and handily available as she daily visited the Horton home, as the family's domestic).

It turned out that Mary was the much younger second wife of Thomas, then aged 50, and five years over the then average male mortality rate; considered to be an old man, and long past a certain capability: in blunter words (and so it might appear) lacking lead in his pencil! And now what of my mother's plight; of being branded as an 'unmarried' mother (no other description was then acceptable – and usually damned with a curl of the lip). At her funeral in 1958 I made what turned out to be a trite remark: 'She was more sinned against than sinned.' Forthright Aunt Kate, of Lincoln, heard this remark, to which she quickly responded:

'Don't believe that,' she said. 'George Horton offered to marry her, time and time again. I well remember his agitation when I visited before the first birth; he was besides himself.' There seems no further doubt about it, my mother had decided to cock a snook at the world.

Perhaps she was still highly emotionally engaged to the man of her dreams. Whatever it was: in a continuous state of living in a past dream, the age difference, or even more down to earth reason – she didn't love the man! So when the branding iron singed, she played the part with all the force she could muster, but make no mistake about this: 'living in sin' was her own 'rightful' choice to live.

So whatever the circumstances of my father's philandering and life-giving, he could not have married his victims anyway. How very careless of him; even if his strict moral upbringing would have enforced marriage as a redeeming way out. Assuming of course that first 'impediment' had not inconveniently existed, and his second pig-headed victim had not declared her 'right' of free decision. Tough on both counts for that deeply frustrated, religionised being.

So many years would it take to put together what came to pass as my own sensitive resolution. By which time my open-eyed innocence would be washed away, in a 'brave new world' of startling freedom. The unthinkable, the un-speakable, bodily feelings (and that includes the questing mind) would no longer be sinfully hidden. And that was a nasty pill for some to swallow: turning a solemn purpose into a recreational pastime, thus undermining for many a most sacrosanct belief; that procreational activity was the only acceptable form of loving.

Now let's deal with those two harrowing evictions; the second one more traumatic: the one from the tied-cottage, shunting my family into the Poor Law institution (still widely known as the workhouse).

The reason for the first was only too obvious: now known

310

as negative equity, caused by a lack of wherewithal to maintain the repayments on a property too highly valued. And what of those lost *hundreds and thousands* forfeited part-purchase, when we were turned out of the place? Gone forever! The price of failure, or making a (forced) poor decision. With hindsight it was obvious: the only sensible way for us was to have abandoned the place; cut the losses and seek alternative accommodation, which we were eventually forced to do anyway – in retrospect it all seems so simple.

Coming to that tied slum-cottage; why didn't we hang on by simply obeying the law? Why did my mother, in what appears to be a touch of reckless madness, forbid my 21-year-old elder brother, Oscar, from reporting to work for the landlord, 'Rawpelt' Henry Smith of Creccy Hall? Who had, after all, offered us a lifeline and a chance for the family to remain intact.

Throughout my lifetime, firmly believing that my mother was culpable, I never thought to question further, and to that I say – more's the pity! Over 60 years passed and just before he died, brother Oscar confessed, by which time my mother was long dead. 'I was the reason for the cottage eviction,' he said. 'I was too scared to work for Henry Smith because of his harsh reputation.'

That was only part of our problem; an upheaval can bring a change of direction which my family badly needed (after all, if we had remained tied to a low-labouring life, we might never have escaped from dreary country-living). But that is not my real point. My brother Oscar, in keeping secret his act of defiance against the landlord, meant that I unquestionably blamed my 'mad' mother. I never came to terms with it and secretly held it against her all her life. And believe it or not – this would in my later life become my only lingering family regret, that I had misjudged her so – that, with hindsight, the truth was obvious: that at age

311

21 my brother must have foreseen the consequence of his action and, being somewhat bolshy myself, I would have understood his reluctance to be an unwilling servant to a tiresome master; in a life as low as the bottom can be.

My other suffering regret, which was much more of a frustration, was the seemingly endless time it took for me to better my rudimentary education. In truth, I thought for years that I was as thick as a plank! But, although I experienced many fits of disturbing healthy anger, my best reaction to help me escape beyond my woes were my attempts to engage in regular bouts of anxious seeking. But that, as most striven folk might agree, sometimes takes a lot of precious time; after the tragic waste of the other unfulfilled time, which we might begin to think that we have somehow unfairly missed.

But that's life! That was what folk kept telling me. And not only that, you've only got one and that you cannot swop; so that undoubtedly means – you are eternally stuck with yourself ... so get your head stuck into books and never stop questioning, especially some of the answers.